T0371167

Deep Listening

Deep Listening

Transform Your Relationships with Family, Friends and Foes

EMILY KASRIEL

Illustrated by the author

Thorsons

In order to respect their privacy, contributors who have chosen to remain anonymous are given only a first name.

Thorsons
An imprint of HarperCollins*Publishers*
1 London Bridge Street
London SE1 9GF

www.harpercollins.co.uk

HarperCollins*Publishers*
Macken House, 39/40 Mayor Street Upper
Dublin 1, D01 C9W8, Ireland

First published by Thorsons 2025

1 3 5 7 9 10 8 6 4 2

A catalogue record of this book is available from the British Library

HB ISBN 978-0-00-865332-3
TPB ISBN 978-0-00-874617-9

Printed and bound in the UK using 100% renewable electricity at CPI Group (UK) Ltd

This book contains FSC™ certified paper and other controlled sources to ensure responsible forest management.

For more information visit: www.harpercollins.co.uk/green

For James,
for everything

CONTENTS

Introduction 1

PART ONE – ARE YOU LISTENING?

What is Deep Listening? 17
Why We're Not Listening – Eight Traps That Catch Us Out 29
How Deep Listening Will Enrich Your Life 45
Why the World Needs Deep Listening 65

PART TWO – HOW TO DEEPLY LISTEN

STEP ONE: Create Space 83
STEP TWO: Listen to Yourself First 107
STEP THREE: Be Present 133
STEP FOUR: Be Curious 159
STEP FIVE: Hold the Gaze 187
STEP SIX: Hold the Silence 207
STEP SEVEN: Reflect Back 229
STEP EIGHT: Go Deeper 255

PART THREE – NAVIGATING YOUR DEEP LISTENING JOURNEY

Deep Listening Ethics 283
Deep Listening Risks to You 287
Questions to Begin 293
How Did Your Deep Listening Go? 299

Conclusion 307

Acknowledgements 311
Endnotes 315
Index 337

INTRODUCTION

A story was unfolding. Just months after the birth of the New South Africa, troops were amassing on the seat of government. As BBC Africa's new reporter, I needed to get to Pretoria fast.

Hundreds of soldiers, former members of the ANC's armed wing, shifted restlessly outside the Union Buildings, demanding to see their president. From here, they could see the lights of Pretoria. Above them, protected by armed police, stood the sweeping floodlit temple. It had long stood as testament to South Africa's turbulent history – from the administrative heart of the apartheid regime to the inauguration of the first democratically elected president, Nelson Mandela. The Union Buildings could be about to witness another monumental moment.

'We've fought too long and hard to be treated like this,' a soldier protested, 'to be oppressed by our new bosses – white officers, our enemy – with food not fit for dogs.' Across the manicured lawn, a group of liberation veterans huddled together, their weathered faces illuminated by the soft glow of cigarettes. 'All of us here are soldiers. But in the MK [the ANC's armed wing], I was a lieutenant – now I'm only a sergeant,' one of them grumbled, his eyes fixed on the expansive sandstone façade of the presidential headquarters. 'Madiba needs to understand. He knows our pain, our sacrifice. We need to speak to Mandela.' His voice rose. 'We fought for him. We need to speak to him now.'

Eyes were cast skyward. Waiting. And waiting. The night grew longer. The rumours swirled and multiplied.

Faintly at first and then with increasing strength, a swish of rotating blades. A helicopter sliced through the inky night. Nelson Mandela, their leader, had heard their cries.

The rigged-up podium was waiting, but remained curiously empty. Looking for the president, I was surprised to stumble across Mandela's tall resolute presence far from the stand, tailed by bodyguards. Armed with his upright posture and transcendent reputation, he slowly wove through the dense crowd of angry fighters, giving a nod of acknowledgement or a raised fist to each person he passed.

'Where do you live?' he asked one soldier, in his distinct gravelly tone. 'Yes, I know Alexandra township, but which street? … Where along that street? … Yes, I can picture that corner in my mind's eye.'

Mandela's attention was finely tuned. He was acutely aware of his responsibility and of the rough years of exile in Angola, Tanzania or Zambia that many there had endured. With his whole being exuding warmth and understanding, the president encouraged the soldiers to share their authentic feelings, their sense of unfairness and intense humiliation. These feelings cut deep as these fighters had found themselves relegated to underdogs in the country's newly 'integrated' defence force.

Over the course of the next hour, Mandela lent his empathetic ear to the soldiers, always without judgement and always with patience, as they voiced their frustrations. As he did so, I could feel their anger dissolving in the warm night air.

Only then did the South African president address the crowd. Slowly, and with authority, he reflected back to them what he'd understood, acknowledging their grievances. 'They are very genuine. You are men and women who are committed to the struggle. Some of you have fought. We are very sensitive to your demands.' Mandela impressed upon these former guerilla fighters the need for discipline and patience. When he spoke, the soldiers were silent. When he finished, in their sweatshirts, zipped jackets and woolly hats, they returned quietly and peacefully to their barracks, satisfied that they had been heard.

It was my first experience of the power of a profound type of listening.

* * *

The story of our life unfolds through our relationships – with parents, siblings, children, friends, neighbours, colleagues, even strangers. These connections are our true wealth. Through engaging with these individuals, we forge our identity, who we are and where we belong, and we make meaning from our short and precious lives. But our relationships have increasingly become frayed and routine; we are bereft of the recognition and understanding that we crave.

And the reason? We no longer invest time and energy in the very fibre that connects us: listening. Almost three in four adults in Great Britain believe that people used to be better at listening, according to a poll taken for this book by the NGO More in Common.[1] Too often, the standard way we listen fails pitifully. An unspoken assumption often lurks beneath the surface: why should we invest in hearing *their* perspective when we are already certain that they are wrong? Our children, of whatever age, aren't sharing what's truly going on in their lives, and we're stuck in dysfunctional misunderstandings with our partners, parents, siblings and sometimes our colleagues too. At work we struggle to engage with people from different generations and backgrounds, people whose beliefs stand in stark contrast to our own. Too often, those attempting to speak to us feel ignored, dismissed, unheard. We avoid those with contrary ideas, talk past each other, or resort to shouting, whether in person or on social media, fuelling the scourge of polarisation.

If only they'd understand. We fixate on trying to explain ourselves more loudly, more often, more insistently. But by concentrating solely on speaking, we're missing the point. Since our days in the womb our ears have funnelled sounds by default, so we take listening for granted. Yet how many of us know how to listen, and then practise this way of relating, so the speaker, the person we're listening to, feels safe to share their true ideas and unleash new thinking? How many of us have the tools to be great listeners when the stakes are high, as they were for Mandela? When we fiercely disagree or when our relationship at home or at work is balancing on a precipice?

This book is an attempt to guide you to enjoy richer and more profound connections through a transformational way to listen in the conversations that matter. I call it Deep Listening. There are no absolute rules – rather inspiration, guidance, stories and evidence to propel you along your own Deep Listening journey. The chapters that follow will give you the desire, tools and confidence to Deeply Listen, challenging you to take risks and go beyond your usual listening, whether you want to nurture more fulfilling relationships with others (and even yourself) or are hoping to help bridge divides in your community. At its heart are the eight steps of Deep Listening, a framework which spans the creation of the right environment to unpacking your speaker's deeper narrative.

My experience as an executive coach and later mediator for the BBC has given me the opportunity to practise the high-quality listening fundamental to my roles. And it is from this first-hand experience, coupled with my extensive research into the work of psychologists and other experts and practitioners, that I have developed this practical framework. When we signed up 1,000 young people from over 100 nations for a BBC British Council Deep Listening project, with the help of academics and a control group, we were able to demonstrate its impact. Participants in this project and many others have helped me to further refine this listening approach.

So, what's the difference between standard listening and Deep Listening?

Standard listening is *transactional.* We often only truly listen momentarily, pantomiming the act of listening as we're 're-loading our verbal gun with ammunition',[2] to use a phrase coined by writer Jacqueline Bussie, getting ready to fire. Then we jump down the throat of the speaker to explain our own ideas, our own solutions, the 'right' answer – interrupting meaning and destroying thinking. Even if we've learned to listen better, we tend to treat the speaker as a resource. We listen to them to extract information, or because it is expected of us. This type of listening blinds us to what is not expressed in words and can leave a speaker feeling brushed aside or used.

Deep Listening is *transformational.* You acknowledge a speaker's humanity when you practise Deep Listening; you grant them respect and empathetic space so they can ignite sparks of fresh thinking. You listen openly to truly learn about them – and yourself. Through an interactive process, your speaker crystallises their ideas and feels witnessed. They can then share a more authentic story that allows you to understand them far more profoundly, even if you still disagree.

When you Deeply Listen, you have the potential to enhance the mental health and self-awareness of your speaker as well as your own well-being. Studies have revealed that good listeners are more capable leaders and strengthen their colleagues' creativity. They catalyse more effective, stronger relationships based on real understanding and trust.[3] Deep Listening turns a person from an object, opaque, perhaps dimly threatening, into a multifaceted human being. And through this type of listening, you develop as a human being. But listening in this way can take a lot of courage. At a primal level, we find it hard to open ourselves up to alternative ideas, even more so when our perspectives clash and we firmly believe that we're right.

In an increasingly polarised world, you need to interact with people who sit round the dinner, board or café table with views that you might find difficult, even abhorrent. You can practise this approach whenever such an occasion arises, with no expectation that you all need to agree. Deep Listening conversations across chasms are essential to functioning families, companies and democracies, enabling us to collaborate, even if we have diametrically conflicting ideas. And the scale of the challenges facing our world demands that we transcend our boundaries to understand them; that we work collectively to tackle them.

Learning how to Deeply Listen is not, however, a ticket to spend the rest of your life stuck in the back-row seats, muzzled, prevented from voicing your own ideas. Whether you've traditionally played a listening role or are accustomed to speaking your mind, cultivating balance is the aspiration. If you have felt silenced, you may need to confirm, before you listen, that you will also have *your* chance to speak. But when you truly listen, others are not only more likely to soften their attitudes, they're also more inclined to be in the right headspace to listen to you.

My Listening Journey

From a very early age, I was aware of the profound consequences of not being heard or recognised. My father, Harry, came to the UK as a child refugee, just before the outbreak of World War II. His birth parents and most of his family were killed in concentration camps. When he died, I was 13. It felt as if I had entered a different land, with oceans of water between me and those around me; friends were too fearful, too out of their depth, to even ask me how I was. While I received much kindness, in the turbulence of loss there were few opportunities to unpack my thoughts or make sense of my world upturned.

These memories have inspired me to embark on my Deep Listening journey, to enable people in divided communities to authentically listen and understand each other, to be curious and connect with people who are strangers to me and to help create a world where people feel truly understood.

Growing up in Britain as a second-generation immigrant, I have always relished my insider-outsider status. I have honed my own listening in myriad situations across time and geography, embracing different opportunities to listen to strangers. I became a radio journalist at the BBC World Service. Every day I was immersed in the world of listening, with my microphone acting as a stethoscope, recording the beat of people's lives, struggles and passions. I roamed solo for the BBC across India, Nigeria and Uganda, interviewing presidents, market traders and musicians.

The enlightening experience of being listened to well by my own executive coach was a seminal turning point in my journey. Basking in their unhurried non-judgemental gaze, I was free to unpack my assumptions. I realised that I didn't have to stick to the role that others prescribed for me. I also became clearer about my own values. It was a liberating exchange, unexpected within the hierarchical walls of a BBC meeting room. I wanted to be able to repay this gift of listening. And that's what led me, in 2013, to train as an executive coach, alongside my day job.

Being coached also sparked a shift in my priorities, placing the pursuit of meaningful change at the heart of my work. I led a culture change across BBC News encouraging colleagues to showcase solutions alongside their reports on problems and conflicts. Fuelled by my own history, I wanted to highlight stories where divisions had been bridged. I created the BBC Crossing Divides season, so news and documentaries, radio and television shows could broadcast reports about how people had come together across lines of race, class, religion, age and politics. Our audiences watched and listened to people from conflicting groups connecting and establishing trust – meat-eaters listening to vegans, black-cab drivers taking the time to understand their Uber counterparts. Briefing colleagues on how to create these conversations sparked my curiosity. I wanted to find out more about how people can learn to listen more profoundly to each other, in spite of their differences.

To deepen my understanding about different ways of listening, I immersed myself in research across psychology, neuroscience, peacebuilding, management thinking, medicine, teaching and philosophy. I pored over papers and studies, first at the London School of Economics and then at King's College London and learned from fellow coaches and mediators, as well as counsellors, psychologists and therapists. I have fine-tuned my approach while training people at a BBC festival in Salford, and on projects with participants in Lebanon and the Baltic states of Latvia, Lithuania and Estonia. Recognising that strong listening is an essential leadership skill, I've been collaborating with the UK Forward Institute for responsible leadership to train all their fellowship cohorts, with participants from companies and organisations as diverse as Unilever, the Cabinet Office and the British Army.

But, as my family will attest, I've still got some way to go on my own listening journey. Writing this book has been helpful.

Navigating This Book

The book is divided into three parts:

Part One explains exactly what Deep Listening is – and isn't. I then showcase eight traps that catch us out and prevent us from being able to Deeply Listen. You, like me, have probably become ensnared by many of these traps, regularly, perhaps every day, often with the best intentions. I then highlight the evidence for the many benefits of Deep Listening – for yourself, your speaker and the world.

Part Two, the body of the book, is your guide to Deep Listening in eight steps:

- **Step One: Create Space.** You begin by creating a place of psychological safety for your speaker. There are also physical changes you can make to your environment, so a conversation feels effortless. Your ambition: Your speaker feels cherished and inspired to explore new ideas.
- **Step Two: Listen to Yourself First.** You can't be open to listening to others until you truly listen to yourself. This step explains how you can begin to forge a more positive relationship to your family of shadows, the unacceptable parts of yourself, so they no longer hijack your most important encounters.
- **Step Three: Be Present.** This step will delve into an elliptical yet impactful aspect of Deep Listening – your presence, which transforms standard listening into a profound encounter. We explore what presence is, and

how you can cultivate it to tackle the internal and external distractions that obstruct true listening.

- **Step Four: Be Curious.** Here we unpack the qualities you project towards your speaker: curiosity, empathy, awareness of judgements and respect. Acknowledging that you don't already know what's in the mind of your speaker can be transformative.
- **Step Five: Hold the Gaze.** This step explores the power of a steady, warm-hearted gaze and other non-verbal cues to communicate to your speaker that they are being heard. We explore how far you can read your speaker's body language, facial expression and tone to understand what they are *not* expressing directly.
- **Step Six: Hold the Silence.** In this step we unravel the many types of silence and the reasons why you may resist a pause. How can you use a rich stillness to centre yourself and signal to your speaker your true respect, giving them the space to think, reflect and share?
- **Step Seven: Reflect Back.** Here we uncover how to crystallise what you're hearing and reflect it back to your speaker. What are the clues that can guide you as you check your understanding of the meaning of what your speaker has conveyed, directly and between the lines?
- **Step Eight: Go Deeper.** This step explains how your listening can illuminate what ordinarily is hidden – your speaker's deeper narrative. This deeper narrative is vital to understanding your speaker – and can include their unexpressed needs and whether their emotions are in harmony or alive with contradictions.

Each of the eight steps closes with Takeaways. We can improve our listening by practising, so each step also sets a Deep Listening Challenge.

Part Three navigates risks and starter questions, as well as ethical conundrums, with tips on how you can reflect on your own listening experience to support your journey.

Throughout this book, I share stories from people who are beacons of the art of listening. We'll hear from leaders like Christiana Figueres, who spearheaded international climate change negotiations at the UN, the head of one of the world's largest advertising agencies, and the CEO of Wikimedia, who oversees the world's largest encyclopaedia. Cultural trailblazers pioneer fresh perspectives, so we'll also gain insights from artist Antony Gormley, Nobel Prize-winning writer Wole Soyinka, choreographer Akram Khan and photographer Platon.

My research took me from Japan to Canada to Kenya, gathering lessons from leaders, Indigenous people and Buddhist monks. I've learned from those who listen in the most extreme environments, in their role counselling religious extremists or negotiating with those on the verge of taking their own life. Each of these inspiring individuals deepened my understanding, and I hope their experience and creativity can inspire you to listen anew.

After you've read the book, you will be better equipped to reflect on the true purpose of your conversations and imagine what your relationships could be like if you authentically, deeply, listened. As you start to question old habits and try new ways of listening, you'll notice that you begin to understand the people around you in a far more meaningful way, and they, in turn, will become more open to engaging with you.

But first, let's look at a Deep Listening conversation in action with someone who has a powerful story to tell.

PART ONE

ARE YOU LISTENING?

WHAT IS DEEP LISTENING?

What does a Deep Listening conversation actually look like? How might it unfold in the real world? The following encounter is between me and my friend Sofiya, who has often worked at the British Library with me, seated at a neighbouring desk. It's not a typical Deep Listening exchange, as Sofiya is so open, articulate and self-aware, but I have chosen it as our

conversation highlights all eight Deep Listening steps and her reflections about the encounter are striking and profound.

For this exchange, I chose to leave the library and walk next door to the elegant St Pancras station hotel. Although we didn't have complete privacy, the plush blue velvet seating absorbed the voices of other guests; we were comfortable, enclosed in our own world (**Step One: Create Space**).

Sofiya's life took a dramatic turn in 2022. Since then, she's lived through danger and turmoil. When Russian troops began their full-scale invasion of Ukraine, Sofiya was working at the British Embassy in Moscow. The Russian state condemned her as a traitor. She was forced to flee her home. I first came to know Sofiya before this time, when she worked with me at the BBC in London. Since her return to the UK, our friendship and mutual trust have deepened. She's often asked for advice, and I've often obliged.

I wanted this conversation to be different, to be a Deep Listening conversation. The agenda was open, to be determined by her. I hoped to feature the encounter in this book, and she knew this. I was also conscious that this ambition could compromise our exchange. I resolved to let go of this distraction, to make our encounter authentic and meaningful for us both (**Step Two: Listen to Yourself First**).

I arrived at the hotel before Sofiya so I could find a quiet spot. I centred myself by turning my attention to my breath. As my phone would record our conversation, I knew I was safe; my mobile could not distract me. I savoured my tea. Slowly (**Step Three: Be Present**).

Emily: What would you like to talk about? What do you feel will be useful and interesting for you?

Sofiya: I want to talk about going home and not being able to go home.

Pause

I've always wanted to live in the UK, here in London. On the surface I'm now doing all the things I've always dreamed about. But what is home? I choose to think of home as the small town near Moscow where I grew up and went to school, and also another small town, but in Ukraine, where I spent all my summers in my grandparents' flat. This other home was always so full of life, love and stupid little family quarrels. And exploring nature with my cousin, with my sister and with my grandparents. There, I felt like a plant who was being watered and exposed to the sun. It was formative.

As Sofiya is talking, I reflect on the idea of home as being universal; our relationship to our home is part of all our journeys. Then I become aware of my mind wandering and bring my attention back to Sofiya **(Step Three: Be Present)**, *wondering where she will go next in her thinking* **(Step Four: Be Curious)**.

As I keep my gaze on Sofiya, her eyes wander, then return to greet mine **(Step Five: Hold the Gaze)**.

There is a silence of perhaps 10 seconds. This prompts Sofiya to reflect more deeply **(Step Six: Hold the Silence)**.

Sofiya: Today I can't return to either of those places. And the difficulty is that the danger is not completely tangible. There is no certainty. If I return, I will or won't face arrest. I feel sad and scared. This fear is in the background, and it also embraces me in every part of my life. It's always there.

More silence.

Emily: So, I'm hearing you say a great deal … *Can I capture, adequately, I wonder, what Sofiya has conveyed through her words and the emotional tone of her voice?* (**Step Seven: Reflect Back**)

You spoke about the excitement you have, living in this country, and yet there is also pain – separation from your small town near Moscow and also from your summers with your family in Ukraine, where you were a plant nourished by the sun. And the constant sadness, fear and uncertainty of return.

Sofiya: Yes. *She exhales.* There's no answer and there's no way forward. My life's been hard. If you were to write a book about it, it would be an interesting book. But sometimes I just want a simple life, with friends, and being able to go home twice a year and stay with my family in Moscow and get my nails done. But … even if I get through the interrogation at the airport, on the third day they will detain me for not filling in my taxes correctly. There are just so many of *those* stories.

This is probably one of the very few areas in my life where I can't do anything, apart from trying to support myself and build a sustainable life in London and minimise the pain of not being able to be home. But my pain is not going anywhere …

I hold the silence and maintain my gaze.

Sofiya picks up energy.

And I'm not sure I want it to go.
I don't think I'll be *me* if I do that.

I'm aware that Sofiya has just had a new insight, which challenges what she said before: 'There's no way forward' **(Step Eight: Go Deeper)**. *Instinctively I feel respect for Sofiya; for the ordeal she is going through, and for the perceptive way she reflects upon her experiences. Though I've always felt warm towards her, my empathy for her is deepening. Until now, she's never laid out so explicitly what it feels like to be her. Perhaps I've never asked* **(Step Four: Be Curious)**.

Emily: So, I'm hearing you say that you've got an ambiguous relationship with this pain. I get a sense that it is physically hurting **(Step Five: Hold the Gaze)**. *For a moment, I quieten and try to sense what's going on for her.* And yet you don't feel that it's right for you to abandon that pain because it also nourishes you. It connects you with part of your identity, with Russia, with Ukraine, with who you are **(Step Eight: Go Deeper)**.

Sofiya: Yes. *She says this with a reflective look in her eyes.*

More silence.

But the pain is also about what will happen if I lose my job here in the UK. On TikTok there are endless stories in my feed of people who were made redundant around Christmas, and they complain about their rubbish employer, as they sit in their parents' home with a cup of tea and a library of books in the background. Me, I can't fail in the way other people can. I *have* to succeed at my job because I *can't* be anywhere else.

The conversation continues.

And then I have the feeling that I'll be OK no matter what happens. I know if this job doesn't work out, I'm sure I'll find other interesting work soon. I sense that my pain is a strength. And I *am* moving on. I think I am really different from what I was last year. This missing home and all the related feelings have made me who I am and have taken me to where I am now – deep inside and actually now on the surface as well. I can appreciate what I've been through.

After some 40 minutes, I ask Sofiya for her reflections on our exchange.

Sofiya: I think that the eye contact helped. I really felt heard. Not just because of the space we're in – it's a really lovely place, but I feel like I wanted to unfold my story (**Step Five: Hold the Gaze**). We ended up talking about things that seemed like they're not related to the start of the conversation, but I think the way you summarised and fed back what I said helped me unlock some extra thoughts and feelings (**Step Seven: Reflect Back**), which I was happy to

> share with you because I felt this safety. I think safety is the keyword (**Step 1: Create Space**). And also, I feel more structured in my thoughts now. It's been clarifying and sort of illuminating. Your questions were based on what you heard, but you also did some inner work before you fed back your reflections. It was interesting to face my feelings from the outside rather than from within.
>
> Our conversation has helped me find those arguments supporting the feeling of being genuinely OK (**Step Eight: Go Deeper**).

As Sofiya reflects, she is able to organise her thoughts, creating clarity. I sense that our encounter has encouraged Sofiya to recognise the ambiguity of her feelings: She acknowledges the pain of exile, insecurity and loss as a core part of her identity, but one that may also be a source of strength, a place for growth. There has been a significant shift.

Cookie-Cutter Listening

In practice, when we listen, we are rarely fully present. Listening is often a hollow, performative act. We go through the motions as we fall into one of the listening traps, distracted by the words in our head, or thinking of our reply, just nano seconds after our speaker's first syllable. We interrupt. Or fidget with frustration, anticipating our opportunity to explain to our speaker what's wrong with their argument. And the chance to demonstrate that *we* know better. The speaker expects us to interrupt, so their own thinking barely has space to form.

Often, you listen only long enough to mentally sort what your speaker is saying into ready-prepared bins: 'I've been there, done that' or 'That's rubbish.' You're like someone who looks at the art in a museum with the sole aim of categorising it – 'That's Impressionism!' or 'That's Minimalism!' – but never truly sees the paintings.[1] In standard listening, you assume that your speaker has pre-baked nuggets of information that they're ready to deliver as soon as you ask them a question. Your role is passive. Whether you're a fantastic listener or an appalling listener, their words and thoughts, you believe, will remain the same.[2]

Deep Listening

The person who first popularised the term 'Deep Listening' was an avant-garde American accordion musician and composer, Pauline Oliveros. I was intrigued to learn that she embraced the term after recording a set of tracks 14 feet beneath the Earth's surface in an underground cistern,[3] aptly calling the album *Deep Listening.* I have often listened to her compositions while writing this book. Her definition was expansive: 'Deep Listening involves going below the surface of what is heard, expanding to the whole field of sound while finding focus. This is the way to connect with the acoustic environment, all that inhabits it, and all that there is.'[4]

Oliveros' focus on profound attention – whether she is directing that to the sounds of people, animals or the Earth itself – resonates with me. Her invitation to go beneath the surface of what is heard is echoed in Step Eight: Go Deeper. In one of her recipes for listening, she advocates that we 'take a walk at night. Walk so silently that the bottoms of your feet become ears.'[5] Her insight that we can listen with our whole body provides an inspiring one for a Deep Listening practice.

My Definition

I would like to be able to define my Deep Listening approach in a single, simple sentence. But this rich and multi-layered process resists a pat definition. Here, I'm going to try to convey its core.

Entirely present and in a safe place, having listened to yourself first, you invite someone to share their thoughts. Guided by curiosity, empathy and respect, you listen to truly understand, letting go of judgements – and any instincts to agree, disagree, obey, solve, or change them. After silence, you reflect back the essence of their words, feelings and underlying thoughts to check that you've grasped their meaning and to inspire more thinking. They go deeper and you reflect, again. On this journey you both understand more fully. They feel heard, met and acknowledged. Irrespective of whether you agree, you both feel more connected.

But Deep Listening is not easy. As third-century rabbi Samuel ben Nahmani put it, we don't see things as *they* are; we see things as *we* are.[6] Ben Nahmani was referring to our dreams, but this insight delivers a strikingly accurate depiction of the way we usually listen. None of us is a blank slate. Our experiences and preconceptions shape what we can and cannot hear in a conversation.[7] It's not easy for the speaker either. As a Deep Listener, it's your role to create an atmosphere of psychological safety, allowing them to move beyond vigilance to expand the range of what they will be willing to say – or even think.

Deep Listening presents an opportunity, never an obligation. Especially when it comes to listening to those who hold very different ideas from your own. Deep Listening is also not right for every occasion. If someone asked you if you wanted some tea and you waited 10 seconds, then tried to reflect back the real meaning behind their words, they might throw you a very strange look, if not worse (and you probably wouldn't get any tea). Deep Listening is most powerful for encounters where the stakes are high, when creating real understanding and trust is critical. But this approach is not all or nothing; the way you use it will depend upon the relationship and the context. Sprinkling in selective elements of Deep Listening can enhance many sorts of conversations: at home, at work, on your commute, with friends and strangers, and even with yourself. And practising Deep Listening doesn't preclude you, at other moments in the conversation, from having your say or probing answers to questions that are important to you. But the focus of this book is on the listening itself.

My Deep Listening approach draws on the work of a wide range of thinkers, writers and psychotherapists, including Carl Jung and Richard Schwartz, along with my own experiences. I have been particularly inspired by the writings of pioneering psychologist Carl Rogers.

Rogers was born at the start of the 20th century. His traditional parents enforced daily prayers and cold discipline upon him and their five other children. He reacted against this stern upbringing by forging a radically different way to relate to others.[8] Rogers believed that therapists and psychologists should listen with an *unconditional positive regard*, accepting the speaker as they were and conveying an empathetic understanding and a sense of safety. There should be no questions, no suggestions, no advice, or any other techniques which directed the client.[9]

In 1974, Carl Rogers gave a talk about empathy to an enraptured group,[10] highlighting the importance of entering the private world of the other and becoming truly at home in it: 'It involves being sensitive, moment to moment, to the changing felt meanings which flow in the other person – to the fear or rage or tenderness or confusion or whatever he is experiencing.'* You cannot embody this approach unless you are truly curious and truly empathetic.

Paying attention to your speaker as well as yourself is integral to Deep Listening. This aspect of my approach draws on the work of mindfulness pioneer Jon Kabat-Zinn, who defines mindfulness, in a jam-packed sentence, as 'Paying attention in a particular way, on purpose, in the present moment, and nonjudgmentally.'[11] Deep Listening attention is also suffused with the wisdom of other mindfulness and meditative practitioners, from Indigenous people to Buddhist monk Matthieu Ricard.[12]

Active Listening – What Deep Listening Isn't

Carl Rogers, along with a colleague, coined the term 'Active Listening' to describe his client-centred, transformational approach of immersing yourself in your speaker's perspective to grasp what they are trying to communicate and conveying back that deep understanding.[13] However, you're more likely to have come across Active Listening in its distorted form: paraphrasing the speaker's message and conspicuously nodding and smiling. There is a chasm between Carl Rogers' definition and how the business world often talks about Active Listening. An

* Carl Rogers was working in the mid-20th century and, like some others who I reference, followed the now discarded practice of using male pronouns to refer to both men and women.

analysis of Active Listening on business websites has highlighted that it has been reduced to a mere set of instrumental techniques 'more connected with coercion and manipulation than with meaning-making and understanding'.[14]

If you manage people at work, you may have participated in leadership training in this type of Active Listening to prepare you for having difficult conversations. So, you explain to a member of your team your worries about their timekeeping. You then give them space, three minutes, or 30 seconds, to express their thoughts and concerns. But your listening is performative. 'I hear what you're saying,' you reply as you go through the motions. And nod. But you're not opening up your ears, or your heart. There is little curiosity. Your Active Listening is hollow.

While some advocates of Active Listening also emphasise staying calm and compassionate, Deep Listening is more profound. You are also listening to what isn't being said and exploring your speaker's unexpressed thoughts while being aware of your own internal responses. Your entire being is listening to their entirety. This is an aspiration, however, and it's unlikely that you'll be able (or want) to listen in this way consistently. Getting caught in one of the listening traps is an inevitable part of everyone's journey.

WHY WE'RE NOT LISTENING – EIGHT TRAPS THAT CATCH US OUT

'You have my undivided attention,' Homer announces to his family over the kitchen table, in a scene from *The Simpsons*.[1] When the camera zooms in to reveal the contents of Homer's mind, however, we see a cartoon jig, with a bird dancing, a cow on the fiddle and a tortoise banging percussively on its shell. Back in the kitchen, Homer remains oblivious to his children. Rather than giving them real attention, he is humming along to the imagined farmyard music. It's not just the tune that is stuck in Homer's head, but Homer himself.

You might not be in danger of a camera opening up your inner thoughts. And you may not be routinely preoccupied with dancing farmyard animals. But you are nonetheless at risk of falling into the same traps that prevent Homer from listening. And, even without the intrusions of a camera, the results can be just as obvious to the people around you, the people you fail to listen to, whose thoughts and needs you ignore, every day.

Some traps are commonly held beliefs which destroy your desire to listen – truly listen – to others. Even if you are able to start listening, you can still fall into other traps that hijack your ability, as you listen, to stay present. These traps can make you, like Homer, hum your own tune, drowning out the full story that your speaker is trying to share. And often, you're not even aware that you've tuned out. I've been thwarted from listening by many of these traps, often in the conversations that matter most, with the people who are most precious to me. When these traps have entangled me in lip-service listening, I've failed to listen properly to close family members, to indispensable colleagues and to strangers who could have revealed new ways of seeing the world, if only I'd been able to really hear them.

When you read about these traps, you might realise you've been ensnared in them yourself, perhaps many times, perhaps every day. You might feel ashamed about the moments when you've blocked what someone was trying to tell you, or when you've cut in and changed the subject mid-stream. But rewind for a moment. Many of these traps reflect strategies that you and your ancestors – going back millennia – evolved to increase the chances that your gene pool would survive and flourish into the next generation. They are not accidental defects. On many occasions, they've served you well. But if you're not careful, these traps can prevent you from achieving the profound understanding and richer relationships that can emerge through Deep Listening.

The first trap is laid by some of our keenest impulses: to achieve our goals and to enhance our status.

I Want to Win

'I've been formally trained to be argumentative and win. I am here to defend myself,' explains Joe, a South African on the cusp of leaving his role in a Cape Town start-up to embark on an MBA at Harvard University. He tells me that he developed an instinct for confrontation while debating at school and honed it through competing at the World Universities Debating Championship. As his opponent was preparing to talk, Joe's whole body was tense, ready to jump. This formidable debater was alert to any chink in his opponent's armour. Anything they omitted to say. Anything he could exploit.

'A lot of my debate training has to do with pretending – creating an illusion of confidence. Never acknowledging what the other person is saying, even inwardly to myself. Though I might feel sorry for my opponent, outwardly I needed to be totally dismissive.'

I met Joe when he participated in my three-week Deep Listening programme. Prior to this course, like many of us, he'd not been aware of his default 'vigilant for victory' mindset. Joe had been raised on rebuttal, listening only to cut his adversary down. The goal of his most important interactions was always the same – to triumph.

You don't have to be a competitive debater to fall into this trap. This is especially true if the person you are listening to holds a completely contrasting perspective or is a stranger who looks or sounds different from you. Or, conversely, is someone close to you who you find profoundly irritating at this moment – a partner, parent or colleague.

'Winning' a conversation in this way causes collateral damage across a relationship. You leave the speaker feeling dismissed or seething, convinced that you have wilfully ignored them. Depending upon your relationship, you may start round two from a position of strength, but with your speaker wary, approaching the conversation with caution and distrust.

I am in Charge

Your role is to explain, to instruct, add value, be right, even at times to dictate. It's in your job spec as boss, parent, elder, teacher, professor, older sibling or supervisor. You need to shine a light, inspire them by laying out your vision. If you don't 'help' them, you are failing to fulfil your duty.

By keeping control and dominating the airwaves, you can safeguard against disruptive ideas that might otherwise skew you off course. If you are honest with yourself, you might feel your authority is threatened by alternative facts or ideas. Often, you mask your desire to voice your opinion with a perfunctory question. You do listen, of course, but you listen presumptuously, impatiently, as you wait for your opportunity to speak. With this mindset, the more authority you wield, the more pressure there is to drive the conversation. To stay in control. If you listen, your dominant status, you fear, will be diminished.[2]

Makiko Shinoda was caught in this trap. Shinoda has served as chief financial officer for many international companies, following a consultant role at McKinsey & Company.

'I was trained, if you don't speak up in a meeting, you're simply worthless. You are not contributing. You don't count. And in my mind, speaking up became equated with not listening, and I came to see listening as being intellectually passive, almost a sign of laziness. The more I strove to be a high-performing businessperson, the more I strayed away from listening.'[3]

Today, Shinoda has become an influential Japanese thought leader. She looks back, with a wry smile, at her old belief that listening is passive. She now advises company executives on how they can set the tone not only through the way they speak, but also through the way they listen.

I Have Expertise (and You Don't)

If you are caught in this expertise trap, (a relation of *I am in charge*), in your eyes the world is frozen. It's as if you have nothing new to learn, because you already know what they are going to say. You're an old hand at this – and you can help your speaker with the invaluable gift of your own opinion, drawing from your superior experience and wisdom.

The expertise trap might be hidden by the tangled vines of enthusiasm and passion. If you're a naturally enthusiastic person, like me, your eagerness to share your thoughts can restrict your listening. Becoming aware of this tendency, like so many of our foibles, gives us options. I've also found it helpful to acknowledge (to myself) that deep down this enthusiasm can mask some arrogance; that my natural exuberance may well be squashing a speaker's reflections, preventing them from sharing, or even generating, their own ideas.

Years of training, experience and accumulated technical knowledge can sometimes frustrate the ability of senior doctors to hear what a patient – or the patient's body – is aching to tell them. Teachers and professors can also get caught in this trap: as individuals who profess to know *the* truth, they can feel an instinctive need to correct anyone who they believe is in some way ignorant.[4]

You might also believe that your speaker's different way of looking at the world is ill-informed, invalid or illegitimate. So, as someone steeped in scientific rigour, you withdraw your attention when a friend describes how seeing a homoeopath has helped with his asthma; and you don't hear him explain how enriching it has felt for him when someone has taken the time to properly listen, understand and offer support.

I Must Prove I'm a Man

'Mother,' Telemachus commands in *The Odyssey*, 'go back up into your quarters, and take up your own work, the loom … speech will be the business of men, all men, and of me most of all.'[5] More than two and a half millennia after Telemachus' command, women in most societies have claimed their rightful place as full participants in conversation. Yet the ancient chorus of gendered roles still echoes in the way we listen; while women also like giving advice, when they listen, men are still more likely to offer their speaker unsolicited guidance on what actions to take, according to a recent study.[6]

While evidence suggests that perceived differences in how men and women listen are more significant than actual differences,[7] your assumptions about gender roles can still hamper your ability to listen. This holds true whether this trap feeds on a belief in a *dominating masculinity* you feel you should aspire towards or a *passive femininity* you feel the need to escape from.

Indeed, in the workplace there is a clear link between gender, assertiveness, and the role of a speaker and listener. Here, men may feel the need to be dominant, authoritative or persuasive to avoid the risk of being marginalised. So, they drill themselves not in sensitivity or receptiveness, but in delivering a strong message. In the words of psychologist Adam Grant, 'How many times in your life have you heard an assertive woman called aggressive? But a man who is insufficiently assertive is considered weak or meek, or both.'[8] In light of the long-held belief that listening and silence are hallmarks of feebleness, you might feel a need to sidestep the danger of being perceived as a good listener, whatever your gender. Listening might require you to recognise your speaker's feelings, or indeed your own – and this can feel like unsafe ground.

Men seem more likely to side-step this dangerous territory altogether and avoid truly listening or learning how to listen better. In the global Deep Listening project that I led there were twice as many female volunteer participants as male ones. Today, when I run Deep Listening sessions, women are consistently more likely to sign up; sometimes, only women sign up.

A survey carried out for this book revealed an interesting gender disparity: American men are much more likely than their female counterparts to cite 'getting other people to listen to them' as a key motivation for enhancing their own listening skills.[9] Men are more likely to view listening as a mere stepping stone to securing their own chance to hold the floor.

I Must Solve and Sort

I recently received a remarkably honest e-mail from Lina, a Lithuanian social worker whom I trained in Vilnius in 2023. She told me that practising Deep Listening at work, supporting a group of teenagers, presented no obstacles. But back at home, she had found it far harder to step into her Deep Listening persona. Lina's partner had been experiencing a tough time at work and had shared – repeatedly – his frustrations about being squeezed dry in the office. He'd suffered back pain after sitting at his desk for too long, staying late in the evening to solve his colleagues' tech problems. But Lina struggled to listen.

'It feels like I have to force my tongue not to interrupt, to convince myself inside my head that I can demonstrate my caring and love through Deep Listening rather than by dumping instant advice like "Why don't you try this exercise to ease the pain?" or "You need to get another job." Sometimes I feel I have failed.'

I wondered what was behind the contrast between the freedom Lina experienced listening at work and the battles, with herself, that she encountered at home.

'Maybe it's because people who are closest to me are the ones who make me feel safe, so I turn off all the filters, so I'm simply honest and open.'

If you find yourself itching to provide a solution, no doubt you're often acting, like Lina, with the most honourable of intentions. Your speaker is sharing their woes with you – whether it's their stroppy teenager, sexist overtures from a colleague, or an old friend ghosting them – because your sage advice will instantly cure their ills. Motivated by my desire to add value to those who choose to share their challenges, as well as assuming that my own solution is ideal, I find this is a snare that often catches me out.

This trap is dangerous because it lures us in with a tantalising piece of bait: our desire to help others, evolved over millennia. Early humans on the African savannah, more so than other creatures, depended on collaboration to survive. Today, the !Kung gatherers of the Kalahari desert also practise a hunter-gatherer lifestyle. These people similarly rely on friends to solve the problem of hunger; their friends share with them their wild game when their own basket is empty.[10]

The temptation to offer advice intensifies if you believe that your greatest value lies in your capacity to mend the lives of others, or if you feel the need to control a situation to stay safe. But if you are ensnared by this listening trap, you and your speaker could both lose out. When you listen to solve rather than to understand, you take on the speaker's responsibility and deny them their agency. This burdens you and disempowers them. Perhaps there is no solution. Perhaps they need to acknowledge and accept that they can't change reality. If you haven't genuinely listened – and even if you have – how can you presume to know what it's really like to be them? Truly understanding your role can free you from this trap and be enormously liberating.

I've found that someone is far more likely to buy into a solution if they've joined the dots for themselves; the value of certain truths relies on their self-discovery. Even if a coaching client comes to me unsure about how, for example, to navigate the BBC hierarchy, a challenge I've faced myself, I've learned to resist pitching my own approach, however brilliant I think it is. I've found the passion and persistence that a client has in pursuing their own solution is far beyond the polite (and quite likely feigned) gratitude I receive when I succumb to merely *solving and sorting*. But avoiding this trap doesn't mean you have to forever withhold your life experience. With your children, for instance, you can always ask: 'Do you need a hug, do you need advice, or do you just want me to listen?'

Another variant of this trap is *listening to cheer someone up*. Here, you believe, your speaker is sharing their sorrows about their obstructive partner or a looming deadline at work just so you can tell them: *Don't catastrophise. Look at the big picture. Others have it worse.* Until you truly listen and acknowledge your speaker's feelings, in all their complexity, they may not feel prepared to move on, acknowledge the 'other side' of the story, or come up with their own reasons why it isn't so terrible after all.

I Don't Have Time

'I get how important this Deep Listening stuff is,' said a senior BBC News colleague with whom I was travelling around South Africa, keen to reassure me of his buy-in as I delivered Deep Listening workshops to journalism students, 'but news is just not like that. We don't have time to have these sorts of encounters.'

Indeed, journalists on tight deadlines (and others out of habit) frequently have a pre-formed narrative, so that when they interview people, they're on the hunt for a specific sound bite to slot into their story. Everything else is ignored. And it's not only journalists that get tangled up with the tyranny of the urgent. You might be secretly thinking: I'm a busy person. I've got to take the bins out. And is the roof still leaking? And did the cat eat dinner? Wasn't there an e-mail I needed to reply to? And wait – I didn't get back to Jon about running this Saturday

… And with all that to juggle, you seriously expect me to follow your mental machinations about whether to stay with your partner?

We're constantly waging a campaign for completion, and we're losing. Despite our best efforts, our to-do lists proliferate and new responsibilities pile onto our already overflowing plates. Time for quality listening is often one of the sacrifices. When I work with people in a professional context, time pressure is the top obstacle to Deep Listening they cite. You might take pride in your squeezed seconds. Lack of time is an indication of what a busy, full and important life you lead. The only way to survive the jungle is to take short-cuts and rely on what you already know or can intuit in an instant.

The challenge is that we think many times faster than we talk. Our brains can digest 400 words each minute, as we often recognise words in conversation before they've been fully spoken, but we speak at about half that speed. As this excess processing power lies idle, listening can feel slow and frustrating, so we become subsumed in daydreaming or planning our response.[11,12]

Another factor underlying the hesitation of leaders to embrace more profound listening is an implicit belief that their current listening practice is more efficient. Standard listening can indeed be quicker, not least because it prevents concerns, challenges and contradictions from coming to light. Lip-service listening sustains the mirage of there being one valid viewpoint, a viewpoint which is alluringly simple, and one which you already understand. Perfectly. Deep Listening takes more time, but it is an investment in the relationship and in true understanding.

This point was highlighted in a conversation I had with Nick Grono, author and CEO of the Freedom Fund, which works to end modern slavery. Grono has intentionally evolved his leadership style to prioritise listening. However, in many encounters, the tentacles of urgency still reach out and grab him.

'I still get impatient. I shortcut decisions, often unconsciously. I jump to conclusions quite quickly. And if I have reached a conclusion, I can still interrupt or signal: Right OK, I've heard enough, let's move on.'

But Grono has come to appreciate that the purpose of many encounters goes beyond simply harvesting facts. He wants to genuinely understand his colleagues' insights and give them a sense of ownership over decisions. And in reality, it's often not a lack of time that prevents us from listening, but the quality of our attention. You can't condense the gift of your undiluted attention into a few seconds of hyper-quality presence, but you can bring complete attention and genuine curiosity to whatever time you have available, and in doing so enrich and expand the minutes.

If I Listen, I Must Obey

'Listen to me!' your teacher yells at you, as she waves her finger in exasperation. It's your first year of school. She shouts: 'Listen to me!' but what she means is: *Obey me! Keep quiet! Sit still! Put your coloured pencils away!* This may have been the very first time anyone has asked you to listen. So, it's perhaps not surprising that ingrained in your subconscious is a belief that listening binds you to a whole set of obligations: your need to defer to your speaker, even collude in your own subjugation.[13] If you listen, you must fulfil all the expectations of the person talking to you.

Amina, who today fights inequality in her role with an international NGO, was brought up to listen – and this form of listening was saddled with baggage. 'As an African woman, I was brought up with this expectation from elders and men, if I truly listened to them, this meant I agreed, and I would take any action that they deemed necessary.'[14]

Growing up in Tanzania, Amina was taught to adopt a posture for listening that emphasised submission. If seated, she was not to cross her legs. She was instructed not to hold her waist in a way that could suggest her own power. 'I was brought up to shrink myself a bit, watching and looking at them but lowering my head.' It's no surprise that she's sceptical about Deep Listening. In your mind, listening might also be so intrinsically tied up with obeying that you find it hard to imagine a type of listening that does not forfeit your own power. A kind of listening where you choose what you do with your new knowledge and understanding.

If you've been denied the opportunity to speak up, if your feelings are being disregarded, when you give the space to someone else to talk, it may feel as if, yet again, they're usurping your power. You need to be heard. In these scenarios, to ensure you get to speak, the other person may need to listen to you before you listen to them. And remind yourself, listening and speaking aren't mutually exclusive roles. Opening yourself to your speaker's perspective aims not to hand them (more) power. It's designed to provide a space for you to understand your speaker, and for them also to understand themselves.

My Brain is Wired to Judge

As soon as a stranger appears – even before they've opened their mouth – you've started judging them. This happens automatically. Your ability to predict and judge is a key function of your brain. Cognitive neuroscientists have described how your brain rapidly extracts information based on your experiences. This understanding enables you to navigate the world around you and to predict what others might say or do. Predicting, automatically, what a person is like is efficient and increases your chances of survival.[15] You can focus on more pressing concerns, for example escaping from that tiger. If you didn't judge, you wouldn't be safe. You wouldn't be able to tell friend from foe.

While modern threats differ from ancient ones – our foes are less likely to be violent predators and more likely to be, say, fellow human beings with whom we disagree about politics – our judging brain has remained the same. And we often believe that our foes are only motivated by money, sex or power. Fundamentally unworthy. This form of judgement feeds on a seductive power trip: you determine (in your own mind at least) who merits reward and who deserves punishment, and you behave as if your certainty is an indication of the truth.

This sneer of reproach, which can be powerful until you become aware of it (and even after you become aware of it), holds you back from truly listening. Instead, you label people in order not to listen to them. Suffragettes, for example, who fought for the right to vote in Britain at the start of the 20th century, were branded (by men) as spinsters, sexually deviant or as mad unladylike monsters.[16]

Your judgements can also distort what you hear when you do listen to someone, whether the person is a distant stranger or an intimate family member. This trap can ensnare even those of us, and perhaps especially those of us, in longstanding intimate relationships, highlighted by these poignant lines from Bella Bathurst's book *Sound*: '… back at home, all our histories just get in the way. Once upon a time, perhaps you thought your wife's views were interesting. Now she talks, and you don't even register she's speaking.'[17] Your speaker will sense your judgements, even if you're careful not to share them, and will become wary of opening up; in their core, it doesn't feel safe. In the words of psychologist Carl Rogers, 'As long as the atmosphere is threatening, there can be no effective communication.'[18]

Breaking free from this pre-judging trap is challenging, as you need to override instincts that have evolved to help you survive. Encouragingly, you can change the way your brain functions, because of what's known as its neuroplasticity, its ability to form new connections between neurons. By paying attention to your thoughts and judgements and cultivating qualities of curiosity, empathy and respect, you can effectively alter your psychological and physiological programming, rewiring your brain.

Once you know what to look out for, it will become easier to avoid becoming ensnared in these listening traps. Before we dive into the eight Deep Listening steps (Part Two), let's turn to the evidence for the rich rewards of mastering the art of listening, to entice you to put it into practice. Studies show myriad benefits for both the speaker and you, in many different sorts of relationships across all domains of life. This approach can also offer you the opportunity to gain a far more genuine understanding of your speaker's mind as well as their heart.

HOW DEEP LISTENING WILL ENRICH YOUR LIFE

'Throw me an onion' or 'Grab some chillies.' The words are tossed across the kitchen in Ana Luiza Ribeiro's São Paulo home as she and her family enjoy their Wednesday communal cook. It's become a tradition with her mother, younger brother, and stepfather, Manoel. Mixed in with the chopping and frying, they're drinking wine and dancing to 'More Than a Woman' by the Bee Gees. With their blend of Italian and Portuguese blood, and everyone a vegetarian, these Wednesday cook-ins are joyful gatherings. And the fiery *peperonata* spices never fail to light up the heart (and the stomach).

But a few times a month, tensions between Ana Luiza and her stepfather would erupt. In personality, Ana Luiza and Manoel are similar, but when it comes to politics, there is a chasm between them. She grew up in São Paulo, Manoel in a small town. She is a human rights lawyer, Manoel is an engineer. Rows about climate change and gender pronouns, human rights and the former Brazilian President Jair Bolsonaro were frequent and fierce.

'We would get mad – like *really* mad. The mood was horrifying. "You're going to be 55 years old someday," he'd say. "And you're going to think just like me." Huge fights. I'd run into my room. For days it felt like time stood still. As if Harry

Potter's dementors were draining any hope and happiness out of the air.'

Ana Luiza and Manoel recognised that they both needed to change, to become less reactive, less angry. So, Ana Luiza signed up for my Deep Listening course. That programme was only open to young people, so they agreed that, week by week, she would sit down with her stepfather and share with him everything she was learning.

Today, some things have changed in Ana Luiza's home. The breakthrough came when Ana Luiza and her stepfather agreed to properly listen to each other; to be present, to stay curious, and to reflect back the very heart of each other's thinking. Most importantly, not to interrupt. They still disagree about politics. But now, when they broach a challenging subject, Ana Luiza finds it funny – watching Manoel, a big man raising his finger, waiting for his turn to speak.

'Yesterday we talked about political leaders and the upcoming elections; we both really listened, and it went OK,' Ana Luiza tells me. She now understands that Manoel sees things from an economic point of view and she through a human rights perspective. She can now see how he comes to his conclusions. 'We aren't trying to convince each other any more. It's been a big journey for both of us.'

Truly hearing each other's stories challenged their ironclad belief – ironically shared – that there is only one way to look at the world: their own. Yet, for Ana Luiza, Deep Listening is still a work in progress.

'It's OK with my family. But with colleagues, I find it harder. It's still stressful and sometimes difficult to listen to those who have very different points of view. But I'm getting better at not feeling like I am losing when I choose not to fight back, not to take the bait.'

Ana Luiza's story illustrates how political differences, like many other types of differences, all too often morph into gaping chasms – and how Deep Listening can help reset. Recognising the power of good listening is important; for thousands of years, it remained buried.

Listening through Time

Since the time of the Greek and Roman civilisations and for most of the last 2,000 years, Western culture has prized speech as a gift from the gods, differentiating humans from other creatures.[1] *To be a speaker of words and a doer of deeds* is the essence of the Greek poet Homer's heroic ideal.[2] Listening, in contrast, has been considered far less significant.

Though the Greeks and Romans dismissed the importance of listening, the ancient Egyptian civilisation valued listening and silence as moral virtues.[3] The Greek philosopher Pythagoras, the man associated with the rigidity of right angles, also, it is said, became an advocate of the more fluid power of listening, inspired by his time studying with the Egyptians.[4] Legend has it that Pythagoras instructed his disciples to undergo five years of rigid silence, listening to him divulge his wisdom. And he addressed these followers in a curious way: from behind a veil, in order to encourage them to listen attentively, undistracted by his body or his gestures.[5]

Today, self-expression is celebrated – if only in its promise. Everyone is said to have a TED talk inside them, a flawless encapsulation of an original idea that they only need to be brave enough to voice. You must learn to articulate your speedy 'elevator pitch' that neatly sums up your aspirations, ready for the moment when you meet that powerful person who can transform them into a reality. Universities, and especially their MBA programmes, prize oratory and the confident assertion of your opinion. The idea that others, indeed everyone, has valuable insights that can illuminate your thinking is seldom countenanced. And most people rarely think about listening as a skill they need to learn and practise.

Before we dive into the evidence about the extraordinary potential of developing different aspects of Deep Listening, there's one piece of research that looks at the impact of this approach in its entirety.

A Deep Dive into Deep Listening: The Evidence

Are you from Iran, the UK, Malaysia or New Zealand? These were the four most popular nationalities among those who signed up to a special Deep Listening project. In total, 1,000 young people from 119 countries took part, including those who participated in the pilot. *Crossing Divides Across the Globe* was launched to celebrate the BBC's centenary, run in partnership with the British Council. I was to train people in Deep Listening from these extraordinarily varied backgrounds on Zoom over a three-week period before they had a chance to test these skills in a challenging conversation with a stranger from another culture.[6]

Which big controversial topic do you feel most strongly about? Does personal success depend on social class? Or do you feel more passionately about social media: overall, is it good or bad for humanity? Should reparations be paid to the descendants of slaves? Once the participants made their choice, they were invited to Deeply Listen – and talk – to a total stranger who felt the absolute opposite about one of these high-stakes topics. I wanted to know if the two participants, perhaps an Argentinean paired with an Afghan, could still practise Deep Listening despite their conversation partner believing the opposite to them.

Given the extraordinary global reach of the project, I didn't want to miss this opportunity to rigorously test whether my approach really worked. Could Deep Listening be a tool to bridge divides? So, I reached out to Netta Weinstein from the University of Reading and Guy Itzchakov from Haifa University, academic authorities in the listening field, and we set up a control group who would have a similar conversation with a global stranger *without* any Deep Listening training.

We were excited to see the results: people who had been trained reported deeper connections with their speaking partners than those who had a conversation with no guidance. Individuals who had been trained were also more likely to say they felt safe to express themselves and felt genuinely understood – even as they discussed topics about which they passionately disagreed. We expected that the Deep Listening training would also make people feel much less defensive, but the results fell below the reliability threshold. In talking to strangers from such different cultures, even with training, participants may have felt a need to stay a little closed to protect themselves.[7]

The Deep Listening connection allowed individuals to dig deeper and unearth more nuanced perspectives about their chosen topics. This self-reflection became a catalyst, participants became more open-minded about the opinions of their partner, sometimes even changing their own. These were the reflections of a young woman from Libya, Rana Bushreida:

'We chose the topic "Personal Success No Longer Depends on Social Class". I agreed with this statement, but my conversation partner didn't. As a debater, I was trained to stick to my idea even when I disagreed. But today I was allowed to listen, understand and even change my point of view when someone from a different part of the world shared their ideas. I love how Deep Listening gives you the chance to deeply see the topic from a totally different perspective.

'When I applied to the programme, I wondered how a three-session training could change me that much. But I am super delighted that it did, in ways I never imagined. I feel I am a completely different person, so excited to have these tools. They've shifted my everyday conversations from being uncomfortable or heated to being informative and rewarding.'

This demonstration of the potency of Deep Listening is backed up by many experiments into high-quality listening.

Speaker Benefits

Your strong listening can boost your speaker's well-being. I find that hugely motivating. Your speaker will feel heard and accepted, less anxious or lonely; instead, more confident and safer – there's evidence that touches on all these gains. Deeply Listening to someone so they can thrive, whether they are precious to you, a client or indeed a stranger, is intensely meaningful. And these uplifting changes support each other in a way that amplifies their value. Much of this value stems from a core need we all share – to be recognised and heard.

We Need to Feel Recognised

This recognition is perhaps the richest reward Deep Listening can deliver. The psychoanalyst Donnel Stern gets to the heart of this universal desire when he writes: 'We need to feel that we exist in the other's mind, and that our existence has a kind of continuity in that mind; and we need to feel that the other in whose mind we exist is emotionally responsive to us, that he or she cares about what we experience and how we feel about it.'[8]

When we Deeply Listen to others, we affirm their dignity as individuals who are fundamentally equal to us, yet unique and irreplaceable, with their own perceptions and gifts.[9] What has a price can be replaced with something else, in the words of 18th-century philosopher Immanuel Kant, 'whereas, what is elevated above any price, and hence allows of no equivalent, has a dignity.'[10] Developing Kant's ideas, a person recognised with this kind of dignity starts to see themselves as someone who has equal rights, who understands that they have a moral compass and can have agency to determine their own life, proposes the more contemporary German philosopher Axel Honneth.[11]

Honneth's point – that recognising someone's dignity can unlock their agency – was highlighted in a research project with Hispanic communities across four states in the USA. The ethnographic consultancy Topos Partnership gathered free-wheeling stories from community members about what their day was like and what made their community unique. When initially asked by researchers why they didn't vote, Hispanic Americans told them things such as, 'I don't want to make a mistake' or 'I don't have the time to properly study the issues.' Following these listening sessions, the researchers noted a remarkable transformation in their interviewees. After sharing their stories with attentive listeners, the interviewees felt more confident about voting, even though they had received no information on the issues. Through the process of talking to these highly trained listeners, the participants gained the confidence to exercise their right to help determine the fate of the country.[12]

Sharing Grief and Joy

Whether you're consoling or celebrating, listening well can help your speaker and enhance your bond.

If you encounter grief and distress when you listen, you might be tempted to come up with consoling words of wisdom or comfort. The Latin root of the word 'console', however, hints at a more powerful approach: *consolar*, to find solace together.[13] Being truly with your speaker, holding them in their pain, perhaps in silence, may be more comforting than platitudes. And being with someone does not require you to cross the boundary into suffering with them. You can contain their pain, providing a place of safety for you both.

On the flip side, if your speaker wants to share good news with you, say they've landed a new job, and you listen with care, curiosity and interest, researchers have discovered that your speaker is more likely to remember and make meaning from that experience, and want to share more good news with you in future, strengthening the fibres that connect you. The very act of disclosing this exciting news to you, a responsive listener, can boost your speaker's self-esteem, beyond the inherent reward of achieving this milestone.[14]

However, be cautious if you sense that your speaker fears intimacy and shies away from emotional closeness. In such cases, their defence mechanisms may lead them to be *less* likely to trust others or feel a sense of psychological safety when they're listened to attentively, especially if the person listening to them is a stranger.[15]

Unlocking Self-Awareness

Your speaker will unlock new thinking about themselves and others when you offer them empathetic Deep Listening, as demonstrated in our global study. Russian-Ukrainian émigré Sofiya benefited from having the space to organise her thoughts, with all their nuances. Although her story is complex, she was able to achieve a greater sense of clarity, which helped her 'find those arguments supporting the genuine feeling of being OK'. It is powerful to allow a speaker the freedom to make sense of their own story, rather than to be given sense by you, the listener. This approach respects the speaker's autonomy, one of our fundamental psychological needs, and sends a clear message to them: You are in control.[16]

The way that someone listens, research suggests, will influence what a speaker chooses to share, how they make sense of an experience as well as the emotions they associate with it. Since memories are dynamic, a speaker's future recollection will be influenced by how attentively they were listened to when they previously spoke about that event, which in turn will affect what they 'know' about their own past and ultimately even their sense of self.[17] What might that look like in practice?

A friend, for example, confides in you that their long-term partner spontaneously quit their job, which was essential to keep their shared household afloat. Bathing in your curiosity, respect and empathy, they feel encouraged to elaborate. As they reflect more, they consider that perhaps they and their partner are not so compatible. Their partner craves excitement and thrives on intense emotions, while they seek stability and value collaborative decision-making. These differences, among other factors, have made the unexpected job departure particularly painful. They wonder what comes next. They leave the conversation still feeling a little hurt, but with greater self-understanding and a renewed sense of agency. On the flip side, if the same individual had been speaking to a distracted listener, they would have been less likely to expand their thinking, and might have remained stuck in a wounded state of helplessness, which is how they may record and then recall their partner's job-quitting episode in the future.

It is motivating to know that your speaker will reap the benefits of being Deeply Listened to. But what about you, the listener? What is the evidence that listening can enhance your own well-being?

Enriching the Listener

I feel honoured, after a coaching session or a Deep Listening conversation in which my speaker has shared something personal. I'm grateful to them for entrusting me with a glimpse of their inner life and soul. It's a privilege and I feel enriched.

As Carl Rogers writes: 'I learn from these experiences in ways that change me, that make me a different and, I think, a more responsive person.'[18]

That has also been the experience of Kyle, who listens in a very specific environment: he lends his ear to fellow inmates in a British prison.[19] 'I was more ignorant before. I mean, judgemental. Don't wanna talk to him, don't need to know him … Listening calms you down as a person, 'cos you realise, that person here's going through this and he's going through that.'

In many British jails, inmates who suffer from distress, despair and suicidal feelings are able to reach out to highly trained fellow prisoners, like Kyle, and talk about their feelings in complete confidence. In fulfilling this role, Kyle has reaped the rewards. Listening to others has helped him become less judgemental, calmer and more empathetic. It has provided him with a sense of meaning. 'When you listen to people it's different. You really help without actually doing anything. Just listening, it's empowering.'

Listening is Collaborating

The newer understanding of listening challenges the idea that a listener is like a reader, scanning words already written, acting as a passive recipient of a speaker's story, peripheral and mute. Your speaker's story is, in fact, a collaboration that they are creating with you. That's a big claim, and it was first demonstrated in a seminal piece of face-to-face research led by Canadian psychologist Janet Bavelas in 2000.[20]

Bavelas and her colleagues set up an experiment. Students were recruited and assigned into the roles of speakers or listeners. Speakers were asked to tell their listening partner, previously a stranger, a true story about a close call that they'd experienced, for example a skiing incident, or nearly losing an assignment on the computer, but where in the end everything had turned out fine.

One set of listeners, however, was given a distracting challenge. While they were trying to listen, they were asked to count the number of days until Christmas, forced to multitask akin to navigating a listening obstacle course. Both the undistracted listeners and those who listened whilst juggling the Christmas countdown were videoed. Moment by moment, undistracted listeners who devoted all their attention to their speaker nodded, winced and looked joyful in response to what they were hearing, as their speaker switched rapidly between horror and humour. As a story progressed, and the undistracted listeners came to understand more, these listeners made many more *backchannel* contributions in comparison to distracted listeners, signalling that they understood both the words and their underlying meaning.

In a similar experiment, the same researchers found that listeners who were distracted and therefore unable to contribute as many backchannel responses led their speakers to tell shorter, less interesting stories with abrupt and faltering endings.

These 'insignificant' gestures and sounds, the backchannel responses, are in fact tangible acts where you make sense of and contribute meaning. Your gaze and smile, raised eyebrows and 'ahhs' play a pivotal role in co-producing your speaker's story.[21] As a listener, you are anything but a passive recipient. Collaborating in this way, not surprisingly, nourishes your relationship.

Relating Well

Deep Listening liberates us from being marooned in our small lives. It deepens connections, helping us meet a need to belong that is fundamental to being human.[22,23] Indeed, the best cure for loneliness is not more frequent interactions, say researchers, but more meaningful encounters[24] – such as those in which you Deeply Listen.

After Deep Listening to my friend Sofiya, I felt a step change in our relationship, though I had previously enjoyed scores of conversations with her. For the first time I had a glimpse of what it was actually like to be her. This experience made me realise something profound: as we dance in and out of each other's lives, we make assumptions about those closest to us. Change can be most imperceptible in those we assume we know best. No need to listen to them because we already know what they think. But our presumptions may be misplaced or past their expiry date. A parent, for example, might assume their adult child still holds the same political beliefs they did in their teenage years, not recognising how their experiences have led them to adopt more conservative or progressive ideas. Recognising how people closest to us have changed signals our authentic interest and respect.

Through great listening, two individuals can forge a memorable connection and a sense of discovery that transcends the everyday.[25] But rather than prizing the outcome of your interaction, you both relish the profound sense of togetherness that emerges during the encounter. Listening well can evoke a state of flow,[26] where you are fully absorbed in a challenging activity like climbing up a rocky path, except in this case the activity involves another person. The interplay of your mutual gaze, your attentiveness as you tune in to each other, the curiosity, empathy and responses that fly between you create and support a special connection. When there's interpersonal chemistry,[27] something magical happens: a blossoming of openness and trust.

If you enjoy trusting, supportive relationships, you are more likely to be happier; the longest-running study on human happiness, conducted by Harvard University, revealed that close relationships are the key to happiness and health.[28] Your cardiovascular, endocrine and immune systems will function better if you enjoy healthy relationships.[29] Enticing?

But Will They Listen to Me?

If I Deep Listen to someone else, are they more likely to listen to me? I'm repeatedly asked this question. As you've read, there are many powerful reasons to Deeply Listen aside from expecting it in return. Focusing on that question, indeed, may actually get in the way of your authentic listening, leading you to become too goal-orientated and transactional, clinging to a 'my turn/your turn' rigid framework. It's easy to understand, however, why people ask this question. It feels unbalanced if it's only you always doing the listening, bearing the emotional load, with your partner or friend doing all the talking. When do you get your chance to relate what's on *your* mind, to give *your* side of the story?

Let's look at the evidence for reciprocal listening. While I haven't yet found research that directly addresses this question, experiments do show a relationship between how you respond to someone else and how they respond to you in return. When my friend Amy, for example, feels that I listen to her well, she's more likely to share her innermost emotions and thoughts with me, and I in turn am more likely to want to be similarly open with her. And if Amy feels truly listened to by me, she is more likely to care about my well-being.[30] When people feel listened to well, their *window of tolerance* is expanded, they're better able to cope with stress and emotional challenges, more able to hold your story in their head as well as their own.[31] And therefore more likely to be in a place to listen to you.

Tuning In at Work

In search of a successful leader who embodies authentic listening, I was introduced to Stephen Allen, who ran the media agency Mediacom that buys advertising around the world. The company boasts $30 billion in annual billings and 8,000 staff around the globe.

When I met Allen, he listened in a way that made me feel relaxed and open to share honestly, a trait he's been proud to develop over decades. When he stepped into the UK CEO role, Allen committed to spending his first month listening to every single company employee, some 200 people back then, for 30 minutes each. Allen's presence, filled with curiosity and a reassurance that nothing was out of bounds, encouraged his new employees to talk honestly about the most important aspects of their work. 'I couldn't believe the number of people, from junior people in the post room to senior leaders, who told me, "I want to learn."' At the time, learning and development were far from mainstream in the fast-paced advertising world. Staff came and went. Rapidly.

'We're not running a f***ing university!' replied a senior colleague, on hearing Allen's plans for a UK company-wide learning programme. Allen knew that the desire to learn was heartfelt and widespread. He stood his ground. 'I'm incredibly proud of how many of those people stayed working with me for 20 or 30 years because I cared about their development, unheard of in the ad business; that and the importance I've always placed on listening.'

Allen's listening leadership steered the company towards an impressive bottom line. He took on the helm of the global business and built Mediacom into one of the world's four largest media agencies.[32]

Allen's hunch that listening impacts on financial performance is supported by research. In the world of injection-moulding factories, one experiment unveiled that when employees were trained to listen attentively to each other, ensuring that they felt heard and understood, the factory was transformed into a well-oiled machine of productivity. Sales went up and profits increased, compared to similar factories where business carried on as usual, without the secret ingredient of listening training.[33]

If employees are listened to well, other research reveals, they form stronger bonds with their colleagues, and feel respected and valued. And employees who feel genuinely heard by their boss are more likely to feel committed and motivated[34] – gold dust for any employer. However, studies also show that some managers are reluctant to be labelled as good listeners, wary of dismantling what they see as an advantageous barrier between them and their subordinates.[35]

Over the last decade, despite these reservations, there's been a sea change, according to psychologist Adam Grant. He's found that many more leaders recognise that to succeed they can no longer rely solely on presenting their top-down vision.[36] The most effective leaders, he has observed, will sometimes start their meetings in a way that challenges decades of practice. They might begin: 'I want to know what other people think. The moment I disclose my opinion is the moment you will probably feel pressured to conform to it. And my opinion is going to change after listening and learning from the rest of you. Let's go around the room and hear from everybody else first.'

Indeed, 'transformational', 'effective' and 'considerate' are the kind of labels attached to people who are seen by colleagues as good listeners at work.[37] And, of course, a business gains from all that crowdsourced wisdom and insight. In one experiment, two teams, each with a leader, were competing to fold the most T-shirts in a 10-minute window. Extroverted leaders carried on with their own vision regardless of their team's ideas. Introverted leaders, in contrast, who were more open to listening to ideas from others, ended up finding out about a faster Japanese T-shirt folding method, thus winning the game.[38]

You may have heard colleagues say, 'I feel emotionally drained from my work' or 'I feel frustrated with my job.' According to an experiment, such statements were *less* likely to be heard in the departments of a high-tech company who received high-quality listening training, compared to divisions who had no training.[39] When I ran Deep Listening workshops with BBC teams, colleagues found themselves opening up. Even though they may have worked together for years, even decades, in these Deep Listening conversations, they felt safe to be vulnerable. As a result, they learned things about their colleagues, personal stories and hidden dreams that allowed them to see the other person as a rounded three-dimensional human being, not just someone who existed to edit their story.

According to another study, nurses were less likely to be insulted or suffer humiliation and sexual harassment in a positive listening climate.[40] It's no surprise that without these harmful dynamics, the nurses' well-being improved.

All these studies into listening are important, but this area of study is still in its infancy. Helpfully, more research is now focused not just on the penalties of distraction, but on the impact of really good listening. Such listening can be critical to unlocking authentic narratives.

An Authentic Narrative

When people are listened to well, they are far more likely to listen to themselves with more care[41] and share a response that is more real, candid and heartfelt. As coach and author Nancy Kline observes, 'If I keep listening with deep interest in where you will go next, you will go next to places I could have never taken you. Places with far more magic and meaning and relevance.'[42] Garnering a more expansive, nuanced story opens the door to greater trust, stronger relationships and more insightful decision-making.

Stories are the currency of journalists, so I've been interested in exploring how Deep Listening can elicit more fulsome and authentic narratives. The case for keeping Deep Listening out of journalism rests on the assumption that there's an objective truth that a journalist needs to elicit, free of their relationship with the interviewee. There is indeed a need for basic facts to answer fundamental questions such as who said what, when and where. But journalists also focus on the perspectives, opinions and feelings of people, mediating between a speaker and an audience. The way a journalist 'shows up' – their manner, curiosity and empathy, all fundamental tenets of Deep Listening – have a huge impact on the authenticity and depth of the story that their interviewee shares.

Benefits: A Delicate Balance

It's motivating to recognise all these positive outcomes of Deep Listening. But these rewards can also cloud your ability to purely listen. If you are attached to outcomes, even the chance to be listened to yourself, this can distract you from being fully present with your speaker. When you Deeply Listen, you need to put these rewards out of your mind.

However, it's a different case when it comes to the bridging benefits that Deep Listening can bring to the world beyond. In an era where we increasingly isolate ourselves from those with different perspectives, the act of Deep Listening to a person who challenges our beliefs becomes not merely a personal undertaking that nourishes our relationship and us both, but also a profound act. When we open our minds (and our hearts) and truly listen to those whose opinions differ from our own, we can play a role in fostering a society less fractured by polarisation. These transformational but less personal outcomes can inspire you and propel your listening. They are the subject of our next chapter.

WHY THE WORLD NEEDS DEEP LISTENING

A Polarising World

The seismic force of polarisation is threatening the bedrock of society – that's the fear of many people across the world. Those living in the USA, Argentina, Colombia, South Africa, Spain and Sweden believe their country is severely polarised; others in the UK, France, Germany, Japan and Brazil fear their country is in danger of polarisation.[1] We pick sides. Where we stand has become central to our identity, especially on social media, where we vent about the alleged evils of the other side. In reducing others to symbols or ideologies, there's a sense that we've lost the confidence to engage across difference. This is particularly evident in the workplace, where leaders are grappling with the challenges posed by intergenerational differences; in several countries age has become one of the most prominent political dividing lines.[2] About one in four Americans avoid listening to people whose views they don't like, according to a poll carried out for this book, and disturbingly, among Generation Z, the proportion goes up to one in three.[3]

When you look closer, however, the data on polarisation points to a more nuanced picture. Between the extreme and often elite voices who hog the limelight with their clashing convictions lies an overlooked 'Exhausted Majority',[4] a phrase coined to describe people fed up with polarisation who want to move past their differences – even in the polarised USA. Other statistics point to a more tolerant attitude towards 'others'. For example, in the UK only one in 20 people now say they wouldn't want an immigrant as a neighbour, a proportion that has sharply declined over the last 20 years, among all age groups.[5] In addition, rather than being split into two opposing camps, opinion in many countries is better described as a shifting kaleidoscope of views. The coloured fragments of glass are reassembled each time the cylinder is shaken, whenever a new issue comes to the fore.[6]

That said, you can't underestimate the fears people have about the impact of societal polarisation, from worsening prejudice and discrimination to slowing economic growth.[7] Polarisation also prevents us from coming together to tackle a host of existential threats that transcend borders, such as wars, pandemics and disinformation. Climate change is an area where genuine debate and real understanding are urgently needed, but in the USA and (to a lesser extent) in Britain and other countries, attitudes have become politicised and thus often polarised.

In some ways, we are psychologically hardwired for this sort of conflict. When attitudes harden, neuroscientist Jay Van Bavel and psychologist Dominic J. Packer write,[8] people begin to see their own interests as being fundamentally opposed to the aims of the other group. 'We start to think that we're not only good but that we're inherently good. And if that's true, then [our opponents] must be intrinsically bad and should be opposed at all costs.'

So, the risk is not just that you may hold very different opinions from others – *ideological polarisation* – but that you then tend to feel negatively about them all as a group – *affective polarisation*. If a society is affectively polarised, people see the group who thinks differently to them as unreasonable and closed-minded, driven by self-interest and ideology, resistant to hearing or recognising *the* truth[9] (meaning the truth that they hold dear). We think we are rational, but in these polarised contexts, we're often driven by judgements and emotions, highly sensitive to anything that looks like a threat to us or our in-group.

For many years, these fears blocked Lebanese teacher Hawraa Ibrahim Ghandour from listening to people in her town in southern Lebanon. She would ignore Muslim women who had unveiled themselves and Syrian refugees seeking sanctuary. For Ghandour, her judgements were a source of indignant pride.[10] 'A woman who has decided to unveil herself is doing something against my religion, and that is not acceptable. Syrians who live in my country are not taking care of their hygiene. Not living a proper Lebanese life.'

Ghandour grew up in a religious family. Her father was determined that she restrict her friendships to those who shared a parallel upbringing, and Ghandour carried those values, and those judgements, into adulthood. 'I could not communicate properly with these people. Maybe I didn't have the chance, or maybe I was just listening to what I hear in the media here, which often stigmatises foreigners and others who are different.'

Ghandour, like many of us, assumed that there was a fundamental difference between us and them. Coach Nancy Kline unpacks this assumption into what she calls core beliefs:

- Who I am is what I believe.
- I am entirely right and you are entirely wrong.
- My values are superior to yours.

- If I become interested in your views, I will have to adopt your values, and so I will stop being me; I will become an inferior person.[11]

These core beliefs are powerful, capable of keeping us swaddled in our separate cocoons, afraid that we will betray our deeper self. And because we feel threatened, when we do meet the 'other', we focus more on counter-arguments than on listening, and thus often leave the conversation more entrenched in our beliefs, our attitudes more extreme.[12]

Disputes within our own family and community can escalate into conflict, fracturing friendships and family ties. People can be left feeling isolated without a sense of belonging, so polarisation can feed into loneliness. A global study of more than 140 countries found that one in four adults felt lonely, with higher rates among young people.[13] When you are lonely, you're deprived of the comfort of being properly listened to, of feeling heard. Loneliness isn't just an emotional pain felt by individuals, it also damages our health. When people feel lonely, they are far more likely to suffer from depression, anxiety and an early death.[14]

It is not only individuals who are harmed; loneliness and alienation also carry political risks, tearing our connective tissue. When groups of people feel dismissed, they experience a loss of dignity and status, a sense of humiliation and shame. Individuals cut off from others yearn for a new way to make sense of the world, wrote Hannah Arendt in her seminal work, *The Origins of Totalitarianism*, and so are much more likely to be persuaded by the temptations of authoritarianism. 'Terror can rule absolutely only over men who are isolated against each other ... Isolation ... is [terror's] most fertile ground.'[15]

Deep Listening Can Inoculate Us

Polarisation is a serious problem. Loneliness is a threat to society and individuals. But through empowering us to have fulfilling encounters, both with those who think differently and those who think alike, Deep Listening can help inoculate us.

Of course, Deep Listening alone cannot solve complex conflicts. Nonetheless, through seeing beyond binary identities, through creating confidence in people with contrasting beliefs to reach out across the divide, through developing more understanding, we can build trust between individuals with conflicting agendas, within communities and between them.

Few settings experience more intensely conflicting agendas than a global climate summit. Christiana Figueres, who led the negotiations for the landmark 2015 Paris Climate Agreement, believes her own practice of what she also terms Deep Listening was pivotal: 'Had I not been practising deep listening, I never would have understood where 195 countries and thousands of stakeholders were coming from. I really wanted to know deeply what they were saying. I chalk up a lot of the Paris Accord to deep listening.'[16]

Figueres sums up her Deep Listening approach as 'pressing the elevator button to go down from the head to the heart, to have a far more powerful heart-to-heart exchange.'[17] She has found that such exchanges have the power to touch the common humanity between people, establishing a shared language of human aspiration. Once that level of trust had been established in the climate negotiations, both with the 500 people who were part of her UN team and with the myriad government representatives in capital cities across the world, Figueres was able to discuss potentially divisive questions.

In contrast, I have found that some people engaged in climate-related work, who are purportedly keen to engage across the climate divide, aren't genuinely listening to people who think differently from them. One philanthropist, who funds programmes to encourage activists to start up conversations about climate, acknowledged to me, 'It's true. We're not really listening. We are stuck in broadcast mode.'

Truly listening to individuals who challenge us with alternative viewpoints whatever the issue, whether or not we are right, is important. As writer and Nobel laureate Wole Soyinka put it to me, it's a hallmark of a fully formed social being. I value Soyinka's insight: listening across the divide is a way of being that we can aspire towards as individuals, and as a society. Encouragingly, when we asked people in England, Scotland and Wales why they might want to learn to listen better, the primary reason they cited was to understand people with different views, a significantly more popular motivation than learning to listen without interrupting, or to be a better friend or even to perform better at work.[18]

I was able to witness first-hand this recognition of competing perspectives in a society under fierce geopolitical pressure.

Feelings were running high in the Baltic state of Latvia just nine months following Russia's full-scale invasion of Ukraine in 2022. Three decades after freeing themselves from Soviet occupation, Latvians feared that Russian troops might reinvade at any moment. And the perceived threat came not only from outside. A third of Latvians speak Russian at home,[19] and these Russian speakers were widely suspected of having split loyalties. The British Council wanted to find ways to help tackle this divide and invited me to Latvia to train people in Deep

Listening, both in the capital, Riga, and the mainly Russian-speaking town of Daugavpils, only 75 miles from the Russian border. It was an opportunity to work with people from both communities together so they could practise with a participant from the 'other side'. After the course, one Russian-speaking participant, Ilona Ustinova, who works in the Daugavpils city education department, reflected on her experience:

'When you Deeply Listen and enable a person to feel safe, they start to trust you and express their deeper feelings. So even in Daugavpils, a city with Latvian, Russian and Polish people, I've ended up having much more profound conversations, for example with people who feel very differently about the war in Ukraine. I used to try to persuade others and now I try harder to understand. Each person has their own story and I've learned to respect that.'

Through practising Deep Listening in an environment defined by tension and suspicion, Ustinova has become aware of her own pre-judgements and prejudices, so she can see beyond them. Knowing a listener is not there to judge or criticise them enables a speaker to feel safe and accepted when they feared they might be threatened or rejected. This understanding becomes the key to unlocking people's capacity to reflect on their own prejudices. As psychologist Carl Rogers wrote: 'In this atmosphere of safety, protection, and acceptance, the firm boundaries of self-organization relax. There is no longer the firm, tight gestalt [whole] which is characteristic of every organization under threat, but a looser, more uncertain configuration … his self-structure is now sufficiently relaxed so that he can [discover] … experiences of which he has never been aware, which are deeply contradictory to the perception he has had of himself.'[20]

Multiple Perspectives

Rogers' point reflects the transformational development that takes place in people who are truly heard. They shift from an autocracy in their head – there's only room for one idea, their own – to an understanding that two perspectives can co-exist – a democracy.[21,22]

Someone who feels less defensive and more able to see both sides of an argument will also be more likely to dial down the strength of their beliefs. This is not a new insight. In 13th-century Japan, Buddhist monk and poet Dōgen Zenji wrote: 'When you say something to someone, he may not accept it, but do not try to make him understand it intellectually. Do not argue with him; just listen to his objections until he himself finds something wrong with them.'[23]

More than seven centuries later, there is now compelling evidence that high-quality listening can enable a speaker to escape from the narrow confines of a fixed perspective. Research has revealed that when speakers are really listened to as they discuss controversial subjects – be it taxing junk food or euthanasia – they become less defensive and soften their attitudes, what's known as dialling down their *attitude extremity*. They no longer feel torn about holding contradictory ideas.[24]

Listening Does Not Signal Approval

The fear that listening to someone with opposing views might signal your agreement can present a significant barrier to listening across divides. In a poll carried out for this book, one in five Americans shared this concern. This worry presents an even greater barrier for young people; Generation Z are twice as likely as older generations to fear that others will assume that they agree if they listen.[25] When I train people, I've noticed an 'aha' moment as they grasp this critical insight: Deeply Listening to someone you clash with does not signal that you share their belief. It does not mean you approve.

Freed from the shackles of this limiting belief, you can open yourself up to your speaker, even if you are worlds apart. You can become truly curious to understand why another person has come to believe these 'abhorrent' ideas, without the risk of being contaminated by them. Instead of fearing a member of an out-group, who should be opposed at all costs, you start to see the humanity in this fellow human being. A South African participant of my Deep Listening global project, Pumulo Ngoma, experienced this way of looking at the world for herself. During the programme, she practised Deep Listening with someone from the Caribbean who believed that we should all be vegetarian. South Africa is well known for its meat-loving culture, and Ngoma often delights in marinated steak and local boerewors sausages around a barbecue, or *braai*, as it's known in her country. Although she was primed to open up to alternative beliefs, Ngoma heard something that shocked her.

'My conversation partner shared how her uncle had a heart attack due to a high meat and fat content diet. I instantly softened. Felt almost out of my body. I was caught off guard. I saw her as a human being with a story rather than someone to win an argument with.'[26]

I saw her as a human being. This is a powerful reflection. When we *other* others, we make them less than human. Deep Listening restores this dignity to the others already in your life and those you are yet to encounter.

With all the positive feedback about the programme, I was taken aback to read this reaction from Yalda, a participant from Iran: 'I think being a Deep Listener just works in democratic countries. In Iran it's rubbish. The government wants to kill us and arrest my people just because of a post on social media. I hate them. I feel so angry I could even kill the government officers, although I would never do that. I'm full of anger and revenge. Sorry to disappoint you.'

When I reached out to Yalda, who has now left Iran to work as a doctor abroad, she cried as she told me that she so wished she could Deeply Listen to those who support the Iranian regime. But until they are ready to listen to her, until she can open up and speak freely about what is inside her heart, she's in no place to listen to them. She makes an important point:

where the listener has no power, or people are caught in the midst of conflict or trauma, Deep Listening might *not* be the right approach. (More about when not to listen and where to draw the line when you decide whom to listen to in Part Three.)

While people with the most extreme views may not be open to learning to Deeply Listen, others who are at risk of adopting such beliefs might still be receptive. Especially if they understand that practising Deep Listening can help them succeed at work, and improve their relationships with their partner, children and parents.

One woman who was open to learning about a new way to look at the world was Lebanese teacher Hawraa Ibrahim Ghandour, who we met earlier. 'I was plagued by fanaticism and intolerance,' she now says, looking back at her pre-Deep Listening days. Through listening and being listened to by strangers from across the world during the programme, she started to question her assumptions. Every morning, Ghandour now shares her first coffee with a new friend, a refugee nurse from Syria. She spends every Tuesday afternoon teaching teenage Syrian immigrants. The way Ghandour sees it, Deep Listening is a glimpse of light that has expanded her horizons, allowing her to see her judgements afresh and learn from others.[27]

With the experience of having these conversations, and the knowledge that they have gained, people like Ghandour are more likely to take a vested interest in the health and welfare of those who live beyond their echo chambers, which is essential for a healthy democracy to thrive. In addition, bringing Deep Listening to disaffected individuals and communities can help increase feelings of belonging and strengthen ties across groups. Deep Listening can fertilise the soil so healthier societies can flourish.

Unlock a More Inclusive World

Social cohesion is nurtured when authentic insights from a wide range of communities, generated by profound listening, inform debate and public policies. Creating the space for those with less power to speak, however, is not the same as delivering on their needs. Indeed, research has indicated that speakers also judge listeners on whether they have followed up and acted upon their wishes.[28] But listening and identifying authentic needs is a necessary first step, and in itself demonstrates respect.

Listening becomes an even more powerful tool for creating change when it is directed towards communities and groups that have historically been silenced or ignored because of their race, caste or gender. 'To be female is to be interrupted,' wrote columnist Renée Graham.[29] Women are listened to less and are far more likely to be interrupted than men, many studies have confirmed.[30] Another group of researchers has shown that people who do not belong to Black, Indigenous or other minority groups frequently fail to truly listen to and understand the perspectives of those who do.[31]

My experience of meeting someone from a specific community who is often not heard, quite literally, serves to highlight what might be possible if society Deeply Listened to voices that have traditionally been marginalised. At a meeting about a Deep Listening event, Reece Waldron, who has a strong stutter, presented research findings. I was surprised to learn that he shares his condition with some 80 million people around the world.[32] During the tea break, Waldron explained to me that there's now a growing recognition of the role that the listener plays in enabling or stifling the expression of a person who stutters, and that 'it takes two to stammer'. If listeners slow down, stop interrupting stuttering voices and avoid finishing their sentences for them, stammerers can leave the interaction feeling heard and fulfilled rather than frustrated and tired.

While not everyone may have the opportunity to learn Deep Listening directly, there may be other ways to spread this approach, such as through the power of social contagion.

Contagious Listening

Social contagion is the idea that your habits, whether or not you smoke, for example, will naturally influence your friends to change their behaviour, which will, in turn, influence others in your friends' networks. Like other behaviours, good listening may well be contagious.[33] Yale Professor Nicholas Christakis has demonstrated through many experiments that positive behaviour is socially contagious.[34] While he hasn't specifically researched my approach, he has pointed to an abundance of social contagion research that closely aligns with the core principles of Deep Listening. He has conducted experiments, for example, that show how acts of kindness and generosity can spread through social networks, creating a ripple effect that encourages others to pay it forward. If I'm kind or generous to you, you'll be more likely to extend that kindness and generosity to the next person, and they to the next. Altruistic impulses can spread even to pockets of people who were previously resistant.[35]

When people have experienced the transformational effects of being Deeply Listened to, they may be better empowered and feel more motivated to offer this opportunity to others – both to the person who has listened to them and also to those in their own community and those outside. If they set the tone of an interaction, this pattern of listening can ripple out beyond their immediate circle. Those who are leaders can have a marked impact. When she negotiated on behalf of the United Nations, Christiana Figueres never discussed her listening approach with anybody. But it was more contagious, she believes, by being practised rather than preached.

'If I bring it into my presence, my way of walking into a room, my way of interacting with people, there's a powerful transformation that happens. I may be aware of it, even if others are not, but in any case, they are touched by it.'[36]

Training teachers to Deeply Listen also presents an opportunity, so they can share the learning with their students to achieve scale. As young people's values and behaviour are in a state of extreme flux, it's a golden window to encourage them to experience the relationship-strengthening advantages of high-quality listening. University students, too, stand to benefit from learning how to listen in this more profound way, giving them the confidence and tools to engage in discussions with fellow students who challenge their own beliefs.[37] Scaling Deep Listening can create a culture change in which we acknowledge people's right to be heard and try our best to listen to them (though not to everyone and not all the time).

A Right to Be Listened to

Speaking and listening are both essential acts of citizenship. There's rightly an increased emphasis on oracy skills at school, but speaking without anyone listening is like talking into a void. Recognising people's right to be listened to is a necessary complement to recognising their right to be heard.

Acknowledging this right also means affirming the worth of everyday voices that so often get muted. When we refuse to listen, we refuse to know. Deep Listening can uncover fresh knowledge and new ideas that can inspire us to tackle entrenched problems and transcend boundaries. But Deep Listening cannot be enforced. We also need to protect solitude: we don't automatically have the right to spout our ideas to any passer-by, if the passer-by doesn't want to listen. As listening needs to be authentic, people need to be ready and open to hearing someone else's story. By cultivating a culture that respects the autonomy of both speakers and listeners, we create space for genuine understanding.

In the world, we build too many walls and not enough bridges. Deep Listening is a bridge across which we can walk to create a culture of understanding, nurture co-existence and build societies more resilient to the pressures of polarisation, with people more deeply connected. With an understanding of the ways in which Deep Listening can enrich you and others in your community and beyond, how can you put these insights into practice? We turn now to the eight-step journey. The journey begins with step one, creating an ideal listening environment.

PART TWO

HOW TO DEEPLY LISTEN

STEP ONE:
CREATE SPACE

In a cold Belfast police station not long after the turn of the millennium, 13- and 14-year-olds were trying on bulletproof vests. These members of a local youth club were here at the invitation of the Police Service of Northern Ireland, who were brandishing their weapons. It was just a few years after the signing of the Good Friday Agreement, designed to end the conflict, but tension was still high – rioting and shootings were commonplace. Even the football team on your T-shirt could mark you out as a threat. Lives were at stake.

The police knew that they needed to encourage a more cooperative relationship with the teenagers, so they reached out to local peace worker and youth leader Paul Smyth. Smyth accepted the invitation, recognising that it was critical that the police and these young people started to listen to and humanise each other.[1]

In the police station, the teens' eyes widened with the thrill of the uniforms and the deadly equipment, but for them the fortress-like station was also a place of dread. Many of these young people had been harassed or even arrested by these same police officers. Police in uniform were intimidating, especially when they towered over you. The cops were always calling you out just for gathering with your mates, eyeing you suspiciously like you were about to cause trouble.

The intention was good, but it wasn't working. The young people would never let down their guard in a police station. The setting was all wrong. Smyth realised that they needed to rethink. He invited the police to abandon their militarised comfort zone and step into a youth club, a far more intimidating space for them. With high-ranking officers and the deputy chief constable among their ranks, there were real risks for the police in entering the club, so they stationed a police unit nearby, ready to respond to any threat of violence.

Perched on the club's scruffy sofas, surrounded by torn peace posters and hand-painted murals of a New York skyline, the police shifted awkwardly. A few sat uncomfortably on bean bags strewn around the floor, like parents in children's chairs at a school parents' evening. The power shifted. The teens moved through the space with ease, settling into their favourite spots, where they sprawled out their limbs. One young man, then others, removed their hoodies. Eventually, some members of the youth club felt comfortable enough to speak out.

'There's no difference between the police and the paramilitaries. Both are out to get us. Both need to be avoided.'

In their own familiar surroundings, the young people were also more ready to understand what it was like to police such a hostile environment. Here, the teenagers learned about police fears – needing to always check under their cars for hidden explosives and being forced to change their route to work to avoid the threat of bullets.

Smyth was ideally placed to be sensitive to the environment. He had grown up in Belfast in a working-class community racked by atrocities and intimidation, bombings and street violence. When British soldiers, police and paramilitaries provoked fear, hate and bitterness, he sought an alternative path. Through taking part in local peace projects since his teenage years, he'd learned how to listen to people with whom he fiercely disagreed.

Twenty years later, Smyth's life still revolves around young people and peacemaking. I was in Belfast to run a Deep Listening workshop with colleagues in the BBC Belfast office, so I went to see Smyth in the centre of the city in his attic office in Mediation House. Smyth told me that he credited the change of scene – from police station to youth club – and the authentic understanding which emerged from it as critical to the growing acceptance of the police by the community, one of the more successful outcomes of the Northern Ireland peace process.

This step explores what you can do to create an environment for listening in which your speaker feels comfortable and safe. We begin with the psychological. Your role is to establish a space in which your speaker feels secure enough to open up and speak authentically, as the teenagers felt able to do in their own club.

The Psychological Realm

A Place of Safety – Not a Landscape of Fear

An unthreatening environment is the bare minimum for any meaningful encounter in order that honest thoughts can flow freely. If you work in a glass office, for example, and need to listen to a team member explain why they failed to meet an important deadline, find somewhere private so your conversation is not on open display. You might not know of a speaker's sensitivities, but be aware of the potential for certain locations or situations to trigger them. Embarrassment and shame are powerful. Try to imagine how the world looks through your speaker's eyes; what feels safe and what feels sinister are highly dependent upon *their* context.

Walk through a space prior to an important dialogue to check if it is suitable for listening. You can take the emotional temperature and ask yourself: How is the speaker going to experience the space? Will this space encourage Deep Listening?

It's a Jungle Out There

What happens if we don't feel safe?

Our bodies have evolved to react instinctively to any sense of danger.[2] While short-term stress may enhance your ability to make quick decisions and run fast, it also sabotages your capacity to think profoundly, or speak coherently,[3] as stress distorts the workings of your prefrontal cortex, the seat of higher-order thinking.[4] When coming face to face with an angry tiger, or an intimidating neighbour who demands to know why you were so noisy last night, you are primed to react with fight or flight; you run away or become defensive or aggressive.

In the business world, when staff feel unsafe, studies have identified that teamwork, creativity and productivity are stifled.[5] Harvard Business School Professor Amy Edmondson has spent a quarter of a century learning how to catalyse organisations in which people feel safe. Not surprisingly, people feel more encouraged to speak up when things go wrong if they know they'll be openly listened to. Edmondson characterises psychological safety as an environment in which people can express themselves openly, comfortable that they won't be punished or humiliated[6] – essential in a Deep Listening environment.

And if a speaker perceives you, the listener, as a safe rather than threatening presence, they will feel calmer. Their parasympathetic nervous system – responsible for resting, digesting and restoring – kicks in, sending messages from their brain through their central nervous system and the powerful vagus nerve, steadying their heart rate.[7]

When I was visiting peace worker Paul Smyth in Belfast, and sipping peppermint tea from a handcrafted earthenware mug, I reflected on how his cosy attic office, infused with his kind presence, encouraged me to feel comfortable and safe despite the dark December night. However, someone in a listening role can deliberately create a relaxed atmosphere to foster a false sense of security which can then be exploited. So, the onus is also on you, the listener, not to misuse a safe space that you have established to pressurise or seduce someone (literally or figuratively) or to lower someone's guard to exert influence inappropriately.

Safe or Threat? First Impressions

People form impressions quickly, often in under a twentieth of a second.[8] As a listener, you must move fast to establish an environment of safety and connection. The photographer Platon is known for his images of world leaders and celebrities ranging from Presidents Bill Clinton to Donald Trump to the boxer Muhammed Ali, as well as human rights campaigners. Such people are often pressed for time, so Platon needs to forge a genuine connection quickly, one that is able to cut through any power dynamic. 'If I'm in the room with a person,' he told me, 'unless they've got a gun to my head, we're equal.'

Platon describes his technique as tuning in to his sitter's frequency, like adjusting the dial of an old radio. While some stations have a very good frequency, as the individual embodies a spirit of collaboration, with others it's faint, and the slightest move can mean he loses the signal. With total focus, Platon uses all his powers of observation. He focuses on someone's eyelash and tunes in to their breathing pattern. He can't touch their hand to feel their pulse, but he's still reading their pulse. 'I need that level of intimacy to tune in to someone's humanity,' he tells me.

Creating that trust is doubly important if Platon has serious reservations about his subject. The photographer recalled being invited to photograph Russian President Vladimir Putin on a winter evening in 2007. Putin's soldiers were watching his every move, in a way that seemed designed to intimidate him. But the photographer had an ace up his sleeve, the fruit of careful preparation. Platon had watched multiple videos of the Russian leader. Most of the footage showed Putin projecting a spirit of toughness: shirt-off, Rambo-esque, black belt. But one video caught an unusual moment: the president smiling as he watched Paul McCartney perform in Red Square. Before Platon pressed the shutter, he spoke up.

'Mr President, before we begin, I have a question for you. I'm a massive Beatles fan. Are you?' Putin's translators shared confused looks with his entourage of advisors. In Russian, Putin ordered the translators and all his advisors out of the room, with just his bodyguards remaining. Putin then turned to Platon and in perfect English replied, 'I love the Beatles.'

In that moment, trust was created, allowing Platon to move his lens an inch and a half from Putin's nose. 'I could feel his breath on my hand as I focused. He did whatever I wanted after that.' Platon has nurtured close friendships with many of the Russian leader's fiercest critics, so it's a strange source of satisfaction for the photographer that the Russian president liked that picture, that it's apparently hanging up in his office.

Consider, as Platon did, how you can create a genuine connection so that your speaker feels recognised in their entirety. And become aware of any anxieties you may be wrestling with. Try to find a way to settle these feelings by accepting them; this acceptance will help to make your speaker feel welcome and comfortable.

Framing and Contracting

By contrast, a speaker can become anxious if they feel uncertain about the answers to certain vital questions: How long will this conversation last? Will what I say be kept confidential? If not, will I be identified by name?

If you have initiated a conversation with someone at work, especially if they have less power than you, it's important to be transparent at the outset about the purpose of the meeting, whether your chat is a social one, an opportunity to explore, or part of a formal process. If your speaker shares needs, requests or complaints, they may assume that you will be able to do something to satisfy them, or at least try. They need to know. You also need to be aware that when you Deeply Listen, your speaker may venture into emotional territory that they ordinarily wouldn't feel comfortable sharing in your presence. They need to have a choice and give consent to the conversation taking a different turn. In coaching as well as mediation, counselling and therapy, being explicit about ground rules is called *contracting*.

It is essential to let people know what to expect before a conversation, believes Peter Coleman, director of the Difficult Conversations Lab at Columbia University. Coleman facilitates and studies encounters between people with starkly opposing views on morally polarising questions, such as *Do you agree with abortion? Free speech on college campuses? Donald Trump?*[9] Without listening guidance or facilitation, he argues, both sides are more likely to leave an encounter more estranged, with their attitudes more extreme. How does Coleman set up these difficult conversations? He clarifies what the participants aren't expected to do: to love or forgive people on the other side. And he provides a more complex framing of the issue – setting up, for example, several of the interrelated dilemmas associated with abortion rather a simple for or against.[10]

Think about who speaks first. In the encounter that I witnessed between President Nelson Mandela and his soldiers, he subverted the conventional power dynamic by first listening to them before requesting that they return to their barracks. Letting the other person speak first can be especially impactful if you have more authority than they do, or if you are enmeshed in a conflict with them or are guarding competing grievances.

Primed for Sharing

Organising regular times to listen in an important relationship can help set the right conditions so you are both prepared to open up. When our children were small, either my husband or I gave them what we called a *whisper* each evening as they were tucked up in bed. A whisper was 10 minutes in which each child had the power to set the agenda; a huge contrast with our incessant daytime demands that they put their shoes on for school, speed up so we wouldn't be late, or hang their coats on the peg.

The whispers evolved organically to give each of our children individual attention. As our children shared a small room, we kept our voices low, so that the conversation wouldn't seep across to their sibling. By defining a regular listening time and a framework with the guarantee of a focused parental ear, they were primed for sharing. And the children talked about whatever they felt was important, from the excitement and fear of our son's stuffed animal, Sheepie, ahead of his first sleepover, to a worm our daughter had found and named Rosie. These were intimate moments where they felt in control and which we all treasured. I still hear the echo of the plaintive reproach of one of their singsong voices if we had inadvertently forgotten a bedtime listening session: 'I haven't had my whisper.'

The Physical Realm

Creating Comfort, Physically

Although we've never met before, I know when David Ole Lesinko has arrived at the Artcaffé in Nairobi, Kenya. Over his smart jeans and brushed cotton shirt, Maasai beads of yellow, sky blue and burnt orange crisscross his chest and encircle his neck. As soon as I mention my research on listening, Lesinko recounts how listening unfolds in his family home. In the rural serenity of his Maasai community, there's only one way in which people share important news: they sit together under the commanding acacia thorn tree to speak and listen. Under the acacia, there is no echo. Under the acacia, all is still. Under the acacia, it is the perfect place to hear. David explains that back home, everyone listens with intense focus. They have no choice, as in Maasai land, there is no second chance to listen.

'When we discuss how our cows will be treated, and you don't understand that we are vaccinating the livestock tomorrow at 9a.m., you can't check a WhatsApp group or call someone. If you fail to really listen, everything will have passed.'

I can sense the pride Lesinko takes in the undistracted listening that his community practises in their rural landscape. But four hours and a world away from the intense serenity of Lesinko's tree, I have to keep asking him to repeat his words. It's not just the cacophony of voices ricocheting off the café's huge glass windows, there's also a noisy traffic junction outside. The gurgling liquid and whistling steam of the coffee machine distorts our voices. I feel frustrated trying to hear Lesinko in that café, and wish we were meeting under the acacia branches.

I am curious to learn more about what sort of places create the best listening environment.

Testing Perfect Spaces

Back home in London, I arrange a visit to an institution called the Person Environment Activity Research Laboratory. PEARL operates from a giant hangar-like structure in the east of the city, part of University College London. Covering an area that stretches the size of a football field, the expansive space allows the PEARL team to simulate real-life environments, such as city streets and train stations. The team tests how, for example, a person's behaviour at a bus stop changes as they tweak the acoustics, temperature or smell.

When I arrive, PEARL's director, Nick Tyler, greets me at reception. His shoulder-length mane of white hair that radiates in multiple angles and his contagious enthusiasm reminds me of the scientist Doc Brown in the *Back to the Future* film. Tyler's ambition at PEARL is indeed futuristic: to create a world where he and his team can design and test environments to create the perfect spaces for humans.

Perfectly Tuned

I don't need Tyler's human environment test centre to appreciate that the Nairobi café was not the ideal place for a profound listening encounter. But he explains that it was the high-frequency feedback from the aggressively rebounding sound waves that was so distracting, alongside the mirrored frequency of Lesinko's voice with the speech of other café visitors. Had I chosen a luxurious restaurant in which to meet, the fabric tablecloths and flowing curtains would have improved our acoustic experience, absorbing the chattering of fellow diners. Our conversation would have felt more effortless and intimate – though less comfortable for my wallet. Then one of Tyler's colleagues adjusts the acoustics in the giant hangar, instantly killing all the ambient noise to create a space with zero echo. It feels unnatural and uncomfortably intimate, as if Tyler is standing only millimetres from my ear, though we are still a few feet apart. So, I wondered, what does an ideal listening space look like?

Tyler bounds up the stairs to where he has built a more intimate room, *The Nest*. Here, staff are encouraged to relax and have cosy conversations. There's a deep, fluffy sound-absorbing carpet and wood panelling to create soft echoes. Wood, I'm told, creates a goldilocks sound environment – the amount of echo is just right. The possibility that others may overhear your conversation can be enough to instil a sense of unease, so this sealed-off cocoon is important for those delicate *tête-à-têtes*. But Tyler isn't happy with the lighting. 'It's on an automatic switch with too much white and blue,' he says with a sigh.

A Dimmer View of Lighting

Fine-tuning the lighting can play a significant role in creating a welcoming listening space. Different lighting conditions can reassure your speaker or put them on alert. In many environments, you can make small adjustments, like dimming ceiling lights and turning on a side lamp or reflecting light off a ceiling or wall. This indirect light is more similar to what we've evolved to feel comfortable with: sunlight diffused over millions of miles. Harsh overhead lighting also makes it harder to read a person's expression, as bright light from above bleaches and flattens out their micro-gestures. Colour is important, too. The clinical bluish-white light, the sort you see in schools or offices, is functional, Tyler explains, but can put people on edge. It's better to install a yellow-pink light bulb with longer wavelengths to create a relaxed atmosphere.

As Tyler and I talk, I'm reminded of the day I arrived in a room in University College Hospital in London to give birth to my eldest. Though lighting was the last thing on my mind, the midwife had a bright idea. She switched off the harsh institutional strip light running across the ceiling and put on the softer glowing yellow light above the baby incubator. Instantly, the hospital room felt more humane. I became a person, not just a patient. I felt safe and more relaxed, so I could focus inwards and manage the long night.

Tyler and his team have also researched the best angles for benches and public seating more likely to promote interactions between strangers. The answer: a relaxed smile of a bench. Sitting, or standing, at an angle of 60 degrees is ideal, he's concluded. Two people can properly see each other, without feeling like the other person is face to face, ready for a fight (or a kiss).

And how far apart should you be? Tyler explains that between 40 centimetres and 1.2 metres is ideal. If we are less than 40 centimetres from each other, most people feel it is too intimate. Beyond a metre or so, we have to raise our voice to be heard, requiring more oxygen and thereby forcing sentences to be shorter, distorting our ability to speak thoughtfully or Deeply Listen.

Avoiding Digital Disconnect

Virtual conversations create unique challenges, with 'Zoom fatigue' taxing our physical and mental energy.[11] There's a time lag between someone speaking and you hearing them when you listen virtually. When you're not in sync, you don't feel close or connected. Not being able to look each other in the eye is also disruptive, as eye contact is vital to building a connection (more to come in Step Five: Hold the Gaze). Without seeing eye to eye, the speaker fears that you are disengaged and uninterested – are their ideas that irrelevant?

I have found it helpful to draw an eye, cut out a small hole in the pupil, and fix this around my laptop camera. This paper eye prompts me to keep my eyes on the tiny laptop camera lens, so my speaker feels that I am listening to them. I also hide my own image from the screen, avoiding a potential source of distraction.

When you can't use targeted smiles and body language, as you can in real life, on a group virtual call, there are other ways to make people feel included and valued. If psychologist Adam Grant notices virtual participants holding back and staying quiet, he makes a point of sending them a private message. 'Hey, I'd really love to hear your voice. I want to make sure that no one is deprived of learning from your perspective. What can I do to make it easier for you to speak up?'[12] Such messages can make the environment more welcoming, so that reticent people feel more confident.

For Comfort and Ease

As you draw up your plan for a successful listening encounter, don't forget to watch the clock (not literally, of course). The mood of both you and your speaker will vary dramatically over the course of the day. One startling piece of evidence I came across was an analysis of the rulings of a parole board.[13] The study found that the judges were far more amenable to prisoners' requests at the start of the day, granting a prisoner parole or agreeing that they could move to a different prison in two-thirds of cases, but this figure steadily declined throughout the morning to nearly zero before lunch. The favourable judgements spiked up again in the early afternoon, after the judges had taken a rest and received a glucose hit on their lunch break. So, when you and your speaker are rested and fed is when you're more likely to be ready to talk and listen. In addition, be mindful of the time available before embarking on a Deep Listening exchange; being cut off can leave your speaker feeling shut down.

Think about your speaker's physical condition, and your own. Perhaps your speaker is elderly, or has limited energy. If so, cushioned seating can make them more comfortable. Those hard-edged, echoey spaces can be daunting if either of you struggles with hearing. For those who rely on lip-reading, good lighting can open up the possibility of a real exchange. If your speaker is on the autism spectrum, turn down bright lights, ensure the environment isn't too noisy, avoid wearing perfume and plan breaks.[14]

If you are listening to a group of people, arrange them in a circle. Their spatial equality promotes the sense that everyone has an equal right to be heard. During negotiations over the 2015 Paris Climate Accord, UN Diplomat Christiana Figueres strategically placed the most critical negotiations in rooms where the furniture could be more easily moved from the standard lecture theatre style, all facing forward, so she could seat people in a square if not a circle.[15]

Beyond these physical and psychological adjustments, what else can you do to establish surroundings where imaginative thinking and more meaningful connections can emerge?

Spaces to Inspire

If your speaker senses that you have made a special effort to make them feel cherished, this can signal your respect far more powerfully than words. When it comes to creating a bespoke conversational setting, the Japanese tea ceremony has few parallels; the thought, intention and attention given to guests are taken to the most extraordinary heights. I experienced this myself when I was invited into the Tokyo family home of Machiko Hoshina.

When I arrive, Hoshina is dusting the ceramic tea bowls with a silk cloth and a carefully choreographed sweep of her elbow, purifying these utensils for me. As Hoshina performs these preparations with meticulous care, she asks herself, 'Am I ready to prepare good tea for my guests?' She checks, 'Am I being present?' Or perhaps, 'Am I ready for Deep Listening?' Hoshina gracefully tucks her white-clothed feet behind her to support the folds of her blue speckled kimono, carefully placing a leaf, just plucked from the balcony, on the fresh water container.

The ceremony is infused with a Zen Buddhist philosophy[16] and this preparatory act represents a symbolic cleansing of Hoshina's heart, preparing a clear, centred self to receive her visitor. Like her mother before her, Hoshina is a certified tea ceremony practitioner. Many of her ancestors were samurai warriors, entertaining other visiting warlords with tea. Over many centuries, the ceremony became a way to frame important encounters. The Japanese prime minister's wife, Mrs Kishida Yuko, hosted a tea ceremony for US President Joe Biden during his 2023 visit to Japan for the G7 summit. According to the Japanese minister of foreign affairs, following the ceremony, the two leaders felt able to discuss their backgrounds and their families.[17]

A Ritual of Care

Before she prepares the tea, Hoshina explains the ceremony's guiding principle: every encounter is a once-in-a-lifetime opportunity. This is conveyed by the Japanese phrase *ichigo ichie*, which translates as 'one time, one meeting'. Ichigo ichie echoes Lesinko's description of listening among the Maasai; his community is also aware that there may never be another chance to learn, should they fail to acquire the knowledge spoken under the tree.

Believing your encounter is a once-in-a-lifetime exchange can transform a mundane, routine chat into something meaningful and memorable. It is possible to demonstrate, with your choice of mug, or what you wear, for example, your intense care for your speaker, signalling that this encounter is unique and deserves your heightened attention.

In the refined atmosphere of her traditional Japanese tea ceremony room, I ask Hoshina how she brings the spirit of this carefully tuned choreography into the messiness of modern family life. She pauses before making a confession: 'If I don't put in a special effort, I drink a gulp of coffee and check my smartphone. Even if we're all in the same room, we often face different directions, so there's no communication through our hearts. We are physically together, but spiritually apart.'

As she reflects more, Hoshina remembers a time when she was able to draw upon the spirit of the tea ceremony to reach out to her middle daughter at a difficult time in the teenager's life. At that time, Hoshina's middle daughter had planned to lead her school's festival and perform with a band. Then, abruptly, the Covid-19 pandemic put a halt to her daughter's dreams, a fate shared by young people across the world. Typically upbeat and cheerful, Hoshina's daughter transformed into an unrecognisable teenager. She stopped eating. No eye contact. Hoshina spent hours creating deliciously healthy meals. But these were rejected, as her daughter retreated into her room.

After months of worry and conflict, Hoshina decided to try another approach. Trading in the traditional tearoom where she usually holds tea ceremonies for their modern family kitchen, she began to purify a tea bowl with a silk cloth. Her daughter observed as Hoshina carefully frothed the matcha with her bamboo whisk, rotating the bowl slowly so the most beautiful design was pointed towards her offspring. Hoshina held the bowl with both hands as a show of respect, in the tradition of her samurai ancestors: with all 10 fingers folding round the tea bowl, they couldn't also hold their sword. Hoshina was also disarmed by this act; she couldn't succumb to the temptation of reaching for her phone.

Hoshina saw her daughter's eyes light up when she bought her a special sweet bean treat that she knew she loved, made with chestnuts to reflect the autumn season. 'I remember it was the first time in ages that my daughter made a nice smile with her eyes and joined the circle with my other children. She ate the treat, enough for just one mouthful but rich enough to be satisfying.' Hoshina reflects that the ritual enabled her daughter to feel safe and protected; part of their family, part of their history. Many of us struggle with encouraging those closest to us to talk, especially when they are feeling down or in a crisis. Through this turbulent time, Hoshina was able to create a space in which her daughter felt able to share. 'She started to tell me about her frustrations with lockdown life. It was a breakthrough.'

The Japanese tea ceremony highlights the potential of applying creative attention to elevate day-to-day encounters when we Deeply Listen. And elevating a conversation need not be so complex. You can ask your speaker for their favourite piece of music and play it as a background for a challenging conversation. You may know without enquiring what's most likely to help your partner feel relaxed. Their favourite Adele track?

Nature's Soft Fascination

Talking and listening in the natural world can be extraordinarily potent in unlocking fresh perspectives and possibilities. It's the slow movements in nature – clouds drifting across the sky, leaves rippling on the trees – that are enough to distract us from spiralling rumination, self-blame and hopelessness, while leaving us enough bandwidth for reflection. Researchers call this capacity to hold our attention nature's *soft fascination*.[18] It's even more calming if you look at a lake, pool or stream.[19] In the natural world, we are able to lift up from the intense focus on ourselves and see our place within a larger system.[20] Even if you don't have easy access to wilderness or a park, you can be inspired by nature indoors, with houseplants and water features, or even through a window in a room or car.

Nobel Prize-winning playwright and poet Wole Soyinka told me that he grew up spending hours in his neighbourhood forest as a mindful place of refuge. He would climb up a tree where he could rest with his thoughts, undistracted. In his poem, *The Forest Bids You Welcome*, he describes their special powers:

Not even the gun's intrusive bark breaks a pact
Sealed since man learnt to milk Nature for his sustenance.
The hunter's breach soon heals, the woods' immensity
Resumes its understanding. Here is where all
Vanished languages of the world converge,
And speak a mono-tongue called Silence.
Each tree is warehouse, cradle and grave
Of earth's mythic beings. The gods keep guard
On soundless narratives from time immemorial.[21]

I feel moved by Soyinka's description of trees as spiritual warehouses, as keepers of soundless narratives, and as listeners. He shines a light on trees as listeners who can understand. Soyinka also evokes the power of nature to elevate us from everyday qualms into a timeless realm. I often found that taking a stroll around London's Regent's Park helped catalyse new insights for my coaching clients, and was a moment of release from the crowded BBC Headquarters in Portland Place, only minutes away. Even better, if you are able to look down from a hill at the far horizon, watching a landscape from a distance can encourage big-picture and values-driven reflections.

Listening on the Move

Professor Nick Tyler explains that a standard walking pace gives you a one-Hertz rhythm, one step per second, that feels comfortable and natural. Walking quicker than that introduces tension into your conversation and can lose the connection with your walking partner.

Going on a journey together can also encourage new reflections, opening up the possibility of leaving old thoughts behind. Like many parents, I found that going for a drive with my teenagers created a space for them to talk openly. In this context, the muted noise of the cars and traffic provided an obliging soundtrack, allowing my teens to speak and share on their own terms or to remain silent.

Playful Spaces

A truly transformative environment needs to be a place in which your speaker can create and share new ideas that they had never dared imagine. It seems fitting, then, to seek inspiration from an artist. *A safe space for stupidity* is how the South African artist William Kentridge describes his studio in Johannesburg. Kentridge believes that to make art he needs to create a safe space where an impulse, even a seemingly stupid one, will be given the benefit of the doubt, where he can 'learn the grammar' of what he is doing and 'see what it becomes'.

I meet Kentridge many miles away from his South African studio, in his high-ceilinged London flat overlooking the British Museum. One wall is entirely filled with playfully executed preliminary sketches in black and white – early impulses which have later become artworks exhibited in museums and galleries across the world. Kentridge hangs these impulses in his home, celebrating the significance of these early ideas before they have even taken shape. Some of his most famous works incorporate tentative sketches. Stupid, in Kentridge's mind, conveys a playful lightness, where the meaning may not be immediately apparent. 'Is it necessary to be stupid?' Kentridge asks. 'You say no, it is not necessary, but it may be essential.'

When I am coaching or Deep Listening to someone trying to make sense of their life, I try to create a space where they can be confident to take hesitant steps and create thoughts, however outlandish or impossible the ideas seem at first. This is a marked difference from interrupting, squashing their ideas before they have fully emerged. The safe environment for Deep Listening isn't, in Kentridge's words, 'a place that's being observed by an audience that says I want to see a finished object,' but a secure space where contradictory, confusing and improbable ideas can be conceived and shared.

* * *

At the end of a tea ceremony, all the bowls and other utensils are cleaned and returned to their original position and the area is brought back into emptiness, ready for another *ichigo ichie* encounter. The space will now be a blank canvas, free of the taint of any previous exchange. In all our Deep Listening exchanges, we too have the opportunity to put our previous disputes aside and begin afresh, as if for the first time. But in order to enter an encounter anew, ready to listen to someone else, we first need to listen to our own shadows. And that's the world we'll explore next – the one inside our own mind.

Create Space Takeaways

Find or create a place of safety | One where your speaker will feel free from any physical or psychological threat.

Contract to cultivate trust | Be transparent at the outset, clarify your intentions. Address how long the conversation is expected to last and what happens with any shared information, if relevant.

Listen before you speak | Unless you are habitually silenced in this relationship.

Get the physical setting right | Avoid glass and metal, which create bad echoes, and seek out wood and fabric. Choose warmer-coloured diffused lighting and stay away from the harshness of overhead and blue-white light.

Ensure you are both rested and fed | Before an important conversation.

Adjust your position or take a journey | Sit at an angle of 60 degrees to your speaker or walk with a slow rhythm so you are in sync with your bodies and with each other.

Turn to nature | Nature can be an enriching setting for a difficult encounter, providing soft fascination and dissolving stress.

Consider playfulness | A place for your speaker to experiment and try out new ideas.

Enable your speaker to feel cherished | With intentional choices. Think of this conversation as a once-in-a-lifetime encounter.

Create Space Challenge

Think about an upcoming conversation and how you can adjust the environment. What will make the space feel safe, comfortable, even special for your speaker? Do they have any relevant physical and psychological needs? How can you show, not tell, that they and this conversation are important to you? Make all possible alterations before you embark on the exchange.

STEP TWO:

LISTEN TO YOURSELF FIRST

Willie's phone rang. It was one of an assortment of gleaming black landline telephones on his desk. The sound perforated my thoughts. He picked up the receiver and answered. Again. And again. When he wasn't bombarded with calls, he reached for a handset to issue instructions to his staff. His voice was wrapped with a thick Romanian accent, brusque and charming in equal measure.

I was trying to talk to Willie, feeling frustrated and increasingly infuriated. But I persisted.

I'd known Willie all my life, as he was a close friend of my late father, Harry. At some level, my father was unknown to me. It was only after his death that I found out that he had been adopted; his birth parents, Max and Esther, were killed in Auschwitz. Harry and Willie were fellow refugees from Eastern Europe. I remember as a young child trailing after them on Sunday mornings as they strolled through the park, deeply submerged in conversation; Willie and my father propelling my sisters, Willie's own children and me, high up on the swings. With my second child newly born, I wanted to spend time with people who had been close to my father.

Willie picked up a phone handset. Again.

'Perhaps you might need to take an urgent call, but this conversation is important, very important, to me,' I blurted out, frustrated, incredulous. 'Why are you interrupting it by choosing to *make* calls *as* I am speaking?' Willie's behaviour was in keeping with his high-octane persona, but on this occasion, I was crushed. His interpretations and insights held the promise of a rare window into my late father's life, but with his disruptions, Willie was obstructing any real shared understanding.

There was a long pause.

'I was very close to your father,' Willie eventually responded, with quiet dignity. 'I feel his loss deeply and it's very painful for me to hear you talk about him.'

As Willie grasped what lay behind his behaviour and shared it with me in a moment of vulnerability, I understood. My anger at Willie's rudeness evaporated, instantly. I felt comforted and connected to Willie and our shared loss. After he acknowledged this pain, no more calls invaded our exchange. He was now ready to listen and share.

Failing to Notice

If you haven't listened to yourself first, you might find, like Willie, that you've closed yourself off from truly hearing what the other person has to say. Memories, strong emotions, prejudices or an unacknowledged agenda can distort an exchange, if you haven't first recognised and addressed these internal challenges. In the words of the poet Robert Frost, 'Something we were withholding made us weak/Until we found out that it was ourselves.'[1] Your shadows, the 'unaccepted' parts of yourself, buried inside, leap out and hijack you when you're trying to listen. If you haven't taken the time to listen to yourself, the part of you which feels young and vulnerable can take over. So, you listen less, and judge more.

I have found that the framework created by the Nobel Prize-winning psychologist Daniel Kahneman can help shed light. He distinguished between System 1 thinking, which acts automatically, driven by your primal instincts, and System 2 thinking, associated with your prefrontal cortex, which is deliberate and allows you to make conscious choices.[2] Without listening to yourself first, System 1 is in the driving seat.

The words of Robert Frost point to the potential of becoming aware of what we have been ignoring in our inner selves – the hidden forces that shape our thoughts and deeds, including the way we listen and react to others. Fortunately, there are ways to acknowledge, accept and disarm your shadows, so they can begin to heal and repair, so they're less likely to invade your important conversations.

Ideally, in advance of a significant conversation, try to recognise any personal baggage that may intrude upon your encounter with this specific individual. It's often far easier and more comfortable for us to avoid looking inside ourselves. Once you feel courageous enough to explore your inner landscape, the impact on your most significant conversations can be profound.

Our Disruptive Shadows

'Morning, f**ko. Ready for another disappointing day?' These sardonic words are spoken by Dan's shadow as Dan lies in bed at the start of the dark, short comedy film, *The Voice in Your Head*.[3] Dan's shadow is dressed in a pinstriped olive blazer and thick gold chain with a hipster beard. The shadow has been recast from Dan's inner landscape into a real-life obnoxious character who stalks Dan's every moment and taunts our hero.

'You know. Your dad *hates* you. Just hates you.' Dan's personified shadow savages a numb and exhausted Dan, prodding his deepest fears. 'It's strange, as it appears that he loves you. That's what it seems like, he's been present and supportive throughout your life, but … he hates you.'

There is no relief for Dan. His shadow picks at his buried doubts and weaknesses, constantly undermining him as he attempts to go about his day. Dan's attention is hijacked by his aggressive shadow berating and distracting him as he attempts to listen to instructions from his boss.

'Why are you listening to *me*?' the shadow reprimands Dan. '*He's* standing right in front of you. *He's* the boss. *This* guy. You're supposed to be paying attention to *him*!'

The film's personification of a troubled and trouble-making alter ego is both disturbing and illuminating. Dan's shadow prevents Dan from being able to listen, something that happens to many of us, far too often.

With many of my coaching clients, the subject of shadows often comes up as clients start to realise how much they are affected by disruptive yet predictable inner thoughts. Like Dan, they hear a voice telling them that they are rubbish, worthless and useless, for example, because in an important meeting their words came out a millisecond too quickly. Despite evidence that they've been able to handle many challenging forums adroitly, that inner voice still reverberates at critical moments, eroding their ability to listen to what's being said.

Sometimes, your shadows may leap up unexpectedly. You recognise, for example, that you're disproportionately troubled by the prospect of another conversation with a less than competent plumber, booked to mend your broken boiler. You first need time alone to register and acknowledge that it's not just the prospect of having a few chilly weeks that's at stake. The reason you feel disproportionately annoyed, angry or fearful is the possibility that this individual has triggered one of your shadows. Perhaps there's an unresolved conflict with your father who frequently failed to meet your expectations of parenthood. Recognising that there may be more to your emotional reactions is the hardest step. It's far easier to ride the high horse of self-righteousness.

Decoding Shadows

Psychoanalyst Carl Jung wrote about our personal shadow as *the other* in us, the unconscious personality that embarrasses or shames us, the sum of all those unpleasant qualities we like to hide.[4]

The metaphor of an invisible bag is one that I came across in the writings of poet Robert Bly to describe how our shadows are formed. Bly tells a personal story. As infants, he and his brother are running balls of energy. But one day the Bly brothers notice that their parents are disapproving. 'They said things like, "Can't you be still?" Or "It isn't nice to try and kill your brother."' Robert describes bags growing behind him and his brother. To keep their parents' love, the siblings put the parts of themselves their parents frowned upon into the bags. By the time they go to school, their bags are quite large. Their teachers also communicate what is acceptable, as Bly writes, 'Good children don't get angry over such little things.' So Robert and his brother take out their anger and put it in the bag. 'By the time my brother and I were 12 in Madison, Minnesota, we were known as the "nice Bly boys". Our bags were already a mile long.'[5]

Each of us has a bag of shadows that remain hidden most of the time, full of largely negative emotions and behaviours – rage, jealousy, shame, resentment, lust and greed – masked by our more acceptable, pleasant self.[6] And when these shadows are suppressed, they can exert a tremendous force over us, making their presence felt most keenly when we come face to face with people whose ideas we find troublesome or abhorrent.

It may be useful to reflect, if you feel able to, what you may have placed in your invisible bag.

Exploring Your Shadows

In a corner of Maygrove Peace Park in London, sandwiched between nearby parked cars and the bough of a maple tree, a sculpture of the renowned artist Antony Gormley sits on top of a large rock nested in crinkled leaves. He's listening with his whole body, a hand up to his ear.

'This was one of my first commissions. It's a lost work in a way,' Gormley observed to me, his tone a little mournful.

Being present and listening deeply are central to Gormley's life and art. When I first met him many years ago, I was struck by his piercing internal stillness, whether he was listening or talking. It's this very quality that animates Gormley's sculpted human figures, which range from lifelike bodies to abstractions made of thin wires. These works populate fields, coasts and grand exhibition halls from the United States to China and New Zealand.

The posture of this listening statue was modelled on Milarepa, the 11th-century Tibetan poet and monk. Milarepa

is always illustrated sitting in meditation with one ear cocked so that he can hear an echo of his own song, Gormley explained to me. It is the sound of his being that the mountains are sending back to him. 'He's one of those people with a very deep commitment to humankind, but in order to understand what being human is, he has to spend a lot of time apart from the human mass. He is actually listening to himself.'

We do not know what Milarepa heard when he listened inside himself. But according to legend, he had a dark past with many shadows to wrestle. The stories tell us that before committing himself to a life of devotion, the poet monk murdered 35 people with black magic in an act of revenge before conjuring up a hailstorm to destroy their crops.[7]

Without sharing such a colourful history, Gormley believes that ultimately all his work comes from grappling with his own shadows and his own vulnerability. 'In our family, there was this supreme being up there,' he says, stretching his right arm upwards, to heaven.

'In a way *he* was the final arbiter. We had to keep to the rules; we had to be effective. Imperfections were frowned upon. I think this idea of having to be an invincible achiever was a very big barrier for me.'

Listening to himself through his work is, for Gormley, a way of acknowledging his own weaknesses, his capacity to be cruel as well as his capacity to love. Looking into the far distance, he adds, 'We are all escaping from our demons, our shadows. But exploring our demons … I think this is a really important job that we all have to do.'

Shadows Signs

The shapes of our shadows are not obvious. We can't look directly into their hidden domains, as they are, by nature, obscured. Therefore, we sense them indirectly, in what we perceive as the loathsome (and sometimes even admirable) traits and actions of others. It's safer to observe our shadows in other people; they often show up when we are listening to their challenging ideas. You might notice, for example, how uncomfortable you feel when your friend mentions his angry exchanges with his parents. This uneasiness could be a sign of your own unresolved issues with your family, stemming from a childhood where open communication and emotional expression were discouraged.

How do you know when your shadows are pulling the strings? Notice when you judge what you are hearing as being black and white, with you 100 per cent in the right and the other person blatantly wrong. You may also feel a sense of loathing towards your speaker as you project your own shadow onto them, in an unconscious effort to banish it from yourself. Another tell-tale sign is struggling with a nagging fear that if you can't insist on the righteousness of your perspective, having your side of the story recognised as *the* truth, it will be catastrophic. It may seem counterintuitive: the more strongly you feel in your gut that you are right (while simultaneously denying that you are in any way emotional), the more likely it is that your shadows are in control. This is not, of course, to deny that you might in fact have a point. But you need to separate reality from shadows in order to come to a place of centredness where you can Deeply Listen to your speaker.

Childhood Shadows

Understanding how our own shadows have come to block our ability to listen can be pivotal in creating the space for a new way to relate. And key to that is recognising the impact of our upbringing. Our sustained and intense journey in the confines of our own family, 'with all its members vying for attention and power, with its alliances, secrets, and resentments,' writes Jungian analyst Karen Signell, has a profound influence on us, continuing to shape the way we relate to others – long after we've left childhood behind. As adults, we slip under the influence of these shadows, which unconsciously guide our actions.

It feels natural because our shadows are so familiar.[8] Our shadows are especially potent in shaping our adult relationships with our siblings; in the words of Jung scholar Christine Downing, 'I am who she is not. She is both what I would most aspire to be but feel I never can be *and* what I am most proud *not* to be but fearful of becoming.'[9]

Stumbling across a childhood shadow was to provide a breakthrough moment for my friend Mark, as we were talking about a relationship that he found inexplicably challenging.

As chair of an English regional energy company, Mark works with a board of directors, including an accountant named Ralph. But their relationship is fractured. Mark feels intimidated by Ralph, even though, as chair, Mark is in authority. When Mark reaches out to Ralph for further clarification on, for example, their cash flow or debt, they usually end up at loggerheads. 'It's as though we are inhabiting two different universes with different languages and rules.' Mark finds it hard to dismiss a feeling that he's being talked down to. He acknowledges Ralph's accounting expertise, yet he can't seem to tap into that knowledge because he feels blocked by his colleague's apparent aura of superiority.

But as Mark is reflecting aloud with me, wondering why he finds Ralph so challenging to listen to, he has a moment of insight. Mark's eyes squint as he looks up. Something in his mind has shifted.

Mark's energy picks up as he describes a sudden revelation about a shadow that has just emerged, in the shape of his brother Noah. With distant parents, and Mark's elder brother no longer at home, Mark's middle brother, Noah, was left in charge. On a wet Sunday, Noah would set up experiments in the kitchen – flasks, a Bunsen burner and chemicals. The harder Mark vied for either attention or explanation, the more Noah would withhold his knowledge and lock out his baby brother. 'Some people say that their older brother is a guide to life, but mine was quite the opposite. Noah resented having me around,' Mark recounts.

As I listen, Mark acknowledges that his relationship with his brother is driving his intense reactions to his colleague; the exclusion that Mark experienced as a child has been brought to life. Mark's shadow has been triggered. Mark recognises that he has been infusing this new professional relationship with long-accumulated pain – a realisation that is both humbling and powerful. 'If I was talking to myself, I'd say, "You need to explore that further." I can ask myself, "Who am I hearing when I listen to that colleague?"'

Before their next meeting, Mark reminded himself that he wasn't a child and Ralph wasn't his brother. That was enough for a real dialogue to open up between them. They're still not best buddies, Mark acknowledges, but this realisation was the beginning of what he hopes will be a fruitful working relationship building on their respective strengths.

When your shadow is triggered, as Mark's was by his colleague Ralph, you may become your eight-year-old self again, with all the simplistic thinking of a wounded child who fears that it's you who is to blame for all the world's troubles. But not all shadows have such a clear origin; your shadows often reflect multiple layers of experiences. What's important is to recognise that these feelings are real. They are not to be dismissed or repressed, as they reveal your hidden shadow world.

Becoming aware of the power of family shadows has been an enlightening experience for Akram Khan. As a dancer and choreographer, Khan has collaborated with artists like Kylie

Minogue and choreographed scenes for the London 2012 Olympic Games opening ceremony. I first met Khan many years ago, after being impressed by seeing him perform at Sadler's Wells Theatre in London. We made a series of BBC radio documentaries together, exploring the interplay between his Bangladeshi heritage, the spiritual Kathak dance he learned as a boy, and his desire to push boundaries and break free. Today, Khan has a growing family, and he told me a story about himself and his son.

The boy is lying in bed.

It's 8.30p.m.

'What do you have to say? Say it quickly,' Khan admonishes his son. 'You know you should be asleep now. You should have been asleep at 8p.m.' Khan has an important Zoom meeting with Google at 9p.m. that he needs to prepare for. His son pleads with his father to give him the time to talk. 'I feel ready *now*,' his son implores. 'But I can't listen,' Khan recounts. 'I struggle. That's when the clash happens.'

The difficulty Khan has in listening to his son is rooted in something more profound than time management.

'I'm not present with my son. That's not his problem. That's my problem,' Khan admits, as he acknowledges how his family shadows intrude upon this relationship. 'You know we don't give birth to a child. I think that's the wrong way of putting it. They give birth to a parent. And I think that this parent that my son's given birth to … he's a bit premature. The father in me is premature.'

Khan has come to recognise that his attitude towards his son reminds him of his own father's behaviour towards him. His late father, Khan explains, was unable to show his love openly to his son, expressing his affection through a punitive harshness. 'My problem is I show love, but not when it matters,'

Khan reflects. 'And when it really matters is when you truly need to listen to them.'

Khan's shadow may distort his ability to listen to his son, but Khan has also discovered that shadows can be a powerful creative force. When he is dancing or choreographing a show, he calls on a whole cast of internal characters, his family of shadows, so to speak, that are present with him on stage.

'When I do solos, I'm never alone. When I need to turn to rage, my father's there. When I need to embody tranquillity or some sort of sense of hope, my mother's there. When I want to turn to something much more complex, a human condition that I don't quite understand, when it's much more grey, I go to my auntie or one of my uncles.'

Just as Khan has learned to identify and work with his shadow personalities, when you are listening to yourself prior to an important conversation (and we're going to get to that soon), try to spot which shadow is dancing around you.

Inherited Shadows

Shadows don't only originate in our own direct experience. I have long been aware of the staying power of shadows that cross generations. When I came across this line about intergenerational shadows in the novel *Homeland Elegies* by Ayad Akhtar, I noted it down. Akhtar's hero reflects: 'As an adult, I would wonder if I'd picked up on some still palpable emotional residue, still carried, still felt by my parents – the raw data of their grief, if you will – that I made my own.'[10]

Indeed, your shadows can be created by trauma and raw unprocessed grief that unfolded even before you were born but which can still intrude upon your conversations and wound your relationships. If one of these shadows shows up, you can ask: 'To whom does this shadow really belong?' And let that question percolate.

Sub-personalities

Members of an unruly internal family is how psychotherapist Richard Schwartz describes our shadow personalities, in the branch of psychotherapy he developed and called *Internal Family Systems Therapy*. Drawing on the work of Carl Jung, Schwartz argues that everyone is born with multiple *personae*, a host of shadows like a family or community. All of them are valuable. There are, for example, sub-personalities who dominate and seem to 'run the show' and serve us well, such as one that loves to learn or another that is keen to please. And we also have shadows that are fragile younger personae who have become hurt or terrified, shamed or abandoned. These shadows, when triggered, have the power to generate painful emotions.

To protect yourself, you lock up these sub-personalities in your mental basement, in a form of exile. When you are listening to someone who thinks very differently from you, you become triggered, and your defences may be breached. Schwartz has used the term *firefighter* to describe a shadow who thinks its job is to protect you and your most vulnerable shadows. The firefighter impulsively jumps in to deal with this emergency, with a compelling urgency. They need to get you away from that place of vulnerability. Away from the shadows that you think you cannot bear. You become defensive, dismissive or angry with the speaker who has triggered you.[11,12]

We all have a set of lively sub-personalities, who, if they're not listened to and acknowledged, can play havoc with our

relationships and our conversations when it matters most, destroying our capacity to listen. Resistance holds us back; so much of the suffering that shadows bring comes from our resistance to acknowledging them. The idea is to get to a place where you can recognise all your sub-personalities, including your firefighters, as valuable, as acting with positive intentions.

What might help is recognising that beyond this group of shadows, we all have a connected *Self* in Schwartz's terminology

(Self as distinct from the ego), which is more spacious and open-hearted. 'Self is the "I am" prior to and beyond "I am this or I am that",' writes psychotherapist Loch Kelly.[13] This Self is intentionally capitalised, as it is far more expansive than your shadows or sub-personalities, and is waiting patiently for you to acknowledge it. This Self, sometimes called 'awareness' or 'consciousness', is the place from where you can observe all your shadows, including your firefighters, with compassion. It is a place where you can bear what has seemed unbearable. It is a place of openness and courage from which to heal your inner and outer relationships. A place which is already free. Which is already whole. Just as it is. Your shadows will still arrive, but with this greater degree of understanding and acceptance, their grip on you will become less fierce.

You can forge a helpful relationship with yourself, sensitively aware of and accepting your own shadows. And if you do that, even if this is painful, then, as psychologist Carl Rogers writes, there is a greater chance that you can form a helping relationship with another person.[14]

Shadows in Conflict

In societies which grapple with deep divisions or conflicts, based upon politics or ethnicity for example, people project uncomfortable aspects of themselves onto whole groups. Here, strangers morph into the enemy in the quest for a scapegoat, someone to attack and blame, to become the carriers of the evil they cannot acknowledge in themselves. In such polarised contexts, true listening is rare.

'Sketch in broad outline the forms of men, women, and children,' the author and philosopher Sam Keen writes, 'dip into the unconscious well of your own disowned darkness with a wide brush and stain the strangers with the sinister hue of the shadow.'[15] Keen highlights the point that to mass-produce hatred, a nation or community must remain unconscious of its own paranoia. The enemy is therefore perceived as real and objective; a nation traces 'onto the face of the enemy the greed, hatred, carelessness' that they dare not claim as their own. Acknowledging that you are casting your own shadow onto a group that you've categorised as dangerous or misguided could render this enemy less threatening. If you can then authentically Deeply Listen and understand the experiences that have led to their beliefs, you may be able to discern the unique individuality of a single face in their midst.

Checking in with relevant shadows before an important encounter avoids dangers that can poison an exchange. Otherwise, if you are suppressing emotional turmoil, it can become contagious, contaminating your speaking partner without either of you becoming aware. So how can you check in?

How to Handle Your Shadows

First, a warning: it may be unsafe to embark on this shadow work, uncovering buried shadows which may have been hidden for a good reason, without support. If you have experienced trauma in your life, are vulnerable or are living with overwhelming emotions, you may not be in the right place to listen to yourself alone. If you are in any doubt, find someone, perhaps a therapist or counsellor, who can support you. If you are in a crisis, YourLifeCounts.org offers links to support internationally.

Return to an Anchor

Even if you are in the right place to listen to yourself, it's best to identify how you might handle any strong emotions before you begin this work. Psychotherapist and meditation teacher Tara Brach recommends finding an 'anchor' for when things get turbulent. Your anchor could be going for a walk, calling someone who loves you, or thinking about a person, place or animal that evokes a sense of safety. It might be a phrase that you can tell yourself, such as 'I trust it's going to be OK', or your breath, or feeling your feet on the ground. Whatever anchor you choose, have it ready so you are prepared.[16]

Knowing that at any moment you can return to this place of safety and ease can empower you to meet whatever emerges with equanimity, at least more of the time. And if the words 'safety' and 'ease' don't resonate with you, find your own words for these qualities.

If you feel you are in a safe space to start to explore your shadow world rather than deny or fight your shadows, you may find that listening to these parts of yourself, especially before conversations where you know you are likely to be triggered, can be life-altering.

Welcome Them All

As a start, your shadows need to be acknowledged and given their place – even embraced, when you feel ready to do so. This is far from easy, as we all feel a degree of shame about our shadows. But ignored, outside your door, they can cause mischief. 'You must invite it to the dinner table, this dubious guest … and see what it has to offer. You cannot leave it outside the door raising a rumpus or sneaking around and causing worry,'[17] writes psychoanalyst Karen Signell. The idea of welcoming our shadows draws on the poetry of the 13th-century poet Rumi, who invites us to entertain these guests and treat them honourably, as they have been sent 'as a guide from beyond'.[18]

Give Yourself the Space

Acknowledging the personal, sometimes heavy, baggage she brings to an exchange allows Dutch listening authority Corine Jansen to protect the promise of a true encounter. Corine has spent many years listening to people in hospital, including those in palliative care. She recalled listening to a man named Peter who was 32 and had just become a father – but he was dying. Peter started by talking about his skin cancer. Then he told Corine about the metastasis in his brain. On this occasion, Corine couldn't have prepared herself.

'My dad died of the same disease, the same combination,' Corine tells me. 'I could not listen; I was tense and distracted, though my father has been dead for more than 20 years.' Corine explained to Peter that she was overwhelmed. She needed a break. 'I know I promised to listen, but I can't right now.' Peter looked perplexed.

'I went out – and cried and cried so hard. I called my partner. "Oh dear lord, this is so painful. I need to get rid of the emotions around the loss of my father."' Her partner responded with wisdom. 'You don't need to get rid of them. Just cry, yell, scream and then go back.'

After listening to herself, taking the time to acknowledge her own anguish, Corine was able to accept her own pain and then put it to one side. She could then be open to Peter, her own experience bolstering rather than draining her empathy so that he, in his distress, could be truly heard.[19] Research supports Corine's experience, indicating that being more mindful of what's happening inside you enables you to be more empathetic and compassionate towards others.[20]

If you are in a place to befriend as well as respect the most troubling aspects of yourself, you will naturally be more open to listening to views you find objectionable and even offensive. I find that when I am able to be curious about, and then acknowledge to myself, my own weaknesses and vulnerability, I am better able to accept my speaker. Recognising that they might be struggling with their own shadows, manifesting as anger, defensiveness or irritation, can help inspire compassion and curiosity. Can you cast this 'other person' as a gift that can help shine a light on your shadows, enabling you, incidentally, to better understand yourself? Through the way you listen, projecting empathy and respect, you can also reassure their frightened self and help all of their shadows to feel a little safer.

Choreographer Akram Khan has evolved a dynamic way to listen to one of his own shadows, who shows up in the form of his late father. He spends time with his father in the studio each day.

'There's a way of standing when I am doing certain exercises, as if I am standing on rice paper. It's so delicate, you don't want to cut or tear it. It reminds me of when I held my father's hand, and I realised he had no strength. I needed to be so careful as his skin was so frail.'

These routines allow Khan to summon up his father and connect with this shadow. His words and movements allow him to show tender love for his father, in spite of the darker memories that still haunt him. In time, Khan hopes that this work will start to unlock what is preventing him from being able to fully listen to his own son.

Another option: invite your shadows to tell their story directly.

Give Your Shadow a Voice

After centring yourself, you can reflect on the significant moments in your life when you first became fearful, anxious or abandoned, and cast your mind back to that time. When that shadow is triggered, you may still feel like a child once again, with the tender vulnerability that you experienced at that time. Perhaps one shadow is keenly sensitive to a lack of fairness, the absence of control, or feeling unappreciated? You may feel shame in owning a shadow who is sensitive to characteristics that make you feel acutely uncomfortable. To deepen your understanding, it may be helpful to move from the confines of the mind to the wisdom of the body. Notice where you feel this shadow. What is its texture? Is it pulsating? Are its edges hard or blurry? Does it have a colour?

You can choose to go somewhere safe where you can't be heard, a private room or, even better, somewhere in nature. In this quiet place of solitude, you can address that shadow out loud and ask it what the world looks like through its eyes. Why, for example, does it feel so strongly?

And now, without judgement, let your shadow speak by embodying it and voicing what you intuit to be its thoughts. Try to listen with warm-hearted curiosity, without judgement. Witness what unfolds. Don't expect the shadow to be rational; perhaps it will speak only with pent-up emotions. Be aware if you become defensive and let that go. Listen instead with compassion, love and increased understanding. You might find it more natural to write or draw these shadow identities as you give them time and space to open up to the light.

I find that if I have this conversation with my shadow, any bracing or tension that I have been holding onto starts to dissolve. A feeling of calm centredness seeps through me.

However, it's time for a reality check. Just because you've had one encounter with your shadow, don't kid yourself that its power to seduce you has evaporated. It's only the beginning of what could be a long and fruitful relationship of understanding that can unfold over a lifetime.

Dancing with Shadows Who Interrupt

The aim is to reach a stage where you witness or even dance with your shadows, rather than acting out against, fighting, denying or trying to annihilate them. It may be helpful to recognise that your difficult, intrusive shadows are only one part of you. There is also the more expansive whole, connected, healthy Self, which is more loving than any shadow. This nurturing part of you has the power to hold all your vulnerable and angry shadows.

Through my meditation practice, I was introduced to the previously-mentioned psychotherapist Loch Kelly. Kelly has incorporated the family of shadows concept into his writing and teaching. He describes to me how he manages his own shadows when they come to the surface during, for example, a difficult conversation with his wife. First he notices that he's starting to feel angry about something his wife has said. A shadow tries to take over; he wants to yell at his wife.

'OK, I hear you,' he says silently to the shadow, and then inwardly addresses this shadow, in a tone a parent would use to comfort a child. "Thank you for trying to help and keep me safe. Is it OK if you trust me and let me handle this? I think it's OK if you don't take over.'

Kelly turns his focus to any physical sensations of discomfort, as they show up, to stay centred.

'I will gradually feel this shift in my body,' Kelly explains, with a gentle smile in his voice. 'My heart will open, my mind will clear and my big agenda – getting my wife to apologise to me – will evaporate.' Kelly's tactic of talking directly to a shadow can be used if one of your shadows tries to pull the strings in a difficult conversation. However, don't be surprised if your shadows keep on popping up. This is part of the dance.

Bringing awareness to such moments allows these difficult emotions to unburden themselves without flooding or hijacking you. The experience can be compared to a clenched fist slowly opening and letting go. Later, you can return to this shadow and explore, with compassionate curiosity rather than guilt-ridden blame, what triggered that part of you.

Welcoming your shadows sympathetically acknowledges their existence and avoids conflict with them. Tentatively, starting to broker peace with your shadows allows your firefighter shadow, desperate to defend your more vulnerable parts, to take a step back. Recognising that shadows have a positive intention can be powerful. This gentler and wiser approach to your shadows, one of acceptance and compassion, may shift an intransigent boulder blocking an important relationship with your partner, friend or colleague. But at other times, we need to accept that our shadows are too strong to let us listen.

'I try to be honest with myself,' listening expert Corine Jansen confessed to me. 'There are some people I just can't listen to.' For many years, Corine tried to believe that she could learn to listen to everyone. However, she's come to recognise that her own childhood – growing up with an abusive mother – has left many long and dark shadows. Corine's internal work on the traumas of her upbringing allows her to profoundly connect with many types of people and offer them a transformational listening experience. But her past has also created some no-go areas that she has learned to navigate around. Corine has learned to respect her shadows.

Appreciating Your Shadows: A Transformation

At the end of *The Voice in Your Head*, the short film I mentioned at the beginning of this step, the hero, Dan, is driving home, at last liberated from his shadow. Out of the corner of his eye, he notices his shadow in an underpass trying to hitch a lift, diminished, pitiful. After thinking for a moment, Dan, with tears in his eyes, opens his car door and invites the shadow in. Though this could be interpreted as a moment of defeat for Dan, unable to evade his shadow, I read it instead as acceptance. We recognise that our shadows will always be with us, but it is possible for us to forge a new, healthier relationship with them.

Having listened to yourself first, in the next step we explore how you can become present and navigate internal and external distractions so you can stay centred during your encounters.

Listen to Yourself First Takeaways

Identify an anchor | Before shadow work, to return to if things get turbulent.

Become aware of your shadows | The unpleasant qualities that we like to hide.

Watch out for signs | Feeling self-indignantly in the right, feeling disproportionately irritated, angry or fearful.

Childhood shadows are powerful | They still exert their power on us as adults, and not just on family relationships.

We can inherit shadows | Intergenerational trauma has an outstretched arm.

We project our shadows onto others | The loathsome traits we judge them for could well be our own.

Get to know your family | Your sub-personalities, those who run the show, those you keep in the basement, your firefighters, and beyond them, your wider Self who can observe it all.

Accept and welcome your shadows | It's a high aspiration, but worth pursuing. Give your shadows a voice and Deeply Listen to them. Bring compassion to your shadows and recognise their positive intention.

Listen to Yourself First Challenge

When you're approaching what you anticipate will be a highly charged encounter, ask yourself: What in me is stopping me from hearing/seeing this person clearly? Name what is invisible but felt. During the conversation, notice if you're not able to engage with what your speaker is saying. Alternatively, if you feel bored, or angry or something throws you, ask yourself: What's turning me away? Did one of my shadows make an appearance? What about your speaker's shadows?

Can you ask (and answer) these questions from your more spacious, more connected, more compassionate Self?

STEP THREE:
BE PRESENT

As Brenda Holder leads the way slowly and intentionally through the steep, scrubby woodland, her dark plaited hair falls back to reveal a set of orange-beaded earrings. Mindfully unzipping her backpack, she retrieves a sealed, transparent plastic bag. With calm, ritual-like movements, she withdraws a pinch of tobacco and gently places it on the deep brown soil. 'We need to acknowledge with respect,' Holder tells me, her words cutting through the sound of the Bow waterfalls behind us, the Earth's gift of inspiration and wisdom.

Holder and her colleague Larissa Heron are members of the Indigenous peoples of Canada, who have evolved a tradition of being present over tens of thousands of years. Holder is First Nation, with Cree and Iroquois lineage. She runs a tour guide business in Alberta in Western Canada, amidst soaring landscapes, fierce bears and healing herbs. Heron is Métis, with Cree heritage; she's just completed her degree in molecular biology.

Though it's late May, the peaks of the surrounding Rocky Mountains are still marked by luminous brushstrokes of snow. I'm feeling a little apprehensive, disoriented, unsure of what Holder and Heron will make of me or if they will choose to share anything meaningful. I am aware that I have much to

learn from these two women and I need to offer them a reciprocal token of respect. Holder and Heron spy a fallen pine log to sit on, edged by juniper bushes and feathery sprigs of wild yarrow. I take out my pen, unpack my watercolour paints and begin to sketch a gift for them, of them. Curiosity wells up inside me. I want to learn about *their* perspective on listening. But I hold back my questions. I am not able to take notes and paint simultaneously. Perhaps they want to take this opportunity to ask me questions about my research.

Holder and Heron respond with a soft, serene silence. I continue to sketch. I'm taking hesitant steps through uncharted territory. Perhaps, I ask them, they might be curious to know about my personal motivations for working in the listening space? They nod. More silence. Then, in an effort to connect, I find myself sharing my family's story. I am aware of the trauma that Indigenous people have experienced here:

their families, communities and cultures intentionally obliterated by the brutal residential school system enforced by the Canadian state over generations. Without a conscious intention, I open up to Holder and Heron about my own violent family history – how my father, Harry, had carried with him the knowledge that he'd been the only pupil in his class of Jewish children in Žilina, Czechoslovakia, to survive the Holocaust. How he had escaped to Britain with his aunt and uncle, who had adopted him. How his parents, along with almost all of their families, were killed. And how this story inspires me in my work in Deep Listening, especially where it is needed most, in divided societies.

Though I'm sharing my strange story with strangers, sitting cross-legged on the woodland floor, their still and centred presence holds me. I feel entirely comfortable. I sense that it is safe to lay down my psychological armour. I do not feel that these two women are shocked by my family's experience, nor do they want to draw comparisons with their own intergenerational trauma or feel the need to come up with a response to help me make sense of my story. They are listening with the totality of their humanity. I feel heard. And even a measure more able to accept my own history.

Awareness and Presence

Cultivating awareness can allow all of us to enter into a state of presence. Awareness is the ability to be conscious of what's happening inside and outside yourself. Presence, simply put, means showing up ready to take in whatever your speaker chooses to share. You are undistracted and in the moment. In the moment with an inner vitality.

I'm also aware that presence can sound a little elliptical and hard to grasp, pretentious even. How does Brenda Holder explain it? For her, presence is experiencing a conversation fully; she is at home unknowing what will unfold, inviting in whoever she encounters and accepting whatever may present itself. 'I don't fear when it comes to listening,' adds her younger colleague, Heron. 'What I need to know and what I need to hear will be just there.' You can imagine how grounding that feels for me, or anyone being bathed in their listening. When you listen in a state of presence, you abandon any preconceived ideas about how you should react. Instead, you are willing to just be. I'm inspired by psychotherapist Richard Schwartz's description of presence as 'luminous moments of clarity and balance'[1] also acknowledging that we are unlikely to be able to sustain an unwavering presence continuously.

The idea of Deep Listening is embraced by Indigenous people across the world, though their cultures are diverse. In the Ngangikurungkurr community in the Northern Territories of Australia, the word for Deep Listening is *Dadirri*, which also includes a quiet, still awareness. An elder and educator from that nation, Miriam Rose Ungunmerr-Baumann relates that her people have passed on this way of listening for 40,000 years. She describes it in these words:

To know me
Is to breathe with me.
To breathe with me
Is to listen deeply.
To listen deeply
Is to connect.
It's the sound.
The sound of deep – calling to deep.

Dadirri:
The deep inner spring inside us.[2]

One way to think about presence is that your thoughts and emotions are transient waves and ripples on the surface of an ocean. They are part of the body of water, yet also superficial and fleeting. They arise and pass away without disturbing the calmness that lies beneath. And rather than scan for danger, hypervigilant to threats, you can effortlessly become aware of the tranquil ocean depths. There is no need to become present, to become centred; you do not need to do anything to create this state of presence. You can just open yourself up to a natural state of wakefulness. Open-hearted presence is Holder and Heron's natural state. 'And when we come from that perspective,' Holder adds, 'listening is not just about taking information in. *Listening is being*.' But is there a contradiction here? How can focusing on yourself, becoming more aware of what's going on in *your* body and mind, help you better listen to another?

The Bonding Benefits of Presence

Most often, we're lost in patterns of thought, carried away as one thought generates another, creating riptides of emotions in their wake. Often unaware, we act out these emotions. So, for example, when your wife tells you about an exciting new colleague who's joined her team at work, you respond sharply, not realising that her joy has exposed your own frustration, adrift in a sea of job applications.

If, instead, you come into a conversation with a finely tuned attention, when one of your own shadows decides to make an entrance, you'll be in a better place to welcome them. Rather than letting them get stuck, you can open the back door and allow them to leave. 'Allow your thoughts to come and go. Just don't serve them tea,' in the words of Zen master Shunryū Suzuki,[3] – or pay them too much respect with a ceremony.

Achieving some distance also helps you experience your emotions as less vivid, less real and less compelling, enabling them to diminish. It becomes easier to stay with what your speaker is telling you instead of reacting or arguing. And researchers have found that your emotional state also matters to your speaker. Our ability to pick up on signs of distress in others, for example, begins in our earliest months of life.[4] Your speaker is likely to sense your anger or disappointment, even if you don't express that feeling in words.

How to Be Fully Present When It Matters

When I train people in Deep Listening, I always include a meditation at the start of the session. I want to give everyone a glimpse of the natural presence that Brenda Holder and Larissa Heron project. Sometimes, though, I notice that eyebrows are being raised and I sense a hidden smirk. I'm conscious that many people feel uncomfortable with the idea of meditation, as if I'm demanding that they levitate serenely above a lotus flower in the posture, and clothes, of a Zen monk. I may feel a little vulnerable, too. I acknowledge that to myself, smile and then invite people to close their eyes, if they feel comfortable with that.

The moments of meditation that I lead are not only a way for everyone to taste the deep, clear stillness that is at the heart of a Deep Listening approach. They are also an opportunity to centre myself, quieten wandering thoughts and surrender any expectations or worries about my own 'performance'.

A Meditation

So, I invite you now to find a quiet place where you can sit comfortably, focus on these words and let go of the world beyond.

Become aware of your posture,
Of your seat resting on your chair,
Of your feet touching the earth.
And your shoulders. Are they tense? You can let them go.

Start to become aware of your breath.
Your breath entering your body
And your breath leaving your body,
Of the start of the breath, and of the end of a breath,
And the space where there is no breath.
A sense of spaciousness, of safety, of being yourself.
A pause.
You may be aware that your mind wanders.
That's what our mind does.
Become aware if you are judging yourself
And let that go too.
The moment of noticing is a moment of awareness.
You can bring your attention back to your breath.

If your breath is not a place of ease for you, you can focus on the ground beneath your feet as you walk. (If you'd like to listen to this meditation, you can find the audio at EmilyKasriel.com.)

* * *

As part of the meditation, I ask participants to remember someone they know who is a really good listener. If no one comes to mind, I ask them to imagine a really good listener. How do they feel in that listener's presence? You might like to close your eyes and try this too.

In these moments, I always imagine Lara Fielden, one of my closest friends since my very first morning at secondary school. Later, we both worked at the BBC, and I gave birth to my children months after hers. During their childhood, they played together in our homes a street apart. In 2021, I spoke about Lara on behalf of her friends – at her funeral.

'When I talked to Lara about something important, she would focus all her attention and razor intelligence, emanating warmth. She listened intently with that quizzical, curious air, face slightly at an angle, and eyes revealing a sharp mind that was seizing the essential elements of what I was saying and making sense of them, all while emanating empathy and support.'

At the crowded funeral reception on Highgate Hill in London, family and friends, press, medical and legal regulators relived impressive professional highlights of Lara's extraordinary life, cut short by cancer. Countless friends and colleagues told me that they cherished similar memories of the transformative experience of simply being listened to by Lara, immersed in the intensity and warmth of her focus.

I miss many things about Lara, but above all I miss being listened to by her. At school and long afterwards, it felt as if anything important in my life hadn't quite taken place until I had shared it with her. Her warm, empathetic, non-judgemental, trusting presence made me feel safe, respected and loved, empowering me with the strength and creativity to navigate stumbling blocks with confidence and wisdom.

Lara was adamant that she wasn't cut out for meditation, but she was naturally mindful and present when she listened. For most of us, however, in order to enjoy the rich rewards of presence, research has shown that we need to consciously practise being mindful.[5] If you want to be able to call upon this presence when your partner confronts you about your spending, or your colleague publicly criticises your work on a project, it's wise to spend time cultivating awareness in more relaxed moments (even if it might feel less relevant then).

Inspiration to Become Still

Let us return to the artist Antony Gormley. 'My work comes out of an attempt to clear all that white noise that goes on in my mind,' Gormley disclosed to me. One of his best-loved works is the *Angel of the North* near Gateshead, whose weathered steel has become a centring landmark for the estimated 33 million people who travel past it by train, road or foot every year. The work is still, in contrast to the busy world that flows around it. Gormley hopes his art can also provide us with opportunities to stop and perhaps change direction, to reflect upon our lives and, if only in those moments when we engage with his art, embrace that quiet calm. The very thing about sculpture, he explains, is that it doesn't come towards you. You have to do all the work. You can use its silence as a listening zone and tune in to what you can hear of yourself in its stillness.

The stillness in Gormley's work is based, literally, on his own unmoving body. For his listening sculpture, his naked body was wrapped in cling film by his wife, the artist Vicken Parsons. She then pressed sheets of soft warm wax all over him until he was completely covered. To create three new standing sculptures, his wife enveloped his whole body with plaster-soaked bandages, cutting a hole for his mouth. During this process, Gormley needed to embody the statue and enter a state of utter motionlessness.

'Once you decide to accept your object status, that you're going to be a *thing*, all sorts of extraordinary things unfold. We're always told that our value lies in achievement, in doing stuff, in being effective, but when I'm wrapped up and being cast, I have to accept that stillness. The paradox is that within that imprisonment, there's an extraordinary sense of freedom and openness.'

Gormley's eyes squint with concentration and then blink, slowly.

Take Time to Move into Stillness

At the BBC, I often had to shift between meetings with BBC executives to solicit their support for my latest project and one-on-one coaching sessions with a colleague. I too felt an enormous freedom in getting into a different space, where my success and failure were not relevant. To become centred before each coaching session, I set aside time to allow any lingering concerns to walk out of the room. I might note anything preoccupying me and ground myself in the larger objectives of my client and of our conversation. I was tuning up, to turn up as fully as I could, to be truly present for my client.

There are other ways to send a signal to yourself that it's time to centre into awareness. As a volunteer for the Samaritans, a suicide prevention charity, Alex offers support to others during their darkest and loneliest hours. He must centre himself before he can wholly engage with anyone in crisis. Before each shift, Alex goes through his own immersive tea ceremony. He puts on the kettle. Minutes after pouring a mug, he leans forward above the still slightly steaming tea. This practice transports his senses into a different micro-atmosphere. In this steamy space, he is removed from what has come before. His eyes can no longer look, his pores sense the wet heat, and his ears feel clouded by the steam, blocking out distracting sounds. You can choose to 'drink your tea slowly and reverently as if it is the axis on which the whole earth revolves,' in the words of monk Thich Nhat Hanh, 'slowly, evenly, without rushing towards the future.'[6]

Think of the members of a professional orchestra tuning their instruments, even if they've played with an identical violin, clarinet and trumpet in the very same concert hall hours before. The musicians are not just going through the motions, nor are they being performative. Instead, they are deliberate and attentive, demonstrating respect for the audience, their fellow musicians and the music itself.[7]

Stillness in Everyday Rituals

In Canada, First Nation tour guide Brenda Holder calibrates her own energy in a daily ritual she calls her *Golden Hour*.

'Nothing is more wonderful to me than getting up at six in the morning, going to sit outside and hearing the news. What do the birds have to say? What can the wind tell us? It gives me so much peace. It's pushing my reset button. I need this time. I crave this time.'

The simple repetition of making a bed, brushing your teeth or washing up – all those ritual things that are repetitive can be opportunities to practise being present. As you brush your teeth, what's going on in your mind? (Aside, that is, from reassuring yourself that the dark circles are just a trick of the light.) Mindfulness pioneer Jon Kabat-Zinn encourages us to sit on the bank of the coursing river of our thoughts rather than getting swept away, and listen to and learn from this current.[8] The invitation extends to you. Take a pause from the page, close your eyes. In this moment of silence, you might like to notice the energy in yourself and in the room, and let it be as it is.

Notice if you desire the world to be different.
If you desire more calm,
As if in the next moment everything will resolve itself
And let that go.
Whatever can arise
Can also pass away.
There's nothing to want. Or grasp. Or crave.
Moment to moment,
Feel your mind dropping back
From even a subtle leaning in.
Recognise the nature of mind already clear of craving.
Experience resting in emptiness.[9]

Embody Stillness

As a tool for centring, your breath is perhaps the most accessible, as it is always with you. I find it helpful to practise the 4-7-8 breath: breathing in quietly through the nose for 4 seconds, holding the breath for 7 seconds and then forcefully exhaling through the mouth for 8 seconds, while I hold my tongue just behind my teeth. I find this rhythm so counter-intuitive that I need to focus all my attention just to keep going for a few rounds, helping my mind become clearer.

It is no accident that the traditional posture of mindful meditation is to sit upright and open, so it is easier to breathe through your diaphragm. Learning to breathe in this way, scientists have indicated, decreases your levels of the stress hormone cortisol and increases your ability to sustain your attention.[10] You might also be able to discern your heartbeat, a rhythm you can't consciously control like your breath, but which, similarly to your breath, reveals the state of your mind, whether frenzied or restful. When you do notice trouble spots, in your mind or in your body – a nagging pain in your neck or left-over anger from that morning – you can welcome these sensations as valid, quietly acknowledging them and promising to return to them, if need be, after your encounter. Tuning in to bodily sensations, how you are from the inside right now, can also enable you to develop a closer understanding of your emotional state. You might notice agitation, clenching or tightness. Perhaps you need to do more centring if you aren't in the right frame of mind to Deeply Listen. If the upcoming conversation is an especially significant one, consider, if you can, postponing.

There's also a simple and intriguing technique for centring that I learned from the former Number 10 communication chief and now high-profile podcaster, Alastair Campbell. I've found it surprisingly grounding. When Campbell thinks he's about to lose his temper, he simultaneously strokes the pad of each thumb with its corresponding index finger, moving in tiny circles – a technique known as thumb circling. He first started this discreet centring motion as a response to intense on-air interviews with Jeremy Paxman, famous for his robust (some called it bulldog-like) questioning on the BBC's *Newsnight* programme. A sports psychologist advised Campbell that the tactile sensation on his finger pads could be a discreet way to get beyond his fight-or-flight mindset. Using both hands engages both sides of your brain, which helps promote a sense of balance and calmness.

Intrusive Internal Chattering

As you pay attention, on purpose, in the present moment, non-judgementally,[11] what do you notice? When I observe my mind for only a minute, I'm always surprised at how often I see it lurching into future planning – I must remember to buy those lemons for the cake on the way home from the library – or find myself sucked back into a memory: Did I listen attentively enough to my daughter when she phoned, excited? Often these thoughts aren't fully formulated or expressed in words, which is one reason I'm not ordinarily aware of them. Instead, these snatches of ideas or images whirl around the back of my mind, interfering with my capacity to be fully present.

For some individuals, being able to manage these internal distractions can be literally lifesaving. Jack Cambria has had a long career as a hostage negotiator in New York City. He told me about the moment he received a call with an instruction: drive to Times Square. Immediately. When he arrived at the top of the Madame Tussauds building in Times Square, Manhattan, he found a 19-year-old man named Larry standing millimetres from the edge. If Larry were to jump, everything would be over in seconds. Intensely aware, alert and attentive, Cambria asked himself: Who is Larry? Why has he ended up on this precipice? As the New York City Police Department's longest-standing hostage negotiation team commander, Cambria had experienced many opportunities to practise being present. To try to encourage Larry to step back, Cambria asked him: 'Why do you feel you deserve a death sentence?' Cambria stayed close to the desperate young man as Larry unfolded his story: abandoned by his father, removed from his heroin-addicted mother, placed with uncaring foster carers, now in New York City, all alone, with nothing and no one.

Distraction, in this moment, was not an option for Cambria. If he had let his mind wander, if he had failed to be present for even a second, Larry might have paid with his life. Meanwhile, Times Square, one of the busiest places on earth, and then clogged with traffic, was now at a standstill. Cambria needed to convey to Larry that he was metaphorically holding him, without the physical harness that Cambria himself was secured with, at the razor edge of this New York landmark.

While he wrestled with his own worries and fears – if Larry jumped, it was Cambria who had failed to save him, Cambria who was responsible – the police commander remembered learning about a concept he found valuable: the chemical hormones behind any emotional reaction would only linger in his bloodstream for 90 seconds. Beyond that, it was his choice whether to create another worrying thought about the future or to observe the thought and exit that emotional loop. Cambria told me how again and again he chose to let go of his worries about how Larry's future would unfold and return to the moment.

Neuroscientist Jill Bolte Taylor, who formulated this idea, encourages us to notice when we feel a strong emotion, and then look at the second hand of a watch. In less than 90 seconds, she believes, by observing ourselves having this physiological response rather than engaging with it, we will notice a difference.[12]

While you might know intellectually that emotions come and go, truly embracing this truth is more elusive when you're lost in an attack of fear, anger or shame. Experiencing the impermanence of an emotion, for yourself, repeatedly, can help dilute the power of emotions over you – when anxiety or anger rear their head in the midst of an encounter. Of course, Cambria could have returned to the thought and re-stimulated the loop of his fears, but with awareness, he was in a better position to make that choice.

Intrusive External Distractions

It wasn't only internal distractions that negotiator Cambria had to contend with on the top of Madame Tussauds that day. Motorists, caught in traffic down below, were enraged. 'Let him jump!' some cried. As Cambria tells me this story, I hear his voice rise and tighten, as he mimics the impatient, irritated tone of the drivers, and perhaps, too, reflects the stress he still feels looking back at that day. When I think of the pressure that Cambria must have been grappling with, at the very epicentre of a cascading crisis, I marvel at his ability to put aside the intensity, in those moments, of these outside distractions.

'If I was paying any attention to the people shouting below, then I wouldn't be able to truly listen to Larry and be present for him,' Cambria reflected. In his training, Cambria had learned about how hard it is to listen to two people at the same time. So he formed a bubble with just enough room for himself and Larry; the rest of the world dissipated, dissolved. Cambria listened to Larry telling him about his abandoned dreams of being a light for kids who were struggling just like him. 'Larry, when you're ready,' Cambria told him, 'you come off that rooftop. I'm gonna give you my business card. I want you to call me and I will try and help you.' Eventually, Cambria was able to help Larry climb over the steel girder and step inside.

In a less high-stakes moment, you may not even notice your momentary sideways glance at the couple sitting next to you in a café, their engrossing argument pulling your attention from the worries that your partner opposite needs to share with you. Developing the ability to tune out distractions is valuable.

Staying Present Despite Distractions

You may have started listening by being fully present, but as the conversation unfolds, you find yourself lured by distractions, both internal and external, that fracture your attention. It's a common worry, especially among young people and those who have ADHD (attention deficit hyperactivity disorder), but it's a challenge for everyone.

Being able to handle distractions is a game-changer. Author Oliver Burkeman warns us about the perilous costs of distracting ourselves during conversations that really matter. He makes the case that attention isn't just one of the tools we use to live our life – attention is our life.[13] Our experience of being alive consists of nothing other than the sum of everything we pay attention to. When we are distracted from the intended recipients of our attention, from the person we want to listen to, we may be destroying a piece of our life and tearing chunks out of our relationship.

Does Your Distraction Have a Message?

Sometimes, you might notice yourself becoming bored with your speaker's story, so you feel compelled to finally call the dentist. Boredom and distraction can sometimes be a way that our mind protects us from listening to information that we fear may destabilise us. In such cases, ask yourself whether there's something the person has said, or something in their tone, which makes you uncomfortable. Is there a part of you that wants to avoid listening, like my father's friend Willie? At other moments, your distraction might be the most important thing you need to attend to just now. The pull of a small child on your sleeve, because they desperately need a hug. When you reflect, you will be able to distinguish between distractions that are unnecessary interruptions and those that call you to attend to what is truly important and meaningful.

Return to the Larger Motivation

Before you listen, the invitation is to check in with your heart's intention, your higher ambition for the exchange. When you take a moment to reflect, you may find that nurturing your relationship is more important than pursuing the victory you had previously believed was your central ambition.

There's an Islamic concept, *niyya*, similar to the Jewish idea of *kavanah*, describing the orientation of your heart. The idea is that we flourish if the intention in our heart is pure. A journalist, Kareem Shaheem, told me about a trip he made to Syria to report on the survivors of a chemical weapons attack. He confessed that he was partially motivated by advancing his career – if the story did well, finding work would become easier. However, he was also inspired by the prospect of listening to and amplifying the voices of the victims of this horror – specifically a father who had lost many of his sons to the poison gas. The journalist knew his life would be in danger in Syria, so he felt he needed to centre his heart's intention so it was pure. If he lost his life, he wanted this loss to be in the purpose of a more expansive ideal.

Once you've rid yourself of these distractions, you might bump into things you've been avoiding, perhaps scars from the past. If this is the case, regain stability by directing your attention to an anchor, perhaps the sounds landing in your ears or sensations in your hands. Getting the right support is also important.

Distractions Diminish Your Speaker's Experience: The Evidence

As we've touched on earlier, if you're distracted this can have a huge impact on your attention and on the experience of the person you are trying to listen to. Distracted listeners diminish speakers' stories without even saying a word, making these stories shorter, with less detail and less coherence. Experiments highlight that listeners who battle with distractions also diminish their speaking partner's self-understanding, so the speaker feels less clear about their own opinions. When you're distracted, you're perceived by your speaker as not only unresponsive, but as disagreeing with them and their story, even if you say nothing.[14]

These studies offer evidence that your own presence, your own self-awareness, can have a profound impact on your interlocutor's experience of the conversation.

The Supercharged Distraction

The most compelling and supercharged distraction for many of us is our mobile phone. One in two people in the UK agree that despite their best efforts, they sometimes can't stop themselves from checking their smartphone when they should be doing other things. The challenge isn't limited to the young – the majority of middle-aged people also say they struggle with this diversion.[15] Designed by some of the brightest and highest-paid minds, smartphones seize our attention with the thrill of a 'free' slot machine, then grip it so tightly that we hardly notice we can no longer escape. The gravitational allure of the shiny glass screen, with its promise of limitless connections and updates, sabotages our attempts at presentness, even when we are not using our phone.[16] This temptation has a profound impact on our ability to listen. Three in four adults, according to a poll carried out for this book, believe that other people are failing to listen to them because they're distracted by their own phone.[17]

My invitation to you is to keep your devices silent and out of sight when you listen – or indeed when you want to concentrate on anything. You can choose to be liberated from their tyranny, at least temporarily. Also, instead of merely stopping notifications on apps, you may want to investigate *Digital Minimalism*,[18] a digital decluttering strategy devised by Cal Newport that has helped me renegotiate my relationship with my phone. What I have found most helpful is the practice of weighing the value you gain from a specific app – how much it actually improves your life – against the cost of your lost time and attention to engage fully with others. This includes your capacity for Deeply Listening. If it doesn't weigh up, the app is terminated.

You might be wondering how you can keep an eye on the time without your phone, if you need a hard stop – to pick up the kids from school or make sure you're home for the start of the big match. With fewer clocks, set a timer on your mobile for five minutes before time is up, so you can remain undistracted and present. There's now time to wrap up elegantly.[19]

There's another sort of ending that can help ground you in your journey to become more present. Spending time with a skeleton.

A Skeleton's Message

I found myself face to skull when I went on a silent retreat at Gaia House meditation centre in Devon. I meditated alone in a beautiful ground-floor room beside huge bay windows filled with giant tropical leaves. It wasn't the plan, but I couldn't avoid the presence of the skeleton seated in the alcove, placed there to cast thoughts into the minds of the meditators. It made me think of all the artists who had painted skulls or hourglasses in their work. The skeleton and I sat looking at each other for many hours over the days of the retreat. My ambition: to become more comfortable with fears about mortality, and thus more able to value the irreplaceable significance of each moment.[20] I found the experience both fundamentally shocking and strangely grounding. The reality of the future facing me and everyone I love was inescapable and beyond my power to change. (The skeleton, meanwhile, is now in therapy.)

The skeleton's message was echoed by something choreographer Akram Khan said to me as I was leaving his south London home. Khan encouraged me to value my time with my mother, Judith, who is fragile and not so young. Aware of the preciousness of family, Khan himself was feeling a little raw, vulnerable and alone. For the first time since his children were born, they were travelling with his wife while he remained on his own, only catching the memory of their footsteps echoing around an empty house. 'I know it's not the last time, but just treat it like this is your last time,' Khan urged me. 'Cherish every moment you're with your mother.' I can communicate how much my mother Judith means to me by being truly present when I am with her. Every visit could be the last. Khan knew there was no possibility of turning back and catching another memory with his father, who had passed away only months before. His parents' proximity, just around the corner from his own home, had granted him a false sense of security.

As you decide on an intention for your encounter, now hopefully centred and present, ask yourself: What's most important to me about listening right now? What do I really want for our relationship? How would I like to feel afterwards?[21] And then, consider what it would be like to want nothing. Remember that at any moment you can return to your safe anchor to ground you.

As Canadian First Nation guide Brenda Holder and I are saying goodbye, she makes a gesture that surprises me. She places the tips of her fingers in mine and then holds my fingers with a timid grasp, and speaks, just above a whisper: 'I must hold you gently. Our hearts are in our hands, and so we are now connecting with our hearts. I do not want to crush your heart.'

These words initially feel a little intimate, but as they settle, they leave me conscious once more of Holder's warm presence. As both women retrace their steps back down the dirt track, I am aware of the gradually diminishing crunch of pine needles beneath their feet.

Having moved into a state of presence, sending a powerful signal to your speaker that they are worthy, worthy of your focused attention, you are now ready to direct that presence towards your speaker in a way that cultivates trust and openness, which we'll unpack in Step Four.

Be Present Takeaways

Cultivate awareness to create a space to listen | Bring attention to your own emotions and centre yourself so you can respond rather than react.

Sense surrounding space | Feel the openness of the space around you, ready to welcome your speaker's whole being. Recognise your mind is already free of craving.

Develop mindfulness | Create your own regular mindful practice for difficult moments. Seek opportunities in daily rituals. Choose an embodied awareness practice. Or your breath. Repeat. Daily.

Tune up before an important encounter | Set aside the time.

Eliminate external distractions | Become aware of anything that might distract you. Place your phone on silent and out of sight.

Become aware of boredom and internal distractions | That may prevent you from listening to uncomfortable thoughts. When you notice your mind wandering, acknowledge the thought and return to presence.

Be Present Challenge

Set aside 10 minutes before an important or challenging encounter. Remove external distractions and turn your attention to external noises and let them go. Enjoy getting acquainted with your breath. Try the 4-7-8 breath (page 145) or listen to a meditation. As the conversation unfolds, notice any internal distractions. How do they show up in your body?

After the conversation, ask yourself: Was I present in the encounter? How did I handle external and internal distractions? Can I centre myself now as I reflect back?

STEP FOUR:
BE CURIOUS

Philip Davies bends down and tenderly strokes a pregnant cow lying in the straw, soon to give birth. She welcomes his steady hand. Davies's pride radiates from his smile as he talks about each animal in his precious herd. They all have names – Mabel, Antoinette, Estelle – names that have echoed through generations of family cattle since the 1950s, drawn from what he calls the foundational herd. Davies is a tall man with an erect magisterial presence, blue-grey eyes, and an authority resting on hands lined by five decades of dairy farming. 'I was born a dairy farmer, milking a cow when I was six or seven – and my father and grandfather before me.' This is Davies's true home, between the valleys and hills of Wales and England, within eye-shot of the Snowdonia peaks.

I feel hesitant, even a little nervous, before I meet Davies. I've come to visit him for a piece I am writing for the BBC website, to see if I can Deeply Listen to him to understand his perspective. As I stand next to him in the tall Wellington boots I've been lent, I wonder: Will I be able to genuinely listen to this man?

'When I was at school not far from here,' Davies tells me, 'some of the boys ordered Chairman Mao's *Little Red Book*. When the books arrived, the headmaster, who used to deliver the post to us boys every morning, would throw them into their porridge. I feel the same about climate change.'

A deep love, appreciation and understanding of the environment that nourishes his treasured cows has not led Davies to accept this pressing global reality. 'Climate change is the biggest load of tosh. It's lies beyond lies,' Davies fumes as he leans his arm on the corner of his cowshed, scanning the newborn calves. I am aware of a fierce, indignant response welling up inside me. The evidence is clear: there is a near-universal consensus among scientists that humanity is driving the dangerous warming of our planet.[1]

I tune in to the vast expanse of sky to centre myself. I notice a conflict between Davies's world view – a deep affection for and connection with the environment and the animals he tends – and the possibility that dairy farming could be harming the planet.

Davies's clear love for his individual cows sparks my empathy towards him, which in turn nourishes my respect for his intimate knowledge of animal and earth and sky. Despite my belief in the reality of climate change, I hope that he feels that I have genuinely come to listen, learn and understand. I hope that my presence conveys that I take his ideas seriously. We'll hear about how he responded to my listening later.

I'm trying to cultivate and communicate, in my conversation with Davies, *curiosity*, *empathy*, *awareness of my judgements* and, finally, *respect*. When these four qualities are woven together with a stillness so alert it's almost pulsating, our listening can elevate conversations into more profound encounters.

To shed light on what it might feel like to be bathed by these four qualities, imagine being listened to by someone who holds, in every fibre of their body, the following convictions:

I'm interested in you as a person,
and I think that what you feel is important.
I respect your thoughts,
and even if I don't agree with them,
I know that they are valid for you.
I feel sure that you have a contribution to make.
I'm not trying to change you or evaluate you.
I just want to understand you.
I think you're worth listening to,
and I want you to know
that I'm the kind of a person you can talk to.[2]

Embodying these profound ideals, co-authored by psychologist Carl Rogers, enhances your unconditional positive regard towards your speaker, which is at the heart of Deep Listening. Internalising these principles, however, is demanding. It's even tougher when you stand on different sides of an argument.

After centring yourself, try starting with one quality and gradually build up the others. The invitation is to begin with the gateway of curiosity.

Cultivate Curiosity

Indifferent listening

As I entered the cavernous office of Ethiopia's head of state, President Meles Zenawi, my overriding imperative was to prove that I was prepared to face up to its occupant – that, and making sure my recorder didn't malfunction. I barely glanced at the three guards in military dress who downplayed their presence, melting into the walls.

Meles Zenawi came with tough credentials. He'd been a fighter in a guerrilla army, spearheading the struggle against Ethiopia's previous regime. As a leader of his country, he was also known for his ruthless treatment of opponents: arbitrary detentions, threats and beatings. The president was now building a reputation as an African leader who could speak on behalf of the whole continent. To demonstrate my journalistic prowess – it was in my early days at the BBC – I wanted to challenge Zenawi on the record about this repression. I had met some of his adversaries in the bar of the Ghion Hotel in Addis Ababa, where they recounted their harrowing tales over local beers.

In my interview, the president began with his vision for Ethiopia, parading his success at growing his country's economy. 'I'd like to be remembered,' he proclaimed, 'as someone who effectively tackled our proverbial poverty.' This topic was not on my agenda, so I quickly moved the subject on to human rights. As the interview progressed, he circled back, trumpeting the mounting production of maize, sorghum and barley. Once more I brought the topic back to the treatment of dissidents. 'What about the US State Department's reports on human rights?' My questions were mere masks, cover for my desire to confront Zenawi. I had very little curiosity or desire to hear his answers, much less to understand him.

I sensed the president was getting angry with my refusal to listen. But rather than expressing his growing rage in words, he literally withdrew, edging farther and farther away from me into the corner of his vast wooden presidential desk. Determined to capture his words, I leaned forward with my microphone, stretching so I could continue to hold it close to the president's mouth and overcome our growing psychological distance. But as Zenawi became more defensive, so did I, and any hint of interest or authentic curiosity slipped between the security guards and out the door. Frustrated, his sentences became shorter. Even less enlightening. Then, he put a sharp stop to our conversation. Early. End of interview.

Zenawi would remain in power for 20 years. When he died, the former US ambassador to the UN, Susan Rice, spoke of his world-class mind and wicked sense of humour. 'He wasn't just brilliant. He wasn't just a relentless negotiator and a formidable debater … he was uncommonly wise, able to see the big picture and the long game.'[3] I think back to how my lack of curiosity led me to squander a once-in-a-lifetime opportunity to explore Meles Zenawi's labyrinthian character. I don't believe I was wrong to challenge the Ethiopian president. What I regret is my failure to demonstrate a genuine curiosity to understand his vision while also holding him to account.

When you are distracted by other imperatives, as I was in Ethiopia, it's easy to stop listening after a few opening words, only paying attention to the gist of what's being said. In such encounters, you firmly grasp the wheel to steer the speaker towards answering your burning questions. This sort of curiosity is a façade – not the curiosity of Deep Listening.

Authentic Curiosity

As your speaker is figuring out your intentions, you need to convey, swiftly, that your prime motivation is to understand them better. Your curiosity sends a message that your speaker is worthy of your time and attention. You validate them as a person, without necessarily validating their perspective. So, what are the hallmarks of authentic curiosity in a Deep Listening context? You acknowledge that the speaker's perspective is different from yours, and that you do not already understand it and cannot infer it. You need instead to encounter their world, with its own tastes and flavours, so you can build a deeper understanding of your speaker and enrich your own perspective. Changing your mind is not the ambition, but it might be an outcome. In the landscape of curiosity, you recognise a gap in your knowledge. When it's filled, you feel relief. But, as researchers have identified, it's also an ongoing and joyous quest,[4] as you wonder about what may yet unfold and where your speaker will go next.

This spirit of genuine inquiry leads Alastair Campbell to move beyond a simple single understanding. Campbell, who was a key member of former Labour Prime Minister Tony Blair's inner circle, disagrees agreeably every week with Rory Stewart, who used to be a Conservative Party MP, holding various ministerial posts. The setting: their podcast, *The Rest is Politics*. Campbell told me about his experience of being listened to by Stewart on a special edition to mark the 20th anniversary of the controversial US and British invasion of Iraq.[5] Two decades ago, Stewart was a young British diplomat working for the US-led occupation authority responsible for the Marsh Arab region of southern Iraq. Campbell was at the heart of an administration in crisis in the chaos following the invasion.

Campbell was reluctant, initially, to relive those challenging days and months. He'd been interviewed too many times about that stressful period. But to his surprise, he and Stewart ended up talking on that podcast episode for two hours. What made the difference? Campbell explained that Stewart was truly curious. Campbell was taken aback by this level of curiosity, knowing that Stewart's circle of friends often chided him, 'You're far too soft on that Alastair, he's a complete bastard.' Campbell shares this with a wry smile. Stewart wasn't trying to catch Campbell out, even if Stewart fundamentally objected to the policies of the Blair government. Campbell found himself being truly open, recognising weaknesses, for example the deep flaws of the administration that they set up in place of Saddam Hussein's. 'We were overwhelmed by challenges,' Campbell acknowledged.

'I've never heard you talk about the war like that before,' Campbell's partner, Fiona Miller, later reflected.

You may find it harder to be curious about opposing viewpoints or topics that don't interest you. That's commonplace. What might help you get back on the road to curiosity is the knowledge that a little curiosity can serve as a priming dose, according to research, sparking further curiosity.[6] If you're curious about, say, a new neighbour's family, and he tells you about his daughter's dream of becoming a teacher, this snippet sparks a greater interest on your part. Your neighbour's world is now a land in which you have gained a foothold, creating an expanding frontier that can help feed your curiosity as the conversation unfolds.

When dairy farmer Philip Davies gave his explanation for the recent warming of planet earth – 'it's part of a regular cyclical long-term temperature change' – my first thought was surprise. How could someone believe this? But instead of responding with dismissal or outrage, I was determined to stay curious. I knew he enjoyed a profound connection with the land. For days, weeks, months and years, he'd been exposed to the brilliance of the sun's rays as well as the anger of 4a.m. sheets of rain. The contradiction between his lived experience and his beliefs drove my curiosity to know what lay behind them. I grasped that being a dairy farmer, part of his generational story, was critical to Davies's identity, and anything that threatened that, including action to mitigate climate change, was difficult for him to embrace.

Muted Curiosity

The personal risks at the heart of Deep Listening can also stunt our curiosity. Oscar Wilde, maestro of pithy observations, perfectly captured this peril when he wrote: 'It is a very dangerous thing to listen. If one listens one may be convinced.'[7] As Wilde intimates, if we are truly curious, beyond learning new facts, we may discover something which disrupts the way we see ourselves. For example, if you are genuinely curious when you ask your partner for feedback about the way you listen to them, their response, if it contains any criticism, might challenge your view of yourself as a kind person who takes the time to understand others.[8]

In other conversations, you may imagine that you already know what will be said next. If you are listening to your child making that same complaint about the teacher who always picks on them, or your friend worried yet again about their demanding boss, you envisage what they will say and stop listening. The Jewish theologian and philosopher Martin Buber had a memorable term for this sort of smug arrogance: *the leprosy of fluency*.[9] Buber coined this phrase when discussing how people tend to translate biblical texts, but this leprosy of fluency can also act as a huge barrier in your listening, preventing you from experiencing true curiosity. When your curiosity is muted, and when you presume to grasp the rich landscape of another person's thoughts, feelings and experiences, your presence and engagement are muted, too. Your child or friend may sense that you are not really interested in them or their story and may cease confiding in you.

If You Were Me, What Would You be Curious About?

For leaders, curiosity is an especially important quality. While many boast of their listening prowess and desire to truly understand their employees, fewer approach conversations with a genuine desire to learn. The Wikimedia Foundation's CEO, Maryana Iskander, is a leader whose curiosity is sewn into her internal fabric. I reached out to her when I learned about her focus on listening as a tool to navigate the start of her challenging role. Leading the non-profit that inspires volunteers across the world to donate their knowledge to Wikipedia is no easy task.

Iskander tells me that she wanted to dig below the surface to understand how her new organisation functioned. When she met members of her new community, she posed a question: 'If you were me, what else would you be curious about?' It's worth pausing for a moment to reflect on this question. Iskander's unexpected query encouraged her colleagues to identify with her desire to know and then match her curiosity by engaging in their own.

So, how can you practise authentic curiosity when you ask questions and listen? Try to pay special attention to anything unexpected that you hear, and notice what surprises you. Your curiosity can extend beyond the facts you are hearing to also encompass how your speaker feels about them. When you notice yourself going into reactive mode, remind yourself: I'm listening to understand more. If your speaker is angry or hostile, there's a way to reframe their negative emotions that you may find helpful: when we receive a gift and decide not to accept it, it naturally stays with the sender. Similarly, if someone is hostile, you can hear them and be aware of this 'gift' of hostility, but choose not to accept it.[10] Another strategy is to imagine that your speaker's words are coming from a positive place; what good intention might be driving them? This alternative focus allows you to remain in a land of discovery, not knowing where they will go next.

You can also be curious about what it is like to be them, to inhabit your speaker's distinct set of circumstances, beliefs, emotions and desires, to enter their unique universe. To reassure you, it is hard for anyone to grasp the complicated experience of being someone else; we can never really understand how another person sees the colour red or feels pain.[11] But appreciating that we all encounter the world utterly differently – whether it's experiences of love or betrayal, parenthood or friendship – can take our curiosity to the next level.

Embody Empathy

I'm inspired by the Turkish phrase 'listening with your heart's ear'. These poetic words were told to me by artist and listening advocate Vuslat Doğan Sabancı, who draws upon the idea in her work.[12] In one of her sculptures, two six-foot high marble ears are intertwined in an embrace. Listening with your heart's ear allows you to connect with the speaker beyond your mind and past your intellect.

Being open-hearted is central to empathy. When you are empathetic, you share the emotional state of your speaker. But you also recognise that they are the source of these feelings; the emotion does not belong to you. You are welcoming the speaker and their world into yours, as a temporary guest. And in this way, you can support the other person without allowing them to trespass on your own boundaries. Acknowledging the distinction between your feelings and those of your speaker,

and understanding that empathy does not compel you to endorse their ideas, can allow you to extend empathy to people with dramatically different perspectives.

Counter-terrorism counsellor Rashad Ali extends empathy to those whom many deem supremely undeserving, working alongside prisons, probation services and the police. His past has given him insights that are invaluable for his current role. In his late teens and early twenties, Ali was a leading figure in Hizb ut-Tahrir, a radical group seeking to establish a caliphate or Islamic rule across the globe. Hizb ut-Tahrir is currently banned in many countries, including the UK, so it's a criminal offence to belong to it. Ali now believes the group promotes a totalitarian ideology, and he is actively involved in undermining it.

Today, Ali listens to young people, mainly young men, who embrace and sometimes act on similarly extreme interpretations of his religion. Some have attempted murder. I meet Ali, softly spoken with a carefully trimmed beard extending into a white flourish below his chin, on a quiet, red corner sofa on the eighth floor of my old BBC World Service office in Bush House, London, now a student café. In the course of his work, Ali has come to understand that empathy is critical. He recounted listening a number of years ago to an Afghan boy, Mehdi, who had arrived in the UK as a child refugee. They met in the boy's new flat. It was a challenging interaction. Mehdi confided to Ali his hostility towards British soldiers. 'They blew up my home. They killed my family. I need justice and I need to free my home from these colonisers.' It transpired that Mehdi was planning to exact revenge.

Ali started by explaining to Mehdi that he wanted to talk to him about how he felt. Empathy, Ali believes, is not about agreeing or disagreeing with someone's position, but rather the ability to understand where someone is coming from and why they think or feel that way. 'You just feel you can connect – it is subconscious, implicit. I believe emotions can be trained, though sometimes I fall short, inevitably, and get annoyed with myself afterwards.' Eventually Ali will pass individuals like Mehdi on to a professional who is specialised in dealing with their specific type of trauma.

There are profound lessons to be garnered from Ali's approach. He reminds us that we need not infuse our empathy with approval, but that it is important to recognise the humanity and uniqueness of each individual we listen to. Faced with challenging conversations, we don't have to take all the responsibility on our shoulders – we can reach out to others for help. As Bella Bathurst writes in her book *Sound*: 'There's a big difference between offering someone a better connection and knowingly taking on another man's poison.'[13] When you extend empathy, you are not required to take on their pain, or their beliefs, as your own.

'I've Been There' Empathy

One strategy many of us use to express empathy to someone sharing a painful story – whether it's the trials of a troublesome teenager, losing a vital customer or the heartache of a miscarriage – is to tell them about a similar experience we've had so they know they're not alone. Though it may come with the best intentions, the 'I've been there too' approach carries a significant cost. It's an interruption that moves the spotlight from them to us. When we start to tell our story, we stop listening to theirs. People often ask how to convey support to their speaker without sharing their own story. I believe that your speaker will be able to sense the heightened empathetic texture of your listening enriched by your similar life experience. Your intensified empathy will be woven into the quality of your kindness; it will emanate through every pore of your body, without you needing to make it explicit.

A coaching client once confided in me about the devastating impact of losing her father when she was just 13 years old. As I was listening to her, I was acutely aware of my intense desire to share my own story of losing my father at the same age. I wanted her to feel that she was not alone. Perhaps subconsciously, I also wanted to derive comfort from acknowledging that shared experience. But I resisted these impulses and remained silent. When she evaluated our coaching journey, she said that she had sensed a deep rapport and a profound connection between us. I believe she felt my understanding, perhaps even more than if I had spoken of my own loss.

Before publishing this anecdote, I reached out to her to check if she was happy that I was including it in this book. I felt a little uncertain, not having communicated with her since our coaching relationship many years earlier. She replied, 'This has touched me deeply. Thank you so much for trusting me with this. Without knowing that experience had happened to you too, I think I did indeed know. And you're right that the unspoken nature of that knowing somehow deepened its profundity.'

Another strategy when you want to extend empathy to anyone you don't know well is to think about how little you know about the challenges or traumas they have faced. Most people will have experienced some type of trauma during their childhood – ranging from parents separating to a natural disaster.[14] Being aware that my speaker is likely to have faced some degree of significant hardship allows me to interpret their words more generously.

Empathy with Boundaries

You need to acknowledge and communicate your boundaries when you extend empathy. Imagine you are listening to a colleague talking about the challenges they are facing with their partner. They misinterpret your warmth as romantic interest. To reset, you can shift the topic to a less personal one. You can also do something physical to disrupt the conversation, like searching your bag for a tissue, or suggesting that you move to a different location. When you are listening to someone you know well in your family, community or at work and you feel in danger, physically or emotionally, it may be harder to put up these protective boundaries. If you suspect that you are at risk, it's not appropriate to open your heart and Deeply Listen. Your safety comes first.

If you feel safe to be open-hearted, your speaker feels encouraged to share a more authentic story, with details that start to illuminate their internal world. You're then more likely to develop an empathetic understanding of their perspective, creating a virtuous circle.

Feeling and expressing empathy is also an antidote to shame. Shame is an intensely painful and complex experience of 'believing that we are flawed and therefore unworthy of love and belonging,' writes former social worker and professor Brené Brown, known for her ground-breaking research in this area.[15] A sense of being alone feeds a feeling of shame, which in turn leads us to fear our own vulnerability, so we avoid close contact. The balm of empathetic listening can help to mitigate shame, by enabling a speaker to begin to trust, creating a deeper connection. You can imagine how powerful any listening intervention might be if it is able to heal even a tiny part of the shame that infects so many.

Leave Judgements Behind

If you are judgemental when you listen, you are signalling to the speaker that they are not safe, as if their identity is being scrutinised and could be found wanting. As if their status or very worth is at stake. To obtain your approval, when they feel judged, your speaker may obscure what they feel permitted to express or even imagine.

The goal, therefore, is to create a place of safety for your speaker, a place without judgement. The poet Dinah Maria Craik evocatively described this place of refuge in these words:[16]

Oh, the comfort – the inexpressible comfort of feeling safe with
a person –
having neither to weigh thoughts,
nor measure words, but pouring them
all right out – just as they are.

The freedom to express themselves without restraint, as Craik portrays, is a precious gift. However, this sense of freedom can quickly evaporate if your speaker senses you are making judgements about their character. Such judgements can come across as threatening, particularly if you are in a position of power, or even if you are not. 'You can't seriously be thinking that's a solution,' you jokingly respond to a friend, and fail to realise how your implicit judgement about their intelligence pierces through their assured exterior to decimate their inner confidence.

Articles about listening commonly urge their readers to be non-judgemental. However, this may be counter-productive. As conflict mediator Gary Friedman put it to me, 'It's just not effective, as judgements are the mechanisms that we use to make sense of the world.' If you tell people to be non-judgemental, they can also feel blamed and defensive, as if they are doing something wrong.[17] Instead, try to notice that judgement in the moment and see it for what it is, before letting it go. Acknowledge that this pause in judgement can be temporary, you don't have to suspend your critical eye permanently. If you discover, however, that you are seizing the lifeboat of *your* point of view as the only safe way out, remind yourself that there are often multiple and equally valid perspectives on any given issue.

Multiple Perspectives

The idea of multiple perspectives is embodied in the Zen rock garden in the grounds of the Ryoan-ji Temple in Kyoto, Japan, reputedly created some 500 years ago by a Zen Buddhist monk.[18] I made a point of visiting this tranquil space during my travels in the country. Sitting there, I noticed the chirping cicadas from the trees beyond, echoing over the surrounding yellow sandstone walls. The sun danced between the clouds, casting fluid light on the 15 island boulders that emerge from a sea of grey pebbles. I became aware of another woman, seated nearby, who was also looking at the rocks but witnessing

slightly different shadows falling on the surrounding tiny stones. I became aware that my point of view was mine alone, not shared. Both our perspectives were true. One does not negate the other.

There is another insight about the value of multiple perspectives hidden in these 15 rocks. In Japan, the number 15 has long been a symbol of perfection. The rocks have been planted so that wherever I stood on the surrounding wooden terrace, I could never see all 15 of them. At least one rock was always out of sight. Likewise, our perspective is always limited. We alone can never possess the complete truth. We always need to listen to others to gain a fuller picture.[19]

The Path of Obliquity

While the larger purpose of a conversation may inspire you, you don't want that purpose to fuel your judgements and distort your listening. One solution is to take what author John Kay calls 'the path of obliquity':[20] that our goals are best achieved when we approach them indirectly. The listening practice of counter-terrorism counsellor Rashad Ali demonstrates how we can Deeply Listen for a specific purpose, in his case, countering extremism, without judgements getting in the way.

At the start of any encounter, Ali is transparent with the people he's come to listen to. He tells them if he is working on behalf of whoever is employing him, whether the British government or an anti-extremist think-tank. But to have a chance to realise these wider ambitions, Ali needs to temporarily abandon his motivation and move with obliquity to a place where his judgements don't impede his ability to Deeply Listen. You can also communicate your wider motivation for having an encounter, to convince your elderly parent to take their medication, for example, and then explain that you are there to listen and understand their concerns. Their feelings are valid for them.

In the Process of Becoming

At the heart of being able to let go of your judgements is an active choice to be free of the person's past as well as your own. You can accept that they are not limited to being the same person as they were yesterday, and neither are you. Can you let go of your prior disagreements, the resentments that you've fostered, and the sins that your speaker has committed? You have the choice to accept, as Carl Rogers frames it, that the individual is a person who is in the process of *becoming*, someone capable of unfolding in new ways and of catapulting to new heights.[21]

People act and develop in ways that we never could have predicted. I can attest to this, witnessing clients dramatically evolve during their coaching journeys. We ourselves can evolve as well. I once harboured a deep-seated fear of speaking in front of a large group. Once the group massed into this larger pack, I thought, it would grow terrifying teeth. When I was invited to memorise and deliver a TEDx UK Houses of Parliament talk, I almost didn't accept. When I got up on stage, I found, to my surprise, that the rows of people looked interested rather than fiercely judgemental. Having survived intact, I now enjoy public speaking. I have come to understand that, however large the audience, it is still composed of unique human beings with whom I can forge a relationship, be it strangely asymmetrical. Reminding yourself of how you have changed may help you believe in others' capacity for change as well.

When you notice the judgements that you've been harbouring about your speaker, and then begin to release them, a new sort of attention becomes possible. You can now enter a place where you recognise that they, like all of us, have a dignity worthy of respect, regardless of who they are or what they have done.

A Little Respect

One evening, when I was nine years old, my elder sister was chasing me through the small corridor of our flat when I fell and hit my head. It hurt. Badly. Our mother was taking a bath, and I cried at the door. When she finally emerged, I recounted, through tears, my sister's terrible behaviour. 'Do you have concussion?' she probed, grasping both my arms. Not knowing the term but liking the sound of it, I nodded. I felt bathed in her concern when she asked if things were blurry. 'Completely,' I replied.

Thus began a longed-for adventure. I received new coloured scented pens, a folder of animal stickers and heaps of attention – as the middle sister of three, it was the supreme treat. At school, I was saved from having to copy paragraphs from the blackboard, onerous because of my mild dyslexia. I was invited to the Royal Free Hospital for three days of intense observation, bouncing on my bed and sharing games with other children on the ward. The only drawback was the humiliation of having to use a potty; I was not permitted to venture past the four corners of my blanket.

Periodically during my hospital stay I was wheeled to a basement clinic where a senior doctor would talk to throngs of eager medical students about me, as if I wasn't present. He placed heavyweight metallic glasses on my face and interchanged the lenses, asking me if I could see more clearly. Sometimes I replied yes. Sometimes no. Randomly. Looking back on that experience, I realise that no space was given for me to express my ideas, thoughts or fears. The trainee doctors milled about me, confused.

Back home again, I started to grow tired of this escapade. I was trapped in my lie. My parents were also frustrated – and increasingly worried. Three weeks passed and they took me for a second opinion. When we entered this new consultant's office, he explained that he wanted to speak to me, and then my parents, separately. I was impressed by his desire to hear from me first and alone, as if he believed that I too could shed light on my plight. But despite his warm and curious manner, I told him what had become my standard story of hitting my head on the wall and everything going blurry.

As I spoke, he looked at me intently, patiently, as if everything I had to say held weight and could help solve the mystery of the crisis in my vision. Being considered an authority wasn't something I'd often experienced as a mischievous nine-year-old. Behind his steady supportive eyes, I sensed that this doctor knew. Yet he still took me seriously and communicated that he accepted me. Next, he showed me a collection of differently coloured dots and asked me to identify numbers in the patterns. It was as if my defences were no longer necessary. For the first time, I answered truthfully. The next day I told my parents that the world was no longer hazy. I could see again.

Looking back, I find it extraordinary that I kept up this lie for so long. Now, as a parent myself, I regret putting my own parents through so much needless anxiety, as well as taking up that hospital bed. I don't know how I could have broken free of the lie without the consultant's thoughtful attention. He conveyed to me that, although I was a child, I was worthy of being truly listened to. I still remember that magical, freeing sense of being respected despite my flaws, despite my lies. It was a huge sense of relief. Feeling respected made it safe to be truthful.

Respect Unpacked

Respect calls for us to acknowledge that other people have ideas and desires that are unique, having lived through experiences that are different from our own. To acknowledge difference and still convey respect you might find it helpful to remind yourself that your parent, colleague, friend or stranger has insights that you cannot imagine. You recognise that there is a gap in your understanding which they alone can fill. You do not respect your speaker for their actions or their thoughts, but instead for their personhood, which is shared by us all.

In Rashad Ali's words, 'We all feel lonely – we all feel misunderstood – we all feel that sometimes the only person who will listen to us is ourselves.' For Ali, the possibility that he can help those vulnerable to extremism move to a place where they can recognise the dangers motivates him to offer sincere respect. Bringing authentic respect to an encounter is also about communicating the idea that you and your conversation partner are fundamentally equal, regardless of your backgrounds, education or roles. This equality entails recognition that their identity or set of beliefs is different, but legitimate in their eyes, and that their insights are valuable. You can imagine how impactful that feels to a speaker, especially if they have entered the conversation fearful of your real or perceived power.

Listening with respect also means being flexible and patient if your speaker is not using their mother tongue. This point is critical for Wikimedia's CEO, Maryana Iskander, as her community is extraordinarily diverse. Wikipedia volunteers create pages in more than 300 languages. 'People who don't speak English as a first language often have to rewire their brains and expend more energy than if they were speaking in their native tongue.' For Iskander, respect is about acknowledging these hurdles and listening with deep intent.

Understanding that others are doing their best, struggling to make sense of the world and make a real contribution to society, are all important aspects of respect, as highlighted by philosopher Axel Honneth.[22] It's about seeing someone in their entirety, as a moral being, whatever their status, and recognising that they have an existence that is parallel to your own. Try suspending your scepticism and choose to see the best in your speaker's intentions, tipping the scales of judgement towards the side of compassion, recognising their potential to unleash good in the world, even if, at first, these assumptions feel like an improbable stretch.

Megan Gonsalves, a Barbadian participant on my global Deep Listening programme, has been drawing on this idea of respect in conversations about a range of topics, including controversial ones like human rights and animal rights.

'Deep Listening has shown me that the pathways that drive people's opinions do not come from a place of malice, ignorance or indifference, even when we fiercely disagree. Their beliefs spring from real experiences they've had over the course of their lives. I now understand how valuable conversations can be when I'm not only inquisitive but I'm also able to put any negative filters aside, and instead offer the person a welcome and an acceptance.'

Reaching for an I–Thou Encounter

When you offer your speaker crystal-clear attention – curiosity, empathy and respect, together with an awareness of your judgements – a sort of magic unfolds, transporting you both into a different space. As the artist Antony Gormley told me, 'The self that is created through our relations with others is maybe the most dynamic, the most plastic and actually the most alive self there is.'

The thinker who has done perhaps the most to unpack this heightened state of connection is the philosopher Martin Buber. He is best known for distinguishing between *I–it* and *I–thou* encounters.[23] I–it encounters are contractual; we each want something from the other, so we treat them as instruments, as objects for us to use, someone from whom to extract value. In these encounters, we assess, compare, sum up and analyse. We treat them as a static, determined *thing* 'that can be broken down into parts, and surveyed, studied or measured'. In I–thou dialogues, we temporarily surrender ourselves in order to step into a new space co-created by us and our speaking partner, standing alongside them. In these moments, we realise that the other person is utterly unique, and so are we. We turn towards their uniqueness, their particular being. There are no anticipations, no preconceptions, no purposes, no aims and no desires. 'Not as though nothing exists apart from him but all else lives in their light,' Buber writes. These relationships are transformational for us both. One feature of these I–thou encounters is that they are transient, flowing and ebbing and flowing back again, through conversations and relationships.

Can we capture and prove the existence of this elusive I–thou chemistry? Uri Hasson, a neuroscience professor at

Princeton, has found a way to peer inside the minds of a speaker and listener during an exchange. His ambition, to understand that listening feeling, which he describes as 'that feeling when you just click with someone. You can finish their sentences. It's almost visceral.' In his lab, Hasson and his colleagues placed people horizontally inside an fMRI scanner (similar to an MRI scanner but focusing on the brain) to measure the patterns in their brains while they either told or listened to a story.

One woman in the scanner was asked to tell a 15-minute story about an experience she'd had during her first year of high school, as if she was talking to a friend. The neuroscientists recorded her brain activity alongside that of people who were asked to listen to a recording of her story. Afterwards, the researchers asked questions to gauge the listeners' comprehension. The fMRI recordings demonstrated that the listeners' brains started to resemble the storyteller's brain, or 'couple' with it – referred to as *neural entrainment*. The better the listeners understood the woman's high-school story, the stronger the resemblance between the speaker's and listeners' brains – in regions such as the *superior temporal gyrus*, which helps us process speech, and the *insula*, which plays a role in our emotions and self-awareness. For the listeners whose scores were highest, who understood the woman's story the best, there was a 'meeting of minds'. During the telling of the story, the same areas of the speaker's and listeners' brains 'lit up' simultaneously.[24,25]

* * *

When I published my article about the farmer Philip Davies on the BBC website, I was uncertain how he would react.

I had placed his perspective amid information about the impact of dairy farming on climate change and the science behind it. When we spoke a few days later, Davies told me that he felt that, unlike previous journalists who had interviewed him, I had genuinely come to listen, without judgements and without an agenda. He said that he had felt heard. I felt moved by his comment, especially given our different perspectives (more to come on how I made sense of his deeper narrative in Step Eight). Now, I needed to check in with Davies again. Would he permit me to include our conversation in this book? 'Of course,' he replied. 'Come and visit me on the farm again, to begin your second book on Deep Listening.'

True, open-hearted and unconditional positive regard can intensify your encounters and deepen your relationships. It is the basis of Deep Listening. In the next step, we'll discuss specific and practical tools you can use to signal these qualities to your speaker.

Be Curious Takeaways

Be curious | Seek to understand your speaker's world and acknowledge that it is unknown territory. A little curiosity can be a gateway to spark more curiosity.

Notice what surprises you | How do you think your speaker feels about telling this story?

Listen empathetically with your heart's ear | Enter their private world and feel at home.

Stay safe | Acknowledge these are their emotions, not yours. Communicate boundaries.

Forgo 'I've been there' empathy | It moves the spotlight from them to you.

Let judgements go | After becoming aware of them. You don't have to suspend your critical eye forever.

Acknowledge the value of multiple perspectives | To gain a fuller picture.

Make positive assumptions | About your speaker.

Cultivate respect | For the humanity of the person speaking rather than because of anything they say or do.

Experiment with I–thou rather than I–it encounters | Recognise your speaker's uniqueness. Experiment with listening without purpose or desire.

Be Curious Challenge

Before an encounter, ask yourself what you might be curious about. For example, you could be curious about how your speaker's background and experience shape their attitudes. During the conversation, become conscious of your empathy barometer. Does empathy flow naturally? What would help you access your empathy? Can you witness your judgements moment by moment? And how does embodying these qualities impact the respect you feel?

After the encounter, ask yourself: Was there anything my speaker did, or about their way of being, that made it especially easy/hard to listen to them? Did I judge them or feel judged?

STEP FIVE:
HOLD THE GAZE

Hawraa Ibrahim Ghandour steps into a classroom in her home village in southern Lebanon, ready to start an English lesson. Today she will be teaching the conditional tense. These students are in their late teens, all of them Syrian refugees, with lives disrupted by war and displacement.

'If I were not tolerant, I would not accept others,' she declares. With this sentence, Ghandour demonstrates the conditional. Can her students come up with their own phrases?

Ghandour pauses. She is a substitute teacher, needing to form new relationships each day. She looks warmly at her group, keeping her gaze kind, her shoulders relaxed, hoping someone will speak up with their own conditional example.

One young man, Hassan, stretches up his hand, hesitantly.

After a moment, Hassan starts to tell a story. 'We can't go out at night. It's not fair that me and my Syrian friends have to be home by 9p.m.' Becoming more agitated, he recounts the intolerance that he and his friends have experienced. His pace quickens. 'In this village,' he tells the class, 'all Lebanese people discriminate against us.' Another student agrees – he's been wrongly accused of stealing chickens. Ghandour knows that it's unusual for Syrian students to share their experiences with her, a Lebanese woman from this village. To encourage them to continue, she maintains a steady gaze.

Ghandour was a standout participant in the Deep Listening workshops that I ran in Lebanon, over Zoom. I'm impressed by her diligence in bringing the lessons about body language to her teacher's desk. As she speaks to me, I can sense her warm and loving gaze, even though we are many miles apart, communicating solely through our screens.

Ghandour has reservations about the number of Syrian refugees her community has absorbed owing to the civil war there, a perspective shared by many fellow villagers. But creating the space for her students to have an unguarded discussion is immensely meaningful to her. She empathises with their disappointment, frustration and anger. 'You need to show them that you are open and trustworthy to encourage them to open up,' she tells me. 'If I look like I am not going to understand your fear, or your pain, or your agony, I'm not going to be a Deep Listener.'

I also pick up on how intentional Ghandour is. The conditional lesson is forgotten as Ghandour builds on the opportunity to encourage others to voice their experiences. In that moment in the Tuesday classroom, she is aware of the direction in which her eyes are cast (straight at her students), the angle of her body on the chair (slightly forward) and the expression on her face (warm and accepting).

When you listen, while you are not speaking, you are communicating without words, often without being conscious of what you are conveying. The person who you're listening to subconsciously reads your signals. But through this exchange, which includes your gaze, expressions, gestures and stance, you are collaborating with them, having a real impact on the story that they will construct, as we learned about in the previous step.

The Gaze

You've probably had the disconcerting experience, at a party, a work meeting or the school gate, when you notice that the person you are talking to is no longer looking at you. Their eyes are sliding surreptitiously beyond you, to scan the room or space, searching for someone more engaging or important to move on to. You feel a touch diminished. Perhaps you've visited a doctor who seems more interested in their computer screen than in catching your eye, especially if they have a difficult diagnosis to disclose. Conversely, when someone's eyes are upon you, their gaze can be so captivating that it almost feels as if you're being touched.

Beliefs about the power of the gaze have endured across the centuries. Anyone who stared at the ancient Greek monster Medusa was transformed into stone, literally petrifying them. The French philosopher Michel Foucault highlighted the gaze of surveillance to describe how a prison functions. 'There is no need for arms, physical violence, material constraints. Just a gaze. An inspecting gaze, a gaze which each individual under its weight will end by interiorising to the point that he is his own overseer.'[1]

The gaze that Foucault describes is so powerful that it penetrates the mind, feeding the prisoners' paranoia and ultimately controlling them. No wonder then that my invitation to maintain eye contact with a speaker is met with hesitation. Some people assume that there is only the Foucault gaze; there to expose, stripping back the layers that people wrap around themselves for protection. You might fear that looking into the eyes of your speaker, and keeping them there, might be misinterpreted as a soul-crushing glare. Others hesitate for a different reason: they don't yet have the confidence to look someone in the eye.

The Quality of the Gaze

Before we look at the physical direction of your eyeballs, let's explore what's beneath your gaze when you Deeply Listen. This is neither a confronting glare, nor a prying gaze to invade their territory, nor a flirtatious invitation. And it is also not a rigid stare, in a competition to keep your eyes open the longest without blinking.

The Deep Listening gaze is supportive, flexible and supple, as if you are encircling another in a gesture of warmth. Your eyes are an instrument through which you can continuously convey the Deep Listening qualities of curiosity, empathy and respect without judgement.

Texture is another way to think about the way you look at someone. I've never learned how to ride a horse (I'm allergic to horses), but if you have, you might be familiar with the advice to use *soft eyes*. When you ride with *hard eyes*, your eye muscles are taut; you are sharply focused, seeing very clearly but with limited range, almost oblivious to your surroundings. In contrast, riding with soft eyes improves your balance, you are connected to both horse and other riders. This gentler gaze also expands your vision and your awareness, so you can take in the entirety of the environment around you.[2]

When you look at your speaker with soft eyes, you are filled with wonder about where they will go next. As a Deep Listener, think about projecting a sense that you are open to receive whatever your speaker chooses to share – however unexpected or outrageous – reflected in your sustained open expression. If you catch yourself straining and becoming too focused on your own agenda, switch to a more receptive soft eyes mode.

Embodying these qualities can be powerful, and can enable a speaker to feel held, heard and connected to you.

Directing the Gaze

Many of us hesitate to look directly into the eyes of the person we're listening to, but academics have found that, of all the cues we use to communicate, a direct gaze is one of the most important. Newborn babies prefer to look at faces that engage them in a mutual gaze.[3] Adults, too, are highly attuned to the direction of a gaze. If your speaker starts a sentence and discovers that you're not looking at them, they will often abandon that thought, disrupting their flow of thinking, only restarting when you make eye contact again.[4]

Mutual gaze, keeping eye contact with your speaker while listening to them, is linked to more activity and flow in the regions of your brain associated with understanding and inferring what other people are feeling.[5] Studies reveal that not only do your eyes convey a wealth of information about what you're interested in, they also hint at your future intentions,[6] for example how long you intend to listen. Even with a stranger, if you look straight at their eyes, rather than slightly to the side, they are more likely to feel close to you and believe that you have things in common, that you are someone from their tribe.[7]

Holding the Gaze

It might feel rather intense if you and your speaker were to stare at each other for a long time. A signal that you are intimate or, on the contrary, you want to fight. In reality, while you try and keep your eyes resting on your speaker, your speaker will often look elsewhere. Then at key moments, when they want to check in with how you're responding, they will return your gaze. This period of eye contact is called 'the gaze window', a time when you insert a nod, or a hand gesture, or you say, 'Uh-huh.' Creating this window with your speaker is a sign that you are working together to co-ordinate your gaze and response, which in itself is a signal of being in tune.[8]

When I coach clients, they will often be silent for a while, and their eyes will move away and upwards as they turn their attention inwards. I try to be fully present, with a Deep Listening gaze. No words are exchanged. Often, in these moments, I sense that something almost magical is happening, that by accompanying them on this journey they will amass the courage to venture down a new path. After a period of time, which can last as long as minutes, they will meet my eyes, and perhaps choose to share a new insight.

When I was listening to the story of my Russian-Ukrainian friend Sofiya, we embarked on just such a journey as she began to think differently about the loss of exile. 'My pain is not going anywhere,' she said, and I held the silence, watching her with warmth and understanding. Her eyes wandered, her focus turning inwards. Then, she met my gaze again, offering an unexpected reframing of her own life: 'I'm not sure I want [the pain] to go. I don't think I'll be *me* if I do that.' Afterwards, Sofiya reflected that she felt comfortable to look away, but when she did make eye contact, she felt a strong connection, which helped her to think more deeply and open up to the possibility of a new way of thinking.

The transformative impact of a direct gaze, if given with the positive intent described above, is well documented, but in some societies it's not appropriate. People growing up in

Indigenous cultures, for example, may have learned not to look their elders in the eye but to keep their eyes downcast.[9] Sustaining eye contact also isn't straightforward for everyone. If you have ADHD, your capacity to pay attention for a long time without being distracted is limited – although with practice, you can improve. If you are on the autism spectrum, looking someone in the eye might be challenging. You might find it easier to close your eyes as you listen. And what if you are without sight or have limited sight, or you are listening to someone on the phone, unable to look at them? What lies behind the gaze, your positive intentions, can also be conveyed through other non-verbal signals.

Your Own Body Language

The photographer Platon uses his body in a deliberate way to signal his positive intentions and to create rapport. Often, he will sit on the floor beneath his subjects, at their feet. 'Depending on how they feel as a person and how I'm reading them, I might be leaning on something close to their knee while I'm chatting to them. Or I will sit back, giving them the confidence to lean forward.' He has refined his body language over thousands of shoots across the world. Platon does not assume that he is entitled to his subject's trust; he has to earn it. He does so by fine-tuning his own body movements, like a dancer, to reflect their body. When Platon's assistant hands him the camera, Platon's body language changes – he will crouch with his shoulders, lowering his camera to his chest. Then he bows. Through his body, he hopes to project a sense of safety and communicate humility despite the obvious power of his camera.

He told me about a project to document the stories of immigrants to the United States. Platon had travelled to the US state of Arizona to photograph a Mexican woman, Fermina Lopez Cash, who lived on the US side of the Mexican border and worked as a house cleaner. When Platon entered Cash's room to take her portrait, she started to cry. She was grasping a framed picture of a boy. The boy was her 13-year-old son, who had tried to join his mother three years earlier. Just days before Platon came to photograph Cash, her son's remains were found in the Arizona desert.

'I put down my camera and I gave her a hug and she sobbed in my arms, even though before this moment we'd never met. She then made a noise that went through my bones. It was the sound of a wounded animal. It was an "aahh" [Platon makes a helpless, guttural noise]. I still remember the vibration of her groan going through my body.'

Just after that groan, Cash pushed Platon, aggressively. 'I want you to photograph my pain. I want it seen. I want people to know what I am going through. Now, in this state,' she demanded.

Platon picked up the camera and took a picture of a mother bent over in grief, with her hair strewn across the picture of her son. The photographer's body language, both carefully calibrated and instinctive, enabled him to earn Fermina Lopez Cash's trust; he communicated to her that she could claim her agency and take charge.

Our bodies are finely tuned instruments, which, when we're listening, signal a world of feelings and expressions to our speaker that will help shape their story and their experience of relating it, mostly without them noticing. Coach Nancy Kline writes that when a listener's empathetic attention is in full flow, they are using every pore of their body to send signals encouraging the speaker to keep going. 'These messages beam from the relaxed warmth in their eyes, from their very occasional nod of understanding, from their electrifying stillness, from their absorption in and of every word the person is saying, *and* of what they are not [saying].'[10]

The term *electrifying stillness* resonates with me. The phrase conveys that while your body might not be moving, it is still charged with an active presence, tuned towards and responding intuitively to what you are hearing, feeling and sensing. Though you are embodying stillness, you are demonstrating your attention in other ways: through your slow nods (quick nods can convey urgency and impatience), your eye contact, your relaxed muscles, your posture, your verbal utterances, 'hmm' for example, expressed in a way to show that you are keen to understand more, and your smile.

A Spontaneous Smile?

If you smile, not only with the muscles around your mouth but also around your eyes, research demonstrates that your speaker is more likely to see you as friendly, likeable and approachable.[11] Your own heart rate and stress levels may lower too.[12] On the other hand, if you try to suppress your facial expressions, your speaking partner will feel less rapport with you.[13]

The impact of a smile on what the speaker chooses to share has been demonstrated in an experiment. Participants were told to watch a film clip – about the owner of a kiosk interacting with customers – and then describe it to two people. Half the participants summed up the film to pairs who'd been instructed to smile, and the other half related the film's story to pairs who'd been told to put on a serious frown. If they faced two frowning listeners, the speakers read the listeners' expressions as a sign of rejection or misunderstanding, so they tended to stick to clipped, concrete descriptions, such as 'Customers enter the store and buy cigarettes.' In contrast, if their listeners were smiling, the speakers felt free to offer more thoughtful interpretations of the film, with inferences about the motivations of the characters, saying things like 'He doesn't trust people any more.'[14] As a Deep Listener, with an authentic open smile, you invite your speaker to go beyond a shallow exchange.

Smiling non-stop, regardless of your speaker's words and feelings is, not surprisingly, unlikely to go down well. You could wait for your smile to spontaneously arise. But I also like the invitation attributed to Buddhist teacher Thich Nhat Hanh: 'Sometimes joy is the source of your smile, but sometimes your smile can be a source of your joy.' To set the mood and calm yourself before an important encounter, a warm empathetic smile can be powerful. One way to cultivate an authentic smile is think of something that brings serenity or joy. It might be a loved one or a beautiful natural scene. Imagine an inner smile radiating from your heart, sustaining and life-affirming. Let that feeling radiate across your face and beyond, to encompass the space around both you and your speaker, as you acknowledge your shared humanity. As the conversation unfolds, feel free to let your smile emerge, reflecting your empathy and understanding. Authenticity, as ever, is your best guide.

People smile in cultures across the world, but culture also informs how we communicate and interpret smiles and other facial expressions. In Japan, to signal that you are pleased, smiling eyes are more important than upwardly curved lips. It's no surprise then that sunglasses are often frowned upon in Japan, but mask wearing has been embraced with little hesitation.

Making use of the insights about a direct warm gaze and open supportive body language can put your speaker at ease. But what about *their* body language? How much can you as a listener glean from your speaker's face, tone of voice and gestures?

Decoding Your Speaker's Embodied Messages

I remember the wise, patient smile on the face of the mother of the household as I listened to her showing me how to stretch out the dough. We were preparing mountain bread in Beit Jann, a remote Druze village 10km from Israel's northern border with Lebanon. The Druze are a small Arabic-speaking minority whose distinct religion originally developed out of the Shia branch of Islam. Researching my undergraduate dissertation on the overlapping identities of the Druze had brought me here; bread-making lessons were an unexpected bonus.

Even without a common language I could interpret urgent signals. One bright morning, in a mischievous moment on a rooftop, I was dancing joyously and innocently with the youngest members of the family to the tin sound of the 80s band UB40 blaring from my cassette recorder. As I looked up to the neighbouring rooftop, I saw an older religious woman wearing a heavy dark dress and a transparent white veil. We had been spotted. The flashing daggers in the woman's eyes communicated her outrage. I felt the guilt pulse through my body, though I never established whether it was the music or the dancing that had crossed the line. Neither was repeated.

If you are sighted, it is likely that multiple times across a single day you observe and draw conclusions based upon other people's body language to make judgements about their emotions, thoughts and feelings, as I did in the Druze village.

For centuries, the idea that we can ascertain the thoughts of others from their body language has been a widely, if not universally, acknowledged truth. Take this example from Jane Austen's *Pride and Prejudice*. In this scene, Mr Darcy has just been delivered an unexpected and monumental blow. His declaration of love, coupled with a magnanimous offer to marry Elizabeth Bennet, has been rejected, despite the inferiority of her family to his own.

> Mr Darcy, who was leaning against the mantelpiece with his eyes fixed on her face, seemed to catch her words with no less resentment than surprise. His complexion became pale with anger, and the disturbance of his mind was visible in every feature. He was struggling for the appearance of composure,

> and would not open his lips till he believed himself to have attained it.[15]

Darcy's anger and internal turmoil are reflected 'in every feature' of his face, and he struggles to bury his emotions. The strength of his feelings is impossible to hide. Yet Jane Austen knew how difficult it is to correctly interpret emotions and intentions from body language; it's a theme running through the whole of *Pride and Prejudice*. Austen's insight is supported by the latest research – more to come on that later. But first let's hear from someone who has developed a degree of mastery in intuiting meaning from the movements of others.

Choreographer Akram Khan has developed an acute understanding of the body. To create a piece of work, a dance that resonates emotionally with his audience, he needs to determine how to move his body and direct the bodies of others. Every quiver of a finger or slide of an elbow is intentional and precisely planned to convey a message.

In contrast to a dancer's carefully choreographed movements, children, especially younger ones, Khan believes, have a more innate and organic connection between their emotions and their physical expressions. Reading their body language is far more straightforward. When a child is excited, he explains, they're jumping across the world. 'My one-year-old literally fell to the floor this morning and put her forehead on the ground. It's life and death because I took her toy away from her. That's her telling her truth. A direct connection.'

True to form, Khan uses his finely tuned skill to try to tackle the challenges he has encountered in listening to his eldest son. Every night before bedtime, Khan's elder children come to his bed, and they act out a new ritual – *jiu-jitsu*. The boys are focused on improving their moves and beating their father.

He's letting them win. But for Khan, 'the purpose is to listen to them'. Khan will notice if one of his sons rolls his shoulder more slowly or is less keen to escape from his grasp. With curiosity and compassion, the choreographer can then ask him what's wrong. 'Today,' his eldest son tells him, 'somebody called me a name. It felt bad, but do you think I'm really like that?' It means the world to Khan that he can tell, through reading his son's movements, when something is upsetting him. And that through this understanding Khan is able to create the space for his son to share those fears.

So, when you are Deeply Listening to someone and want to use clues in their facial expression, gestures and tone to gain a sense of what they really mean, how certain can you be that you are interpreting them correctly?

The Accuracy of Non-Verbal Cues

You may be aware of a memorable fact that's been lurking in the shadows of communications research – 93 per cent of communication is non-verbal. Of that, we deduce 55 per cent of what we understand from a speaker's face and 38 per cent from their tone of voice. Verbal communication, it seems, accounts for a mere 7 per cent of the meaning we glean as someone speaks. This statistic has been widely cited in textbooks, academic articles and many popular online posts. I remember the sweeping self-assurance with which a trainer at a BBC management course instructed us that only 7 per cent of our communication depended on the words we used.

The striking statistics raised questions in my mind. I needed to know what the research was based on and how robust it is. The trail led back to 1967, when Professor Albert Mehrabian at the University of California, Los Angeles, embarked on a mission to investigate what happened when there was a clash between the meaning of a spoken word and the speaker's body language and tone of voice.

Mehrabian and his team conducted two different experiments with psychology students, each a piece of the puzzle. The first study asked participants to look at a written word such as *great*, *really* or *terrible*. Simultaneously, two women spoke the same word, but in a positive, neutral or negative tone of voice, regardless of the word's actual meaning.[16] In the second study, participants were shown photographs of women trying to express *like*, *neutrality* and *dislike* through their facial expression. At the same time, participants heard a voice say the word 'maybe' in a tone that conveyed liking, neutrality or disliking.[17]

Extraordinarily, neither study compared, side by side, the power of the speaker's words, tone of voice and facial expression. In the second paper, Mehrabian mysteriously combined the outcomes of these two distinct experiments, assigning different weights to their results (without revealing how he did this) to deliver the widely quoted statistic: 7 per cent verbal, 38 per cent tone of voice and 55 per cent facial expression. Mehrabian himself believed that his research was often misinterpreted and misrepresented, arguing that it would be absurd to suggest that the verbal portion of communication made up only 7 per cent of the message. 'Suppose I want to tell you that the eraser you are looking for is in the second right-hand drawer of my desk in my third-floor office,' he wrote. 'How could anyone contend that the verbal part of this message is only 7 per cent of the message?'[18]

While these studies are now seen as flawed, and their application seriously limited, Mehrabian was instrumental in highlighting the role that non-verbal communication can play. But the question remains: how do the different ways we communicate stack up? What does more recent research reveal?

Mehrabian's study highlighted facial expressions as being more significant than tone or the actual words in conveying meaning. But recent findings suggest the contrary – the facial expression of your speaker may be misleading. Though Mr Darcy might have struggled to conceal his outrage in *Pride and Prejudice*, people can often mask their true feelings when they speak, giving a smile, for example, when they are feeling anything but positive. There are also large differences in the way individuals use their face and body to express their feelings. Some speakers are dynamic, swirling their hands about, while others sit stock still and project a poker face. By becoming aware of the baseline of your family, friends and colleagues, how they normally behave, you may be able to use non-verbal clues to help discern their mood. It's harder with a stranger you're encountering for the first time.

Indeed, it is not that we can't interpret what people are thinking or feeling from their facial expression and therefore should completely disregard this clue. It's that often we may be wrong about the meaning behind the speaker's expression, according to psychologist Adam Grant.[19] For example, if I see someone smile, I might interpret that expression as a sign that they are happy or pleased to see me. They might instead be experiencing what psychologists call *duping delight*, excited that they're about to take advantage of me and get away with it (surely not). On the flip side, someone might look anxious, and I assume that they're upset with me. In fact, they're worried about whether they're going to be taken seriously or be able to snag the last doughnut on the plate.

Reading the Tone

Your speaker's tone of voice, in contrast, is worth paying special attention to. It's a more accurate way to tell what they're feeling, compared to the expression on their face. You can imagine the range of inflections in your voice that you could use when you asked someone, 'What's the problem': dismissive, suggesting that the speaker should not bother responding, or empathetically inviting them to elaborate. To elicit more information, you can ask yourself: What does their tone of voice evoke in me?

As a coach, I find that a strong sigh can often be a sign that something important has shifted in my client's thinking. Take Sofiya's deep exhalation at the moment she recognised that there was a chasm between the person she had been and the person she had become. This exhalation from deep inside her body seemed to be a release not only of stale air but also of stale thinking.

A tone of voice is harder to mask than a facial expression, which is why it's easier to interpret someone's emotions on a voice-only call,[20] when you are not distracted by their face. But even with tone it's hard to be certain that you are accurately reading your speaker. There are, however, some clues. Comparing anger, joy and sadness, research suggests that anger and joy both tend to be expressed in a tone that is louder, higher-pitched and spoken with a faster speed in comparison to sadness. Listening for the range of tones can help distinguish between joy and anger; someone who's joyful in contrast with someone who's angry is more likely to speak with a greater spread between their highest and lowest notes.[21]

What about gestures? Proof that we can accurately interpret gestures, such as moving hands or nodding, is less convincing.

Speakers make gestures because they think that they're helping listeners understand them better. But the evidence is more mixed, based on an analysis of more than 60 studies about how accurately we interpret these physical expressions. Gestures can help in some situations, for example if your speaker wants to give a sense of scale and points to a nearby object as a comparison – 'It was a raging river, that high' – or if you don't speak the same language as the speaker. Otherwise, especially when your speaker is talking about an abstract idea, don't rely on the power of gestures to enhance your understanding.[22]

Not surprisingly, there's been a lot of research into how much gestures give someone away when they're lying. From uncovering fraud to preventing acts of terror, there's a lot resting on the capacity to reveal when people are or are not telling the truth. You might guess that you will see signs of nervousness, your speaker averting their gaze, touching their nose or shifting around. But in reality, research indicates that to determine if someone is lying, these non-verbal cues are unreliable.[23]

The Tapestry of Signals

There is no need to be hypervigilant, paying attention to a thousand things simultaneously, just because you know about the myriad ways that your speaker can communicate their thoughts and feelings. Most likely you will interpret their signals as a pattern, as a whole picture.[24]

Meanwhile, you can use your eyes, face and body to signal to your speaker that you are listening to them with attention and curiosity. Being roughly aware of your own gaze and body, and how they relate to the gaze and body in front of you, can help you enter a dance of increased trust and understanding.

Being roughly aware is the point here. Letting go of any self-judgements about your own body language can also allow you to be more natural. Even here, too much effort to come across as relaxed can be self-defeating. To be natural, as Oscar Wilde famously quipped 'is such a very difficult pose to keep up.'[25]

Having established that accurately interpreting your speaker's meaning is far from guaranteed, we'll turn in Step Seven to how you can check in with them to learn if your hunches about what they are saying and conveying with their body and words are correct. But before we do that, we need to give them some space. So, in Step Six, we will turn to the extraordinary power of silence.

Hold the Gaze Takeaways

You are co-creating your speaker's narrative | Through how you respond, in expression, gaze and tonal acknowledgements to what you hear and understand.

Become aware of your body | How are you communicating with your body, breath, shoulders and hands? Can you convey a warm empathetic non-judgemental curiosity?

Hold your gaze | Powered by your internal smile, electrifying stillness and grounded, open posture.

Cultivate soft eyes | Empathetic rather than hard and goal-oriented.

Become aware of your speaker's body language | Tone is a more accurate signal of their feelings compared to their gestures and facial expression.

Can you come to a place | Where you and your speaker's non-verbal signals are communicating seamlessly to transform the encounter?

Hold the Gaze Challenge

In your next conversation, become aware of your own body language, and in particular your gaze. As you listen, see if you can keep looking at their eyes with a soft, warm quality. Notice if you feel uncomfortable. Be aware when their gaze wanders and then returns to you. Afterwards, reflect. Did the mutual gaze strengthen your rapport?

STEP SIX:
HOLD THE SILENCE

As Hannah starts to make sense of what Adam, her brother, is telling her, the shock reverberates through her body. His deed is taboo, disregarding the religious values they were brought up with, the trust of his wife and the future of another woman.

Hannah stays silent.

I met Hannah when she took part in one of my programmes. In her experience, gaining the confidence to step back and not speak, to stay silent, has been life-altering. Adam has not shared this heavy burden with his wife, anyone in his family, anyone in his community. Until this exchange. It's a long call. At first, Adam is angry. Angry with the world and angry with himself, telling Hannah that his life is destroyed, that perhaps it should end. Hannah listens in silence to the tale of how her brother met a woman while working in the Netherlands, as his wife of 10 years remained at home in the Middle East. How he became closer to this other woman. And now she is pregnant.

Hannah feels outrage at a world that allows one person, even if it is her brother, to shatter the trust of his wife, whom she knows well, and to fundamentally alter the life of the woman he slept with. Hannah has a powerful impulse to tell Adam that he has acted like a criminal. She knows she is judging him.

Silence.

Hannah gives herself a pause. She centres herself. 'I'm watching myself. I know I'm a very emotional person, there's a tornado swirling inside me. I also know silence is better than speaking if I'm angry. Better than speaking when I'm fearful.' Hannah reminds herself that we are all human. We all make mistakes, sometimes serious ones. So she continues to be still. To settle herself, Hannah reflects that if she wasn't perceived as a strong listener, someone he could trust, Adam wouldn't have told her this heavy news. She feels shattered. But also grateful for the opportunity to listen to her brother, to be with him at this vulnerable time. Hannah waits until her brother has told all his story, till she has heard all his worries, till the end.

And more silence.

Hannah reflects that sometimes silence is more potent than judgement. She didn't condemn Adam, but neither did she reassure him or make light of what he had done. In the space that Hannah created, Adam was able to pause. And, in that pause, he could reflect and confront tough choices. Perhaps, as a starting point, though this might risk his marriage, just perhaps, he could be open with his wife and tell her the truth.

Hannah tells me that she is proud of herself. That if she hadn't taken up Deep Listening, she would have behaved in a very different way. And that without her silence, a silence that allowed her brother to develop trust in her ability to truly listen, he would have not been able to share and begin to imagine a way forward.

Using the Presence of Silence

There was no interrupting in the silence that Hannah offered, no attempt to devise a solution. The silence held the space for her to witness her condemning judgements and let them be, to feel an acceptance not of what Adam had done, but of him as a brother, with all his weaknesses. And this accepting silence gave Adam the room to acknowledge his life-changing deed and start to think about how to navigate his future.

Silence, as acoustic ecologist Gordon Hempton writes, 'is not the absence of something but the presence of everything … It is the presence of time, undisturbed. It can be felt within the chest. Silence nurtures our nature, our human nature, and lets us know who we are.'[1] This is a powerful reframing of silence, challenging the idea that its presence is defined by its emptiness. Hempton captures the physicality of silence, and its nourishing potential to transform our understanding, and that includes our understanding of ourselves.

Silence is integral to Deep Listening. Interestingly, *silent* and *listen* are made of the same six letters. When you Deeply Listen, after your speaker has finished a thought, I invite you to try to wait for three, five, even ten seconds, while you hold your warm gaze steady in their direction. They may give more insights or consider, without words, the implications of what they've just shared with you. Naturally, the opposite of Deep Listening silence is interruption, stealing from your speaker their time to think.

This step will unravel the many different threads of silence and address any resistance you may have to an extended pause. We'll explore the evidence for the impact of a respectful, empathetic silence on your speaker, on yourself as a listener and on the depth of your connection.

The Wide Spectrum of Silence

Silence is the absence of words, not the absence of communication. The writer Paul Goodman unpacked its many messages in *The Nine Types of Silence*: 'There is the *dumb silence* of slumber or apathy; the *sober silence* that goes with a solemn animal face; the *fertile silence of awareness*, pasturing the soul, whence emerge new thoughts; the *alive silence* of alert perception, ready to say, "This … this …"; the *musical silence* that accompanies absorbed activity; the *silence of listening to another speak*, catching the drift and helping him be clear; the *noisy silence of resentment and self-recrimination*, loud and subvocal speech but sullen to say it; *baffled silence*; the *silence of peaceful accord* with other persons or communion with the cosmos.'[2] [emphasis added]

Before we explore the more generous silences that Goodman highlights, let's dive into some of the disruptive undercurrents of silence, and their capacity to stir up ripples of unease, disquiet and distrust.

Our Resistance to Silence

Silence, I acknowledge, has a bad reputation. There are *conspiracies of silence, deafening silences* and *epidemics of silence*. Silence has been seen as a symptom of fear, defensiveness or even deviance.[3] If you are silent, you worry that people might interpret your absence of words as weakness, an inability to generate new ideas. You fear silence will be interpreted as a sign that you've lost interest or are bored. You have, you believe, an obligation, an imperative, to fill that gap and keep the conversation going. When you cover up an embarrassing silence you think you're empowering your struggling speaker to find the words. You support them by completing their sentences, reassuring them, conveying that you are on their wavelength and know exactly how they're feeling. Consider the following dialogue between Billie, a patient, and her sister, Rose, who has come to visit her in hospital.

Billie: The doctor's just told me I seriously need to think about having this surgery. But … *Billie clasps her arms across her body, tightly.*

Rose: Oh, don't worry! You're in great hands. I've heard your surgeon's really experienced. You'll be back on your feet in no time.

Billie: But I'm not sure if I'm ready for this. There's just so much that's …

Rose: That's a bit new? Trust me, everything will be fine – honestly. I've had countless friends go through this and you can too.[4]

Rose minimises Billie's feelings, then races to simplify a difficult dilemma, instructing her sister how to act. Rose doesn't give Billie time to wrestle with and make sense of her fears about the operation; instead, she jumps in, denying the possibility of reflection and genuine sense-making. While her tone feels patronising, Rose was probably genuine in her desire to be helpful and comforting. Like Rose, I used to frequently interrupt or complete people's sentences for them, both in an effort to be helpful and to avoid a pause which I was convinced would be awkward.

Awkward silence. When I lead Deep Listening workshops and I bring up the importance of silence as a core element of Deep Listening, I often hear this phrase. As we reflect upon our first practice, participants always recount their discomfort with sustaining silence. People fear that their speaker is primed to misinterpret silence, that silence will break any connection that they've created, as if uninterrupted sound waves are the only precarious thread linking them to each other.

Silence carries other risks too. Perhaps you avoid silence in the hope of preventing ideas you find difficult from being expressed out loud, such as criticism of your parenting skills by your own parents, for example. There may also be perspectives which are hugely challenging, about an alternative grasp of a conflict from across a political divide, for example, or the belief that AI will surpass human intelligence and come to control us. Rather than allow space for your speaker to create and voice these 'disturbing' ideas, you avoid these people altogether or slash the silence and charge in with your alternative and superior arguments. Your version of the truth is preserved and prevails.

Controlling Forms of Silence

People with less power can be prevented from speaking up and raising concerns; they are effectively being silenced. I was explaining my Deep Listening work to Amina, who works in policy and advocacy for a US NGO. She was sceptical about the rewards of silence and explained why.

'Amina, come to my room and bring me my purse,' Amina remembers her mother telling her. Amina's mother trained her daughter to sit still and listen until her instructions were over. No asking questions. No possibility of an opinion. No answering back. Only silence. Amina grew up on the Tanzanian coast, in a traditional family. Here, she tells me, silence was central to the way that children, in particular girls, were brought up to behave.

Amina arrived home from school one day, accompanied by an older cousin she'd met on the way. There was a lunch portion ready for her, cornmeal with cooked sardines and tomato, alongside a dinner portion of beef stew and rice. Amina ate the sardine lunch and offered the beef dinner to her elder cousin.

'When my mother returned, she was ballistic with rage. How could I have been so greedy and eaten two portions of food? I knew the highest act of disrespect was to open your mouth when your elder was talking to you. So, I did as I was supposed to do: I listened in silence. Even as my mother beat me.'

When the same cousin came around at dinner-time, everyone realised what had happened. No one thought to question why Amina hadn't spoken up earlier. As Amina is telling this story today, I see her still taut with indignation at the unfairness of being punished for her hospitality, denied the opportunity to speak the truth.

Amina, who now has children of her own, identifies as an African feminist. Being forced to be silent for so many years motivates her to help others speak out today. Amina is full of respect for some aspects of the tradition in which she was raised, but reflects that this type of silence forced upon children and women sits uncomfortably with her values. Indeed, the imposed silence that Amina describes is designed to amplify the voices of a select group and suppress the voices of others, depriving them of the opportunity to question or challenge the status quo. It is not the silence of Deep Listening.

If your own experience of silence feels painful, imposed upon you by people with more power, I invite you to recognise that a Deep Listening silence has an altogether different timbre. You cultivate a Deep Listening silence out of choice. You have agency. As a Deep Listener, it is you who makes an active choice to create a spacious place for others to think freely.

The Silence of Deep Listening

Within a Deep Listening pause, you embody, with the help of your open-hearted gaze, the essential elements of a Deep Listening approach – curiosity, empathy, respect and awareness of judgements – as well as a healthy dose of active patience and acceptance. And as a reminder, this is an acceptance of the other person's humanity, not of their views.

With silence, your speaker's expectations of being interrupted are subverted. They feel recognised when they thought they would be ignored. Dutch listening authority Corine Jansen describes the silence of her listening as a place of safety for her, where she is able to fine-tune her body as her instrument, to be receptive to her speaker:

'This silence is a unique point in history. Your speaker is here, with tiredness, with pain, with thoughts and feelings – but I am also here, and I choose to be here with my whole being, as much as I am able. There is nothing else. This is the beauty of listening *with* a human being instead of listening *to* a human being. It's an ethical choice, to accompany someone as they find their own narrative.'

You may have experienced a *companionable silence*, perhaps when you are walking with a close friend in a wood or along the beach. Comfortable in their presence, you don't have to talk to prove that you are at ease. This is the polar opposite of an awkward silence. There is no tension or animosity that you feel compelled to try to dissipate with words.

There is a close relationship between cultivating a Deep Listening silence and cultivating patience. Writer Oliver Burkeman defines patience as an 'active, almost muscular, state of alert presence'.[5] He describes an experience of patience, which could also be used to describe a Deep Listening silence, as 'tangible, almost edible … as if it gives a thing a kind of chewiness'.[6]

There is no judgement in a Deep Listening silence. When I was being listened to by Canadian tour guides Brenda Holder and Larissa Heron, during the long pauses I felt no pressure from them to deliver a fascinating insight. In their luminous silence, I knew I would be accepted whatever ideas I chose to share.

'Silence is golden, a place of learning,' Heron explained. 'I am learning now, as a young adult, you don't have to fill the space. If you let it be, things will come to fruition. In our Indigenous world, we are far more comfortable with silence. Silence is the space in which we exist.'

In that rich silence, both you and your speaker have the space to generate not only new thoughts, but also, as Heron expressed, to allow things to come to fruition, for meaning to emerge.

You will know how powerful silence is when it is used judiciously by a speaker. Think of Dr Martin Luther King's famous speech, 'I have a dream', and its long pauses. These pauses not only projected confidence and gravity and allowed the rapturous applause to die down, but also gave time for the audience to comprehend the implications of his pivotal vision and connect with it in their hearts. When you listen and offer a healthy pause after someone has finished speaking, you are similarly indicating that you genuinely desire to understand the richness of their words and thoughts. Silence is a valuable tool to send a powerful message to your speaker – one of respect.

Elevating Your Connection

Silence signals that you are not trying to dictate terms and control the agenda of this encounter. Instead, the conversation will have a more natural rhythm, allowing both your bodies to slow down. Scientists have identified that silence reduces your heart rate and your blood pressure,[7] so practising these pauses can be a powerful way to create conditions in which more reflective thinking can unfold.[8] When you are both more reflective, especially when you find yourselves in dispute, each of you is more likely to be able to see the other person's perspective.

The intentional pause after your speaker has finished a thought is also a moment to rise above the clutter and racket of busy lives. Through creating this generous reflective space, you provide room for you both to tap into something more meaningful and profound. In the silence where you wait to know what they will think and say next, trust is generated between you.

Silence is Golden

In negotiations, silence is popularly perceived as a tactic to intimidate. But recent research in a paper titled 'Silence is Golden'[9] challenges this belief. One or both participants in a negotiation were asked to be silent for 20 seconds after the person with whom they were negotiating had finished talking. Contrary to expectations, this extended silence did not lead to one party gaining at the expense of their opponent. Instead, the *if you gain, I will always lose* mindset was replaced with more reflective, thoughtful and deliberative thinking on both sides. In this more creative state, the parties could then together generate solutions with mutual benefits – many more *win-win* outcomes. The 'Silence is Golden' work draws on the ideas of Nobel laureate Daniel Kahneman[10] and his distinction between automatic System 1 and more deliberate System 2 thinking. Silence can provide the space and quiet for both parties to move to a System 2 way of thinking, which in turn can craft golden opportunities to expand the pie.

Practising a Deep Listening silence may even have a life-changing impact on your most important relationship, as Maria, a Mexican woman who'd taken part in one of my Deep Listening programmes, recounted.

Maria used to be a serial interrupter – jumping in early, full of emotion, without waiting for anyone, especially her husband, to finish a sentence. Her husband also mirrored a symmetrical habit of breaking into her words. Differences quickly burgeoned into arguments, of which there were plenty, as there was no buffer between home and work. Maria's husband was the CEO of a business that employed more than 180 people in many cities. She, his project manager.

In the office, Maria was a perfectionist, and she cared. 'I always speak from my heart, so I would challenge anyone who isn't being very professional, if they are arriving late, for example. It's my husband's business, so I feel very loyal towards him.' Not everyone in the office welcomed Maria or her supervision. She felt that people were coming 'from under the table' to complain to her husband about her.

One evening her husband said he needed to tell Maria something important: he needed to sack her. When Maria heard the news, she was stunned.

'If it was me before this course, it would have gotten into a *big* problem. The worst thing is I love to interrupt. And I always feel my husband should prioritise my needs, whatever they are.'

Maria felt the urge to let loose. But in that moment she cast her mind back to the Deep Listening steps. And she recalled the practice of silence. Maria paused for 10 long seconds. The seconds gave her a space that was pivotal in empowering her to hold back. The pause also created an opening for her husband to explain more. Rather than it being him pushing for her dismissal, it was a client who was insisting that Maria must go.

Maria was able to step out of pure reactivity during her long pause, giving her husband time to elaborate. This client came from a prominent family in an important city for the business, and his support was vital to enable the company to survive. Her dismissal was the only solution. Maria's husband guaranteed that the move would be temporary.

Today, when Maria looks back at that moment, she feels that the silence transformed what came next. Without the silence that allowed her husband to give her the critical context, that incident could have threatened the trust between them or even led to their divorce. Maria's silence not only created the space to allow her husband to explain his dilemma but also enabled her to move into a more reflective frame of mind in which alternative perspectives could be entertained.

Silence, however, does not land so softly and powerfully with every speaker. People who are depressed may be more likely to interpret silence as a sign of rejection, and may feel more anxious when someone grants them a few seconds of silence than those without that condition. Depression can lead people to imagine that someone is silent because they are not interested in them or don't care about them.[11] Other conditions might also make silence feel threatening or uncomfortable for your speaker. So, if you don't know the speaker well or you feel your silences are being misinterpreted, cut back on their duration, or check your speaker's tolerance for pauses.

Transformational Pauses

Silences mould sound. I came across this phrase in George Prochnik's book *The Pursuit of Silence*,[12] and it captures the power of silence to shape whatever comes before and after it. A silence can not only stop you from saying something you may later regret, as in Maria's case, but it gives you both a chance to consider the meaning of the words that have just been spoken. A rich, expansive silence is also fertile soil for your speaker to mould the thoughts they will generate next and the words they will share.

If you don't give your speaker that silence, the silence filled with your warm-hearted attention, they may be restricted to the same ingrained mental grooves. However, when you focus and guarantee that you will not interrupt, they can feel secure, so their mind is gifted the space to soar. In that unimpaired creative space, if your speaker stumbles across an obstacle in their thinking, they silently ask themselves a breakthrough question so their mind can continue on its way.[13]

I learned more about transformational silence in a somewhat extreme setting (the same place I had encountered the skeleton). When I told friends that I was planning to go on a silent retreat, some reacted with laughter or told me, 'I give it an hour.' The 'rules' at Gaia House, a silent meditation retreat centre which was formerly a convent, touch on the puritanical: 'All retreatants are expected to refrain from engaging in conversation with others, including writing notes or non-verbal interaction.'[14] When we passed someone in the corridor, we were to cast down our eyes to avoid the rich exchanges possible with eye contact. It was no surprise that we had to hand in our phones. Even reading or painting were out of bounds for the duration.

By chance, my first retreat was due to start only days after the sudden loss of my close friend Lara, and I contemplated cancelling. But perhaps, I thought, this space might allow me to start to inch towards comprehending her death?

In keeping with the rules, I was silent as I sat down at meals with other retreatants, perched on a cushion for hours through group meditations, took slow mindful solitary walks in the surrounding gentle hills, and carried out my allotted daily task: chopping the garden-nurtured carrots and beans. A thick intentional silence filled the grounds and seeped into the bodies of everyone present. Our default was an intense stillness. Internally, I started to adapt.

Without the auditory distractions that ordinarily intrude and dissipate my focus, I began to hone in on acute sensations in the most precise and unlikely places. The pattern in the grain of the wood on the edge of a door frame, the smooth roundness of a garden pea against the roof of my mouth, the piercing islands of stillness between birdsong. When one of the retreat leaders talked to the group about practising compassion, his tone sounded a little smug. I felt a resistance. I was alert to an almost physical surge of irritation flying across my chest – before it dissipated.

As the days slowly, slowly unwound, I felt as if I was entering a new realm where the world unfolded differently. Despite my recent loss, it contained a modicum of comfort. In my rawness, the idea of spoken words came to feel intrusive. When it was time to break the silence, I was still in a place of pause, simultaneously drawn to discovering more about my fellow participants but also hesitant about walking away from this richer place of being, back to the reality of the gaping absence I felt from the loss of my friend.

I'm not assuming that you now feel so inspired by my retreat story that you're tempted to sign up to a month-long silence tomorrow. However, there are elements of that silence that can infuse your more momentary listening stillness and allow you to absorb what you are encountering in a generous and thoughtful way.

Silence Serves Both Sides

I was coaching a broadcast editor who allocated work shifts to her team, which included a demanding presenter. The presenter was insisting on hosting the weekday shows and evading all weekends. My client found this impasse difficult to navigate. We decided to do a role play, and I started off playing the part of her entitled presenter. She played herself.

In the presenter's role, I began by stating my need to avoid presenting on Saturdays and Sundays. When I paused, for a micro-second, the editor came in immediately with a slew of well-reasoned arguments: the significant audience for the weekend slot, the fact that presenting the Sunday show would advance 'my' career, and the need to balance the needs of all her team members.

Even though I was only acting, I was surprised at how aggrieved I felt. Her failure to give me space to think and articulate *my* thoughts left me feeling interrupted and shut down. She had believed that if she could correctly communicate the sensible rationale behind her shift allocations, her presenter would surely understand. Until I gave her feedback, she was unaware that she was interrupting me. We then flipped roles, and I played her, once without granting significant pauses, and then again with silences. I witnessed a sea change in my client, as if a new thought had taken root. She became calmer and more present, less like she was still in dispute with her on-air talent. When we met next, she related how she had since held a constructive conversation with her presenter, allowing them to come to a compromise. The silence had enabled her presenter to feel heard. He was then ready to listen.

Time to become aware of any biases that you are holding about the person speaking can be another advantage of a long pause. For example, if you're interviewing someone for a job, are you judging your speaker rather than what they are saying? Have you subconsciously categorised them into a group that is not one in which you belong or feel entirely comfortable?

Silence buys you time to diagnose 'What's really going on here?'

Silence can also give you time to broaden your perspective. In his influential book on negotiating, *Getting Past No*, William Ury advises that you *go to the balcony* in challenging situations.[15] Silence can give you the essential few seconds to clamber up the stairs and, from this higher point, take a wider perspective on things that seemed close-up and personal. Naturally, a Deep Listening silence is not there to give you time to prepare a witty and damning riposte or generate an impossible-to-answer killer question.

Easing into Silence

If you're still a little hesitant about embracing silence, here are some ways to become more comfortable with it. But before you do, take a moment to consider the length of time you choose to remain silent. I am aware that if you work in a hard-nosed environment, granting pauses during a work meeting may feel wasteful. Hollywood executives who were attending a Deep Listening session laughed at the idea of leaving even a split-second unused. What mattered to them was swift thinking and a sharp (and witty) retort.

The advice I gave them was to experiment and see what happened. The same invitation extends to you. Take three to five seconds (or longer) after your speaker has finished speaking, depending upon the situation.

When you are making your first forays into the land of silence, however, you might want literally to count to 10 in your head after your speaker has finished. This may feel like a clumsy and awkward eternity at first, but it may be helpful to get comfortable with the feel and texture of a significant pause in order to enjoy its empathy-building power. People tend to overestimate the time that they are silent, so for example when people were asked to pause for 20 seconds in one 'Silence is Golden' experiment, it was extremely rare for conversations to include even one pause of over 17.5 seconds. When you use silence, notice if, during this time, you start judging yourself or fantasising about how your speaker is judging you – and let that go. If you come up with something that feels truly important to say and you are desperate to share it, jot it down to return to later.

Take a sip of water, slowly. That's the technique used by Wikipedia leader Maryana Iskander to enforce a few seconds of silence on herself in difficult discussions. She finds that this silence helps dissipate negative energy, granting her time to consider what might be triggering her or the implications of what her speaking partner has shared.

With limited impulse control and attention that darts from topic to topic, people with ADHD can find it harder to stop interrupting. Asking for understanding from others, taking notes, keeping interruptions short and posing questions to encourage people to continue after an interruption are all strategies that have helped people with this condition.[16]

While I can't claim to have entirely left my interrupting behind, two things have helped me on my journey to cut in less and create more space for silence.

The first is finally comprehending that, at a deep level and encased within the shell of any interruption, is a kernel of arrogance. If I interrupt, I must believe that I matter more than my speaker, that my next question and the alternative direction I shift the conversation to are worth so much more than anything they think or say.[17] The second is that the practice of giving people a spacious silence for their thoughts to unfurl, as I have done with my coaching clients (frequently, for over a decade) and with members of my family (on occasion), and witnessing the new insights that have appeared, has transformed my relationship with silence. Try it and see if you too experience your speaking partner generating ideas beyond anything you would have imagined, perhaps also wiser and more salient.

To encourage you, although silence is most often the practice that initially meets the most resistance, it is also the behaviour which my Deep Listening graduates tell me has made *the most* transformational difference to their lives. A final reward of a Deep Listening silence is the space it grants you to make sense of what your speaker has just shared, as we'll explore in Step Seven, Reflect Back.

Hold the Silence Takeaways

Silence is not defined by emptiness | Silence can be luminous, nourishing, inviting.

Become familiar with the spectrum of silences | Notice their different textures: hostile or generous, demanding or centred.

Notice if you resist silence | Unpack. Do you fear an awkward silence? Is it your duty to fill it in? Do you butcher silence to block challenging ideas?

Notice what emerges in a Deep Listening silence | New thoughts, ideas, meanings, connections, respect and trust. Silence moulds sound.

Note if you have more power in any exchange | What are the opportunities you can use to bring in silence?

Use the pause of silence | To become more centred, aware of biases and take a broader perspective.

Tone down silences if your speaker is depressed or has other conditions | Check in with them.

Hold the Silence Challenge

The invitation is to practise warm-hearted silences for a week, leaving these 3- to 10-second pauses as often as you can. After each opportunity, reflect on how the silence impacts on whether your speaker takes a new journey, if you learn something unexpected, and if there is any change in the quality of your relationship. Depending upon the context, you may choose to tell your speaker that you are practising silences or take these pauses unannounced.

STEP SEVEN:
REFLECT BACK

When we listen, our minds are making rapid assumptions. Probably all of us have been in a conversation where we are guessing to fill in the gaps and assuming we've understood. We then go into the world and act upon our 'new understanding'. People often don't articulate exactly what they mean at first, so later you might discover that the story you've taken from the conversation is entirely at odds with your speaker's intentions. As it is said, 'The single biggest problem in communication is the illusion that it has taken place.'[1]

Imagine this typical scenario: Your manager, Sam, tells you to prepare a presentation. Eager to impress, you craft a lavishly ornate, 50-slide deck late into the night. Come the meeting, you confidently set up your presentation, but Sam looks confused. 'We only have 10 minutes.' You frantically condense your *magnum opus* into a brief summary. Had you confirmed your understanding of Sam's original request, she could have had an opportunity to confirm, deny or clarify, preserving your energy and your dignity. But, as we'll discover, there is far more to reflecting back than checking facts.

In this step, we will unpack how to reflect back in a Deep Listening way, to sift through the meaning and feelings behind what the speaker has said, to encourage elaboration, and to allow your listener to enjoy the profound impact of hearing their own beliefs encapsulated and presented back to them.

Reflecting back in four stages:

Stage 1: You Deeply Listen to your speaker.
Stage 2: You reflect back what you think they mean.
Stage 3: You check to see if you are right.
Stage 4a: Your speaker replies with a resounding YES! when they feel you've fittingly summed up the complexity of what they think and feel. You now know that your speaker knows that you know.
Stage 4b: Or, and this is more likely, you haven't quite captured what they meant to say, so your speaker gives you a half-hearted *yes* … or corrects or clarifies. Or they elucidate with more extensive and expansive thoughts.

You again attempt to sum up their thoughts, Stage 2, and the cycle is repeated. Until you reach Stage 4a. When you've truly understood your speaker, and they know it, this may be an opportunity for your speaker to listen to you.

You might be thinking that reflecting back sounds robot-like and patronising. You are not alone. Mindless repetition of the last words that the client had said was how some people in the wider psychological community caricatured Carl Rogers' empathetic reflective approach. This damning response left Rogers feeling shocked, appalled and misunderstood.[2] It took many years before he gained the confidence and authority to talk and write about this aspect of listening and its critical role in enabling the speaker to feel truly heard.

You don't have just one attempt at reflecting back, as you read earlier in my conversation with my Russian-Ukrainian friend Sofiya, when I reflected her ambiguous feelings about home many times. It's an iterative, spiralling process that leads you to a state of deeper understanding so you arrive in a place where you are together on the same page and both know it, having built up a shared story of your speaker's truth, even if your beliefs diverge. This process goes beyond merely confirming a shared understanding of your speaker's words. It is about the creation of meaning.

If you have established a safe environment for your speaker, they may feel secure enough to tentatively try out ideas about which they are not yet sure. As you crystallise these ideas in your reflections, it helps your speaker clarify what they actually feel.

There's no need to channel your inner parrot and repeat back all your speaker's words verbatim. Rather, you make a stab at summing up the essence of what you *think* they mean. That includes your understanding of their feelings and of what's been left unsaid, not just the words, but under them, amidst them and beyond them. We will discuss later how you can read your speaker's cues, but essentially you're guessing. And don't worry, you don't have to be correct. What's more important is that your hunch leads the speaker to find a more accurate way to describe what they mean, as they ask themselves, 'Well, if it's not *that*, what *am* I feeling?'

The invitation is to surrender your agenda as you attempt to crystallise your speaker's meaning so you reflect their underlying reality, not yours. They are in the driving seat. Therefore, don't follow your nose with follow-up questions. (I confess, as a curious journalist, this was truly challenging for me at first.) Instead, focus on reflecting back what you understand them to be saying, feeling and meaning. Then, through iterative steps, you get to a deeper version of their story, which is itself a kind of question.

'Tell me more' is the one invitation you can extend that functions like a question. 'Tell me more' prompts your speaker to think about what's behind what they last told you, to go deeper and begin to ask themselves more questions. And it's up to them to define what the more is, so they stay firmly in charge. Stay away from 'What else?' 'What else?' prompts the speaker to shift sideways into another story with more surface detail, taking away their opportunity to reflect more deeply.[3]

Open to a New Truth

The Brazilian lawyer Ana Luiza Ribeiro, who we met earlier, found that reflecting back, peppered with 'Tell me more', transformed her professional relationship with Angelo. Angelo runs an NGO that provides families with after-school English, maths and sports lessons, funded by the foundation where Ana Luiza works. 'We live in really different realities, Angelo and me. He lives in a poor community in Recife, Northeast Brazil. I live in São Paulo.'

Huge storms had been raging across the state of Recife. Ana Luisa was aware that homes, furniture and livelihoods had been destroyed. As Ana Luiza had just completed a Deep Listening programme, she'd taken the time to listen to herself before a call with Angelo, so she was conscious of her assumptions.

She started thinking she had to send food to his community straight away. 'It's pretty scary, we tend to mix what they are saying with what we feel and understand. And in my humanitarian work, we tend to think when someone is vulnerable, everything we give them is useful.' On this occasion, Ana Luiza chose to empty her mind and move to a place where she could be open to Angelo's truth. She began the conversation: 'What's going on? How can I help?'

Angelo spoke of the horrific destruction in his region, the ongoing torrential rain, the stress everyone was under. No one was sleeping properly, as the river had stormed inside their bedrooms. Through an iterative process of reflecting back, Ana Luiza came to understand that the community needed funds for mattresses and pillows. 'Tell me more,' she prompted. Angelo explained that they also needed bedsheets and towels. He explained that another donor had already stepped in, and there was now enough food.

Reflecting back not only allowed Ana Luiza to send Angelo what he needed most, but it also changed their relationship, allowing it to emerge from a hierarchical straitjacket. She felt that by giving Angelo her focused attention, and being curious about *his* story, what it was like for *him*, and reflecting back her new understanding, it changed the power dynamic. 'It was as if I ceased to be this distant, high-up, important, rich person.'

By demonstrating her understanding of Angelo's reality, without allowing her agenda to intrude, Angelo told Ana Luiza that he felt she recognised him as a partner, with knowledge and expertise. Through hearing his own thoughts reflected back to him, Angelo said that he experienced a deep sense of being recognised.

Break out of a Script

Such powerful signals are often absent. Our conversations frequently follow a predictable format, one that is tired, that ignores the richness of a unique moment. You play out a part as if you are in a play, as a manager, friend or parent. You act and talk in that script, asking expected questions or trying to push a specific agenda. When you reflect back to someone what you understand them to have meant, it breaks free from that script. They are also encouraged to depart from their script and speak more authentically. You both shift into a more profound exchange of meaning, beyond the prefabricated conversation that everyone expected.

You hear your partner's key in the front door. You ask how their day has gone. *Fine*. You don't express any interest in their pre-packaged response and launch into your own worries about your cat/parent/weather/political leadership/rubbish collection. You could, instead, truly listen to their reply with curiosity and reflect back what you feel they are experiencing in that very moment: 'I sense [from your tone of voice] that your day was somehow … exhausting?' Now you're showing real curiosity, and they will recognise that. It is as if the line separating the two of you has been rendered more permeable.

Though reflecting back is potent, don't feel you need to reflect back everything, or in every conversation. Sometimes silence can be just as powerful.

Take Note

Should you make notes to help yourself remember key words and phrases? When you first begin to Deeply Listen, you might feel you should, after you've checked with your speaker that this doesn't make them uncomfortable. When I first qualified as a coach, I took copious notes. These gave me reassurance. What my client said was important. I was listening. I could prove it. You, too, might be tempted. If so, the invitation is to relinquish any keyboard and screen and restrict yourself to a notepad and pen, jotting down significant phrases rather than creating a verbatim transcript. Deep Listening is not about capturing every detail of someone's story. It's about listening to understand, and slowly going deeper.

I invite you, when you feel ready, to take a radical step and give up these simultaneous notes entirely. Trust yourself. Free from any pressure to capture your speaker's whole narrative, you can begin to trust yourself to pick up on what matters and leave the details aside. Not writing can be more powerful than writing, allowing you to be fully in the here and now, communicating your presence with your whole being. In addition, if there's not much trust and you take notes, your speaker may feel that you want to take control of their story, extracting what you will for nefarious purposes.

Making notes does have value in some contexts, notably professional ones. If someone is complaining about the lack of follow-up to their earlier complaint, for example, writing full notes conveys that the individual and their story are important. You want to record all the details, as they could be vital as you go on to attend to their concerns.

The Challenge of Choice: What to Reflect Back

When you reflect back, you will alternate between:

- Summing up and paraphrasing what your speaker has said – without many details.
- Honing in on specific words and phrases.

Take the following conversation from a Deep Listening demonstration I held at the International Journalism Festival, in the hall of a medieval castle in Perugia, Italy. I needed a volunteer to assist. A man shifted uncomfortably to the front of the vaulted room. I invited him to tell me something about his name.

Bjorn: My name is Bjorn, which is a Swedish name, but my mother is French, and I live in England.

Pause.

Emily: So, I am hearing that there are a lot of international influences, but you have a Swedish name, is that right?

Silence.

Bjorn: Yes. That is exactly right.
Emily: Tell me more.
Bjorn: Not just international, but messy in other ways as well. My mother is Jewish, my father Swedish Protestant. I am neither. My wife is Italian, my children are even more confused than I am.

Silence. I nod.

Emily: You told me about your melting pot. And you are quite … proud about being able to touch all these different identities? *I ask hesitantly.*

I sense Bjorn is thinking. His focus turns inwards as he reflects.

Bjorn: I think I am … proud. I'd not really thought of it as pride before. I'd thought of it as fact. But it is a fact which makes me and my team.

Silence.

Emily: There is pride, in something you've almost taken for granted? *I offer, as a question.*

Here, I am attempting to reflect back Bjorn's thoughts and also his feelings, though he hasn't used words to articulate them. How did I choose what to reflect back? You will get better at identifying the most significant ideas, until it becomes semi-intuitive. There are also some clues to listen or look out for:

Observe where an expression is coming from. If your speaker seems to connect to a deeper part of themselves as they speak, use their exact words and phrases, with their intonation and rhythm.[4] Ask yourself whether this is something new for the speaker that has not yet been heard. Words which come immediately before or just after a pause can be significant, as this pause can be a sign that the thought is being newly formed. In contrast, when someone speedily recites a chunk of background information in an atonal uncaring voice, you can sum up these ideas with just a few words.

Key words and phrases. Watch for phrases which are emotionally charged, like *I hate them*, and look out for superlatives, such as *the hardest thing I've ever done*. If they use a metaphor or simile, however odd it sounds to you, like *climbing out of a dark river*, make sure to reflect that back. Chances are it will be packed with meaning for them, even if you can't yet interpret its significance. These standout words or phrases are handles that help you get a hold of the suitcase of their story.[5] If one word in what you hear seems heartfelt – It was *horrible*, for example – you can reflect back that single word on its own: *Horrible?* – inviting your speaker to reflect and expand. Highlighting an important word can be a way to unlock new thinking and leaves less room for your own agenda to intrude – if you are worried that this might be a risk.

Assumptions. In my coaching, if I sense that an assumption is oversimplified – 'I always struggle to meet deadlines' – I can pick that up by simply reflecting, *Always?* Inserting the word 'yet' after a negative assumption is another way to identify and question a preconception. Your speaker tells you, 'I'd love to learn to dance, but I can't imagine daring to take a class.' You reflect … 'Daring to go to a class – yet?' introducing the idea that their assumption might not be true forever. This reframing *yet* may open the door for them to step through and learn to salsa. There's an element of challenge and direction in a 'never' or a 'yet' that goes beyond merely reflecting, so be aware of your tone and use this approach judiciously. I would only consider picking up on an assumption if I'd established enough trust.

Voice. Pay attention to words and phrases spoken with real energy, when your speaker's rhythm halts or pauses, shifts in intonation, when it stumbles, stutters or changes pitch.[6] These are all clues, highlighting what is significant for your speaker. As we learned earlier, tone of voice is often a more accurate signal of meaning than a frown or smile.

Body posture, facial expressions and gestures. While it may be hard to determine your speaker's feelings from their non-verbal signals, they can provide clues as to what's important to them, and sometimes allow you to discern what is merely hinted at, partially expressed or left unsaid.[7] You might, for example, reflect back to your speaker: 'You don't seem comfortable in that chair?' inviting them to elaborate or clarify (and maybe find another seat).

This book is focused on listening to an individual. If you are listening to a group, you can watch out for shared clues. The collective energy of the group, its *corpus*, can help you determine their overall mood, even if within it there are diverse and contradictory opinions. When I work with a group of leaders and I pick up a shade of scepticism, I've learned to name it. 'I sense that in your workplace you don't feel confident about including your speaker's feelings when you reflect back.' Ideally, if I am correct, someone will speak up for the group. I can then properly understand and address their hesitations.

Emotional Reflections

With a group or an individual, unless you are sensitive to their emotions and include these, people won't feel truly heard, however well you reflect back the details of their story. Imagine the following scenario:

A software developer, Charlie, is on a virtual catch-up with you, her manager, and says, 'I've finished debugging that code.' That's straightforward, and together you can determine the next steps. However, if Charlie instead says, 'I've finally wrapped up debugging that blasted code,' though there's no difference in the content of the message, the meaning has shifted, altered in an important way for both Charlie and you, her boss. Assume you were to simply acknowledge that you now understand that the job has been completed. Would Charlie feel that she had successfully communicated her message? What might she do with the frustration she felt? Would she feel free to raise any other concerns? Be motivated to work harder on her next project?

Now, on the flip side, if you were to recognise the heart of the message Charlie has told you, you might reply with more sensitivity: 'You must be relieved that it's finally behind you, huh?' or 'Had a pretty frustrating time of it?' or 'I imagine you're not up for another round of that' or anything else that communicates to Charlie that you've genuinely heard and understood her. It doesn't necessarily mean that you need to change her next debugging assignment or that you must spend an hour listening to Charlie complain about how the code was filled with basic errors. With this new information from Charlie, various things *could* be approached differently, but not necessarily.[8] Even if your speaker has not expressed their feelings verbally, you can pick up on their emotions. You might hear intimations, like those given by Charlie, or you might deduce your speaker's sentiments from reading between their words, their tone and the way that they are showing up.

The psychologist Carl Rogers believed that listening was most effective when you paid attention to the feelings and emotions behind people's words, and where you could discern a pattern of feeling behind what was being said.[9] Reflecting back emotions and the feelings underlying them enables your speaker to feel heard, so they can begin to open up to the possibility of change, argued Rogers. Today, this belief forms the bedrock of many types of therapy and counselling. When you include your speaker's emotions in your reflections, it helps your speaker understand themselves better, helps you imagine what it actually *feels like* to be them, and strengthens your relationship, as your speaker will feel that you truly get them.

Returning to my conversation with Bjorn in Perugia, I reflected back what he had said, and also what I had intuited that he was feeling; in his case, a distinct sense of pride about his multicultural family. When he reflected on the idea that he was proud, it was as if he had just put up a picture and was looking at it for the first time *in situ* as he surveyed it from different angles. Through my listening and reflecting back, Bjorn was able to acquire what seemed like a new insight into his hybrid identity, and I sensed that he took pleasure in this new understanding.

You might also find that your speaker expresses something with a vital energy or shows signs of vulnerability, yet when you sensitively reflect this back, they vehemently deny possessing any such feeling. In my coaching experience, when clients are emotionally charged about something, but firmly reject the possibility of these feelings, either I have misinterpreted them in some way, or they're not yet ready to acknowledge these feelings. In such cases, I generally step back and move on.

Meta-Reflections

When you feel you can't take in any more information, you can draw together what you've noticed and sum up your overall understanding. You, as a witness, can step back and see this larger pattern. When I coach or mediate, I often find that such a *meta-reflection* serves to inspire a mental shift in the speaker as they perceive their experiences in a new light. A critical part of meta-reflection includes your speaker's emotions, especially if you've noticed a significant shift. Another way to think about the bigger picture is through a prism of music.

Two notes played or sung at the same time can be either harmonious or discordant. Become alert to whether you sense a harmony behind what your speaker is saying, if everything they express points to a feeling of joy, or if you sense contradictory emotions. You might reflect to your partner, for example, 'You talk about your intense love and gratitude towards your mum, but I sense that perhaps you also feel some … perhaps bitterness towards her at the moment – is that right?' Reflect this contradiction not as a challenge – keep an eye on your tone – but as something that they may want to think more about.

When you accept their contradictory emotions, they can start to accept these feelings, which seem to pull them in different directions, *without feeling torn.*

Striking the Right Note

It can be challenging to strike the right note when you reflect back, so it's helpful to hone your tone.

You want to convey to your speaker that you are authentic and not formulaic, so be alert to overusing a single phrase or sounding patronising. Pose your reflections as suggestions, rather than definitive statements, to allow them to agree or clarify. It's best to avoid starting every reflection with 'It sounds like you're saying …?' Effective reflections need to hold your listener's attention and demonstrate variety. You might try, 'So if I understand you correctly …' or 'Let me see if I got that …' or 'I sense that …', or 'I imagine that you might be feeling …' You can also offer your reflection as a statement with a question mark at the end. When you're unsure, you might use, 'I've probably not quite got this right, so please correct me, but it seems like you're a little fearful of seeing Max again?'[10] Above all, find ways that feel natural for you.

Convey the impression, through your tone, that your interpretation of your speaker's message is tentative. You're trying on borrowed finery; these clothes don't belong to you, and you're unsure if they fit.

Your summation doesn't need to be perfect. As you reflect back, you're trying to imagine how the speaker sees things, using their frame of reference. Your purpose is to see if your understanding has value for the speaker and to stimulate them to articulate their perspective with greater precision and nuance, the way it truly is for them. So, if your speaker brushes your understanding aside or corrects you with their interpretation that is closer to their truth, it's important not to let your ego become fixated on the need to be right. You can let go of your formulation without attachment and instead embrace the reformulation that is theirs.

You are active throughout, on the edge of your metaphorical seat, curious to understand the core meaning hidden behind their words. By demonstrating your sincere desire to understand their thoughts, without hanging on to your own interpretations, you gain their trust.

At this stage, you may be worried that these guidelines sound intrusive, embarrassing and out of place in the context of many relationships. You are right to be concerned. Have you established enough trust to allow you to hazard a guess about your speaker's inner world? You might like to ask your speaker's permission. Begin by treading softly in your initial reflections, constantly taking the temperature. Your tone hesitant, rather than adamant.

If you sound judgemental when you reflect or use words that are stronger than your speaker themselves has chosen, they may feel alienated and even threatened. How would you feel if someone reflected, with a smattering of judgement, 'Hey, you *do* look upset'?

To avoid coming across as judgemental or threatening, centre yourself before each reflection. Release a long breath to let go of any tension in your voice by letting it soften, allowing it to release. When you make a sound, you bring two vocal cords together and then apart. Without tension, your vocal cords can come together in ways that are supple and gentle. The timbre of your voice can then infuse your reflections, so they are more likely to be welcomed by your speaker.[11]

Psychologist Carl Rogers set himself a listening challenge that I find inspiring: 'Can I let myself enter fully into the world

of his feelings and personal meanings and see them as he does? … Can I enter it so sensitively that I can move about in it freely, without trampling on meanings that are precious to him?'[12] Rogers highlights the importance of treating the thoughts of another with careful respect. If someone chooses to share with you even a glimpse of their precious inner world, it is a privilege. Acknowledging that privilege, both to yourself and to your speaker, is meaningful.

Have You Truly Heard?

Your speaker won't always tell you whether you've successfully captured their thoughts or if you're wide of the mark. So how can you tell? If you've taken a wrong turn, your speaker will bristle with annoyance, perhaps squeeze up their face or raise an eyebrow, writes clinical psychologist Neil Friedman. They may then repeat what they'd said earlier or change the subject abruptly, staying at a superficial level. In contrast, when you've accurately reflected back, you'll notice your speaker relax a little. When they next speak, they'll venture beyond their previous ideas into new territory.[13]

Reflecting Back Disagreeable Ideas

As we've heard, it can be challenging to hear ideas that don't align with our beliefs. We often interpret what we hear, based on our thoughts, feelings and expectations, automatically. So, what can you do to avoid confirmation bias, hearing only that which confirms what you already believe? One creative solution is to purposely set yourself the intention of searching for evidence, as you listen, that proves you wrong. A warning: this takes practice and dedication, as you need to override your habitual neural pathways.

Beyond hearing the sound waves, it's even more demanding to take the next step and reflect back to your speaker demands that you find reproachable, for example. You may feel a surge of resistance preventing you from honestly articulating their arguments because you are convinced that they're mistaken. So, you gloss over uncomfortable opinions, or ignore them, cherry-picking ideas that echo your own beliefs. I'm certainly guilty of this when I'm not being intentional about my listening. However, letting your beliefs drive your reflections in this way will lead to your speaker feeling frustrated and sidelined, and you will be hampered in your search for genuine understanding.

The ambition is to authentically drive towards *their* truth. Therefore, do not distort their meaning. And be aware of the trap of putting a spin on their words so they're more aligned with your own perspective.

Say you passionately believe that cyclists are a menace on the roads. Your neighbour tells you how new regulations enshrining safe routes for cyclists are finally giving her the confidence to cycle to work. Her partner Jamie's drive to work, however, has been slowed down by the introduction of the new cycle lanes. You might be tempted to play down your speaker's newfound enthusiasm for two wheels and choose instead to highlight Jamie's frustration with the traffic: 'Sounds like these cycle lanes are really annoying Jamie.' Instead, the idea is to reflect both these perspectives and relay what you sense your speaker feels about holding this competing narrative. 'I sense that you're proud of finally feeling confident enough to cycle to work, but also perhaps conflicted – the same cycle lanes that bring you freedom also curtail Jamie's. Is that right?' It will be easier to embrace an open-minded curiosity if you have taken the time to listen to yourself first, so you're aware of how much you have riding on this.

Of course, your ability through this iterative process to get closer to their truth in no way implies that you subscribe to their beliefs. You may need to reassure yourself of this, as at first it may feel truly uncomfortable. One way to ensure there are no misunderstandings is to reflect back with care, using phrases like 'So you feel …' rather than presenting their ideas as universally acknowledged truths that you support. Through this deeper understanding of their perspective, you might end up refining your own. But the end goal of Deep Listening is not to change your mind, so free yourself of any such pressure. Reflecting back their belief in their ideas does not make them your own.

When you are listening to someone with a conflicting perspective, focus on any pain they may be experiencing, listen for their suffering, make space for it and reflect it back. This has been a strategy climate change negotiator Christiana Figueres has used in countless conversations with people whose agendas, at first, seem to clash with her own. She gave me an example. 'Farmers are in deep pain. So, it's about asking questions to understand that pain and how they're experiencing it. It's about making space for the pain, the suffering, without dismissing it, because if there's anything that is common to all humans, it's our suffering. That is our common humanity.'

Another form of selective reflecting can rear its head in conversations between parents and their offspring. For example, your son Jake tells you, forlorn:

Jake: Oliver didn't send me a Happy Birthday.
You: You've had plenty of lovely birthday messages (*reassuring tone*), no need to worry about that.

You may have the best intentions, showcasing the positive to your child to save them from pain. But they could experience such a response as a negation of their emotions, a dismissal of their right to have these sentiments, leaving them feeling muffled and alone. Indeed, research indicates that such 'disagreements' between children and their parents are quite common, especially when children share emotions of fear and anger.[14]

By contrast, if your child feels you're attuned to them, as your reflections are sensitive and ring true, this will be an invitation for them to disentangle what's behind their mood and explore their feelings in a safe way.

Jake: Oliver didn't send me a Happy Birthday.
You: You didn't get a birthday message from your friend Oliver, and you feel … a little … sad? Is that right?
Jake: Yeah, really wanted one from him (*sniffles*), he's always sent me one before. Always.
You: Feels hard not to hear from Oliver, who was always there for you?
Jake: (*More sniffles*) All the people round here, they don't know me like Oliver. He was, like, knew me forever. Same with Tom. It's different here …

Silence.

You: Sounds like it's been hard, making new friends, not quite feeling at home in the same way here?

Jake: Yeah … mmm …

Silence.

(*Tone shifts*) But I got Jan's party next Saturday, and Rohan says he's going to bring in his card on Monday.

In this conversation, Jake is exploring why being ignored by his old friend Oliver is so unsettling. He misses the certainty of belonging. Once he's acknowledged his feelings, Jake shifts spontaneously to talk about new friendships. Through your openness and your acceptance of his sadness, Jake no longer needs to insist upon his difficult feelings. Your child, on their own, may feel validated and secure enough to bring in a larger perspective, or you might need to help lead them to this point, depending on their age and maturity.

The transformative power of hearing your own views reflected back has been demonstrated between groups who hold two very different perspectives. Attitudes around immigration in Phoenix, Arizona, had become polarised following a controversial anti-immigration bill, so neuroscientist Emile Bruneau and a colleague chose that city to conduct an experiment.[15] People from two different communities in Phoenix were recruited: the English-speaking white community and the Spanish-speaking Mexican immigrant community. The researchers began by establishing a baseline, measuring what white Americans felt about the newer arrivals: how much did they agree, for example, that *Mexican immigrants are generally thoughtful and honest?* The Mexican immigrants took part in a parallel process. Did they agree that *if I saw a white American grieving over a lost family member, I would think about myself in that situation?* In the main body of the experiment, people from each group communicated their opinions with their partner from the 'other side' who reflected their thoughts back to them.

Following the experience of being listened to by a member of the other community, attitudes were measured again. Having been heard, individuals from both communities were found to identify with the 'other side' more strongly and feel more positive about them. The most compelling aspect of the study was this revelation: when members of the *less* powerful group, the Mexican immigrant community, expressed their ideas and felt understood, they experienced a larger positive shift in their feelings towards the white American community than the white Americans experienced towards them after they had been heard.

The key takeaway here is that when you're in a conversation where your speaker may perceive you to have more power than they do, or your speaker is lacking in confidence, it may be even more impactful for you to listen to them and then reflect their perspective back. These individuals are *less* likely to have opportunities to feel heard and *less* likely to assume that their opinions matter or that they will be given an open-minded hearing by those who carry more financial or political weight.

More broadly, including information that challenges your perspective as you reflect may feel counter-intuitive, especially at first. But when you successfully achieve this feat, even just once during a conversation, you feel a wonderful, transformational sense of the early stages of mastery. Not only have you been able to put your own agenda aside temporarily, but you've entered dangerous territory and survived intact. Inwardly, you can smile.

The Power of Authentic Reflections

Sometimes you're so busy zeroing in on a certain aspect of what your speaker is saying that you miss what's most significant. The 'noise in the room' which initially seemed like a distraction might actually be the core meaning of what your speaker is trying to express. I stumbled into this trap in my conversation with Bjorn in Perugia. Bjorn shared details of his family, but as the conversation unfolded he tried to turn the tables and switch the spotlight to me, asking me questions: 'What about you?' 'What about your name?' I ignored these 'interruptions'. The medieval hall, with the multitude of reporters watching, made me tense. I was trying to demonstrate Deep Listening – me listening to him – so I omitted to include, in my reflections, his apparent discomfort.

If I had felt more centred, I could have taken a step back and attempted to answer or acknowledge what lay behind his questions rather than ignore them. I might have reflected, with hesitancy: *From your questions, I sense you feel imposed upon. Perhaps you'd rather not share any more, is that right?* – leaving Bjorn to confirm or correct me, enabling a deeper understanding between us to emerge.

By helping your speaker explore, clarify and articulate their thoughts (ideally, not in front of an audience of international journalists), you are providing something of value. Even if you've missed the mark, they will sense your desire to understand.

If you successfully encapsulate feelings that your speaker has not yet acknowledged, your reflections can be supremely validating; their world has come to make more sense, to you, and to them. Most people rarely have the experience of hearing someone attempt to disentangle and elucidate what they are straining to clarify in their own head.

Someplace inside, someplace deep inside,
we all want someone to listen to our heart's song.
We want to sing an aria of our pain; a ballad of our love;
a medley of our anger, hurt, sadness, joy.
We want to give voice to what is inside each and every one of us:
the particular ways we have been blessed and hurt by life.
We all long to be heard.[16]

These lines by clinical psychologist Neil Friedman get to the heart of why authentic reflecting back is so powerful. This practice can respond to a fundamental need that nests inside each and every one of us. But sometimes we want to go beyond reflecting back thoughts and feelings, and venture into accessing and reflecting back a speaker's deeper narrative. This is the subject of our final step: Step Eight.

Reflect Back Takeaways

Your reflections are powerful | Checking in with your speaker that you've understood correctly sheds light, encourages elaboration and conveys respect.

Crystalise the core | What you think is the essence of what the speaker has told you. Your ambition: to tap into *their* meaning.

Include emotions | Whether they've been spoken, intimated or expressed non-verbally, even if they are negative or painful.

Watch out for metaphors and superlatives | And phrases with an emotional charge.

Reflect back | Offer with humility your summation of their meaning and feelings and what may have been left unsaid.

Check in with your speaker | To ensure that you fully understand them. Ask them what you've missed or got wrong. Don't get hung up on being right.

No need to take notes or reflect verbatim | The focus is the essence of what they are saying and thinking.

Include meta-reflections | Be alert to wider patterns and harmonic or discordant emotions.

Reflect back authentically | Even if you disagree. Especially important if you have more power than them. Include the 'noise in the room'.

Respect their boundaries | Be humble in your reflections.

Repeat | Continue to reflect back until you get a resounding YES from the speaker. You can then ask additional questions to deepen your understanding of their story. Ask, 'What more?' rather than, 'What else?'

Reflect Back Challenge

During an encounter, try to reflect back the core of what you've heard, iteratively, until your speaker feels completely understood. Check that you've captured the words, emotions and notes between their words. Notice if you stray into advising or trying to cheer them up and inadvertently downplaying their pain. Afterwards, ask yourself: Was I able to find a way to reflect back that felt natural, that increased understanding?

STEP EIGHT:
GO DEEPER

'We all have an official story, a visiting card story' that we present to the world, believed writer David Grossman. But if we are fortunate enough to find an attentive and empathetic listener, a 'sympathetic witness', they can encourage us to reveal the layers, the story that lies beneath the surface and the story that lies beneath even that. This underneath story can allow us to climb out of the prison of our official story and 'bring us into tighter contact with our life'.[1]

The far-reaching transformation that a sympathetic witness can spark is inspiring. A Deep Listener can be a catalyst for a speaker to uncover the deeper narrative that drives their thinking, so that the speaker can then step outside the confines of the official version of their life and into a new story. If together a speaker and listener are able to make sense of even a fragment of this narrative, it can elevate their understanding and enrich their relationship, creating a profound bond.

Stories matter.

A Deeper Narrative Uncovered

I listened carefully to the story of dairy farmer Philip Davies when I went to interview him, even though I opposed his views about climate change. I noticed that he frequently referred to catastrophes that had shaped his long farming history. 'I remember foot-and-mouth disease devastating the herds around here in the late 1960s,' he recalled. 'I was at school. The start of October. And I went to play sport. I could see fires all the way from Manchester, fuelled by burning cows.' Davies vividly remembered the day the vet put down three of his cows in his own yard because of mad cow disease. 'It was a tragedy,' he lamented.

I awoke early to walk through the dry, thigh-high corn on the second day of my visit to the farm, trying to make sense of Davies's outlook. He denied that humans have had a significant role in warming the planet and downplayed the scale of emissions caused by dairy farming. The open landscape centred me as I tried to understand Davies and make sense of his deeper narrative. I noticed the pride he felt in the intensity of his lifetime of labour, alongside his disappointment at the lack of respect given to such toil. I felt his fear when he looked to the future. He was getting older. If his farm wasn't clean of tuberculosis, could he sell his cows and retire? Davies's sense of injustice was visceral.

'We feel voiceless and weighted down. Farmers are the most optimistic people I know, but scratch under the surface, we are carrying disappointment and anger. We've been silenced by everyone pointing the finger at us. "You naughty people, you are ruining the planet."'

Climate change was yet another example of the 'faceless men in dark corridors', in Philip Davies's deeper narrative, looking for a scapegoat, someone to blame. Over his working life, farmers like him have had to grapple with reduced milk prices and a panoply of plagues: foot-and-mouth disease, mad cow disease and now TB. As ever, those 'government mandarins' would seize on the usual suspect – farmers. Though we didn't see eye to eye on climate, and I did not change my mind, I came to understand more. Too often, I and other city dwellers are oblivious to the extraordinary effort that Davies and other farmers dedicate to producing the food that nourishes our bodies and binds our families together. In Davies's narrative, the idea of climate change had been manipulated by politicians and bureaucrats who had no lived experience of the earth's natural cycles.

When Davies listened to my interpretation of his deeper narrative, it rang true.

To explain the relevance of deeper narratives, I've been drawn to the metaphors of writer George Steiner. He likened the way we normally communicate to a form of shorthand, as if our whole self were 'a plant deeply and invisibly rooted, or an iceberg largely underwater'. When we speak to others, we most often talk *at the surface of our selves*.[2] Your speaker, like all of us, has a surface story which they unwittingly rehearse and perfect, ready to present to others when they are asked standard questions about themselves. But that surface story may have little to do with their deeper narrative, which is drawn from their authentic self, reflecting their true feelings and aspirations. And if you're able to penetrate this surface layer, this superficial topsoil, and stumble upon their deeper narrative, you may discover more fertile ground from which to nurture real understanding.

Of all the Deep Listening steps, this is the least concrete and the most demanding. You need to let this deeper approach sit with you. Maybe it's not a place you or your speaker feel comfortable exploring right now. Or you might be tempted to venture into this territory. Rather than probing any individual parts of your speaker's message with an array of tools, going deeper requires you to step back so you can let the whole of *you* (your whole being) listen to the whole of *them* (their whole being).

Your presence listens to their presence.[3]

Be Alert to Clues

The following are a few pointers to alert you to your speaker's deeper narrative. They all reflect aspects of a whole rather than individual clues to be checked off.

Feelings and Emotions. While I've used the terms *emotions* and *feelings* interchangeably throughout this book, when you are choosing what to reflect back, a distinction between feelings and emotions may be helpful. *Emotions* can be characterised as an often unconscious physical sensation or reaction we have to something in the environment, and *feelings* as the meaning we make of the raw emotions as we process them.[4,5] For example, your cousin experiences a wave of anger pulsing through her as a high-end SUV vehicle snatches the parking space she was patiently waiting to back into – that's her emotional response. Then, as she's telling you about this outrage, she *feels* hard done by, part of a pattern, you sense, in which she feels unable to secure what is rightfully hers.

While you are listening and reflecting back your speaker's feelings, you can also consider their feelings about their feelings. These are their *meta-feelings* – a sense of how 'safe or free or proud (or ashamed or horrified)' they are to claim a specific sentiment.[6] Say you're listening to your partner talk about work and how their contribution towards an important pitch for new business was unacknowledged. They're wondering whether this job is really right for them, disappointed about not being able to play a more senior role in the new division. You also notice, though they haven't articulated it, that they feel uneasy, or even guilty, about having these feelings, as if they *should* feel grateful for still having a job after the multiple redundancies across the company. These meta-feelings of privilege and guilt are an aspect of their deeper narrative.

What is their meta-feeling, you ask yourself, their response to acknowledging these thoughts and feelings? Be inspired by the idea of moving beyond the limits of what is already known – by you and by them.[7]

Words That Are Unsaid or Downplayed. You can become alert to meanings that are implicit or only hinted at. Being tuned in to these clues can save lives, as Alex, a volunteer with the Samaritans, has experienced. He recalled a night shift during his training period.

'I answered the call. The person sounded kind of alright. They mentioned that they were having a bit of a hard time but didn't sound too bad. My mentor, who was listening in to the call, passed me a note: "Suicide in progress?" I thought, Blimey, that's weird, the caller hasn't said anything like that at all. I don't get it.'

Alex's mentor had honed her intuition over 20 years of listening to such calls. She picked up something that Alex hadn't spotted. Through the exchange, it transpired that just before reaching out, the caller had taken steps to end their life. Alex's mentor was relying on her instinct, the caller's tone, and not letting the caller's spoken words obscure their real meaning.

A few months later, Alex was on shift when he answered another call with the greeting, 'Hello, the Samaritans.' The caller didn't say much. So, Alex asked, 'How are you doing tonight?' They replied, 'Not so good.'

'Honestly, the way that they said, "Not so good," I just knew that they were probably in a very bad way, actively suicidal. As the call unfolded, it became clear that, unfortunately, I was right.'

I was curious about what, on this occasion, had alerted Alex. This caller spoke quietly. And after these three words they didn't follow up or begin to explain what they *did* want to talk about. In Alex's experience, if a caller says, 'Things are really terrible,' they might be struggling with enormous challenges, like finding out a partner has cheated on them or worried about their rising debt, but it is a different depth of feeling. Hidden in this caller's three soft words was a struggle to articulate something that was beyond bad. The caller was only able to hold out a tentative finger to Alex, they were feeling so desperate and alone. They did not fathom that Alex or anyone else would understand. So, they held back. Through the conversation, this caller eventually recognised their need for more help.

Alex knows that when he hears a caller's story, he is never to say, 'I understand' or 'I get what you're saying.' It is often too hard for anyone to understand.

The only thing we can do is attempt to understand.

Perspective. Pay attention to the perspective that your speaker chooses to use.[8] They may use the *first person* when they are more confident about owning an idea. For example: 'I knew that my partner was going too far.' The *second person* is often used when they want to draw you in: 'Of course, you'll understand …' Using the *third person* conveys a distance, a disassociation with the thought, for example: 'It's terrible that they're allowed to get away with it.' When they feel ambiguous about owning up to an opinion, they'll imply that such sentiments are universal, using an expression like: 'Obviously, *everyone* needs time away from their partner.'

The Whispering. The ambition is to fine-tune your physical ear as well as your *gut*; in the words of psychoanalyst Samoan Barish, '… an ear that heeds the whisperings as well as the shriekings of a patient's utterances'.[9] Greater volume doesn't necessarily suggest greater significance. New utterances that hint at a deeper narrative may be softly murmured.

Trailing into Silence. When your speaker's tone shifts and their voice trails off into silence you might assume this transition signals that they've lost confidence, or perhaps given up. But it could indicate a breakthrough moment, be a sign that your speaker is now ready to free themselves from stale beliefs and enter a realm of new possibilities.

Two researchers demonstrated this breakthrough moment when they interviewed women who had difficult relationships with their mothers. These were relationships that were demanding to remain in, yet hard to abandon. The daughters alternated between describing their maternal relationship with a hopeless and judgemental third person 'It's broken' and at other moments reflecting, 'But she's my mother,' with an implicit self-criticism, as if they should get along because they were bound by this ultimate bond. These two feelings were in sharp conflict. The women felt hopeless and stuck.

Then, one woman, Meredith, began tentatively stepping into the realm of not knowing. Anticipating her mother's death, she reflected: 'She's alive and breathing, and there'll be a time when there's nothing else more I can do, when she's dead. So, if she's alive, I feel like I just can't quit. I can't [*pause*] – I have to continue to hope, and what I … what helps me do that is, at times, to divorce myself from what I know … and I just have to be like a human being that almost [*pause*] is more innocent than I am. Like, I have to … [*sigh/pause*] *I don't know …*'[10]

Sounding less certain, Meredith began to question her longstanding conviction that her relationship with her mother was both beyond repair and also irreplaceable. This new reflection created the space for Meredith to envision a new relationship with her mother, one might imagine, one that could potentially both have boundaries and be forgiving. By listening with what's been termed your *third ear*, hesitant and conflicted messages from your speaker may become clearer, giving you genuine insight into their deeper narrative.

Your Third Ear

The term third ear was coined by Theodor Reik, one of the first students of Sigmund Freud in Vienna. Reik was later to become Freud's protégé, friend and defender, and an influential psychoanalyst in his own right. Our third ear senses what is unspoken, lying in our speaker's unconscious. The idea is that our '"instincts", which indicate, point out, hint at and allude, warn and convey, are sometimes more intelligent than our conscious "intelligence".'[11]

To use your third ear, as Reik suggested, you need to seize the messages that travel from your speaker's unconscious to your own. This involves tapping into your own unconscious. The insights gained from listening through your third ear are rich but subtle. 'These small fish that escape through the mesh,' Reik believed, are 'often the most precious'.[12] And the invitation is to trust these messages, and offer them back with humility to your speaker.

Getting comfortable and proficient with your third ear takes time. The deeper narrative discloses truths but defies pressure. You will understand these messages by letting the process unfold rather than trying to engineer it. That may sound obscure, and indeed it is, quite literally. The best way to penetrate this secret language is by looking into yourself and witnessing your own reactions, often sensed in your body, to decode what's at the centre of your speaker's world. Through experience, you will become aware of your own sources of intuitive knowing.

Here's an example: I am hearing from a close friend, Will, about how sad and frustrated he is that at work his colleagues have failed to grasp his profound grief over the loss of his dog. After a silence, it's straightforward for me to reflect back Will's thoughts and feelings. In that pause, however, I could listen through my third ear, sensing what arises in my body, in my mind and in my emotions. Here I sense confusion; why is Will choosing to share these feelings with me? It feels uncomfortable in my chest. I feel strangely judgemental about Will and his loss. I let that sit. I then have a sense that Will's story might relate to me – perhaps it is *me* who has fallen short. Mulling it over, I feel guilty about my own infrequent messages to Will over the last few months. I can then check in with him: 'You sound sad and angry about your work friends. I'm so sorry' and then, 'Perhaps I also haven't been the sort of friend you have needed during this time?' I'm giving him the opportunity to voice any feelings about me, or unspoken needs, or to dismiss my hunch. Here, I am listening to my own feelings for what they can tell me about Will's. He confirms my speculation, and we smile, together.

Waiting for the Meaning to Reveal Itself

As the world of deeper narratives requires you to navigate your own subconscious and unconscious territory and that of your speaker, you may need to wait for the meaning of a deeper narrative to make itself clear, rather than actively exposing it. This meaning-making process shares parallels with some types of art-making, so I turned to artist William Kentridge to explain to me how he goes about creating. He gave me an example from his studio.

'Take 10 small squares of black paper. These are just 10 pieces of black paper. But if you start putting them against each other, even overlapping, suddenly you might say, "Oh those three pieces are like a person leaning forward." That's a new image revealed that I recognise from the way the squares are aligned. This art-making is very different from if you were to say, "How do I make a person leaning forward?"'

I like the playful approach that Kentridge brings to his creativity, which is also relevant for exploring deeper narratives. This creative focus invites you to suspend your analytical powers to embrace unknowing and possibility. Kentridge's process, like surfacing the deeper narrative, is a form of coherence creation, making sense of fragments, and painting a picture or telling a story from what emerges. It relies on our capacity to recognise rather than our ability to know.

Seeing or hearing something as if for the first time, rather than cradling the answer in advance, can help you. Be alive, like Kentridge, to what emerges. Rather than finding meaning, let the meaning find you.

Sense-making is the gift you offer your speaker. Even when you get it wrong, your guess is in the service of your speaker. They feel that you have the best intentions. You want to see if your interpretation helps them understand themselves more clearly. They can correct you, and with increasing confidence, learn to navigate and make meaning, and come to understand their own truth.

A Land of Values

On your journey around the landscape of deeper narratives, you will encounter the land of values. And this may be difficult terrain. When you're listening to people with whom you resolutely disagree, a judgemental thought might pass through your mind – *they* lack values, by which you mean the values that are most cherished by *you*. I find social psychologist Jonathan Haidt's work useful here, highlighting a smorgasbord of values.[13,14] Other people are also driven by values, just different ones from our own.

Haidt and his colleagues identified five key moral foundations that underpin the most commonly held values. Each of us will cherish different values and these will evolve over time.

Care and avoiding harm. Protecting and caring for children and other vulnerable beings is imperative. The relevant virtue is kindness.

Fairness and avoiding cheating. This could be triggered by economic inequality, unfairness due to unequal contributions or marital infidelity. Relevant virtues are justice and trustworthiness.

Loyalty. This value may show up as cherishing your nation or sports team and being alert to those who you believe betray this loyalty. Relevant virtues are patriotism and self-sacrifice for the group.

Authority. This drives a person to obey figures of authority and resist those they perceive as subverting this order. Relevant virtues are obedience, deference and respect for traditions.

Valuing sanctity and purity. People who embrace this value have a deep-rooted sense of the immense worth of what they cherish most. Relevant virtues include temperance, chastity, piety and cleanliness.

Haidt later added:

Liberty and challenging oppression. This can manifest as standing up for communities you feel are being threatened.

Drawing on these examples, reflecting back the values you believe are driving your speaker may be helpful, using the same respectful tone discussed earlier. Understanding that your speaker is motivated by a different aspect of a value driving you may help you understand and connect with them, even if, for example, you sit in different political camps. If there is enough trust, people generally respond well to hearing that their thoughts and actions are driven by values.

Another aspect of a person's deeper narrative is their unexpressed needs, such as an unfulfilled longing to be seen and validated.

Reduced Lives

Have you ever visited a doctor and felt short-changed? They hear you describe what's wrong and within the space of five minutes have diagnosed your new condition and given you a prescription to ameliorate your symptoms. But you still feel unsatisfied, even a little disappointed. It's an affront to have the full complexity of your body and your state of health boiled down to a simple ailment. Samaritan volunteer Alex often encounters this sort of speaker. 'They don't want, necessarily, their lives to be really simple and summarisable. They want or need the social company as well, which is why they're calling. And they want recognition of what they're going through. And so, for me, really good listening means going beyond summarising and being clear. The bigger ambition is to allow that person to feel truly heard.'

Alex's callers want him to acknowledge and reflect back their life in all its messiness, a life which isn't resolvable through a pat response. They want to hear someone else recognise their contradictory thoughts, and to reflect back that their story can't be reduced to its simple essence. There is no easy solution.

With speakers grappling with depression, trauma, serious illness or grief, like Alex's callers, they may feel so overwhelmed by their feelings that they don't tell you their story in a linear way. Only through disconnected dots. Through your silent empathetic listening and your hesitant sum-up suggestions, you can help them create some coherence, some strands of meaning. Perhaps you can help them move from being trapped inescapably in their anguish to seeing and embracing their pain from a place not quite so close, from the perspective of a witness. Such a shift can be liberating.

The Range of Deeper Narratives

Unpacking the deeper narratives of those around us can enhance relationships and understanding across many settings. Our understanding of the big events, strong bonds and closely held traumas of our partner's childhood can help us to imagine how it feels to be them and bring us closer. Diplomats may seek to understand the national deeper narratives of their allies and adversaries in the service of furthering their country's own interests while enhancing the relationship.

In my own field of journalism, engaging with a speaker's deeper narrative can help unpack the authentic thoughts of interviewees, as I found with my encounter with dairy farmer Philip Davies. Exploring his ideas at this depth gave me space to consider the nuances of his position, rather than adopt a reductive approach that simply labelled him a 'climate sceptic'. However, there's tension in using Deeper Listening as a journalist, tension between our need to find a story and a desire to be non-directional. Journalists typically come to an interview because they want to learn more and gather information for a piece or programme and showcase a specific viewpoint. There's no getting away from that agenda. However, the agenda can be temporarily set aside, after the journalist has communicated it to their interviewee, so that the journalist is open to whatever unfolds. Reflecting back, in an iterative process, allows the journalist to check the speaker's facts and sentiments and their interpretation to see if it rings true, and to give the space for a new understanding to emerge.

Another arena where increasing attention is being paid to deeper narratives is medicine. The pioneer of the developing field of Narrative Medicine is Rita Charon, a doctor, literary scholar and leader of the Narrative Medicine programme at Columbia University in the USA. Charon draws on a close reading of storytellers such as Henry James and Alice Munro to Deeply Listen to her patients.[15] She argues that the skills of an attentive reader – who pays attention to imagery, plot, voice, time and space – are transferable to listening.

Charon illustrates the point by means of a story, drawn from her own relationship with a patient she supported for nearly a decade. This patient had endured two cases of breast cancer. Following her successful treatment the second time round, she developed a hounding fear that the cancer would come back. She would reach out to Dr Charon or other specialists almost weekly, convinced that the cancer had returned. It would have been easy for Dr Charon to draw upon a conventional medical approach and reassure her patient that her cancer markers were now at standard levels and her mammogram results were normal. But instead Dr Charon paid close attention to this woman: 'I remember so clearly the day she described powerfully her sense that something was waiting in the wings, as if about to pounce. I remember leaning against the sink in the examining room, listening to her words, taking in her panic at this invisible pursuant.'[16]

Reading the doctor's description of her patient's inner world communicates that she has absorbed what it feels like to be her patient, drawing on the woman's metaphors, tone and mood.

The doctor then reflected back – 'wondered aloud' – if dying, the certainty of it and the fears around it, was what her patient truly dreaded, rather than the cancer. This led to a candid and fearless opening up about death itself. 'She realized that the recurrence of her breast cancer had tormented her with the unspoken – until now – certainty that she would at some point die.'

This conversation about the 'lurking fear that had yet to be perceived' – her death – paradoxically brought peace to this woman, for she at last grasped more clearly what lay behind her suffering.

If Dr Charon had solely repeated to her patient her encouraging medical signs, her patient's mind would have been far less likely to reach a state of ease. Following this conversation, and further work together on this deeper narrative, Dr Charon's patient no longer felt the need to make weekly visits to the doctor. And Dr Charon believes that their conversation about death deepened their relationship in a way that was unattainable within traditional medical practice.

A Feels-as-if Story

The emotional truth of a deeper narrative, such as the one that Dr Charon unearthed with her patient, is highlighted in the term sociologist Arlie Hochschild uses to refer to the same concept: a *feels-as-if story*. Hochschild defines it as 'the story feelings tell, in the language of symbols. It removes judgements. It removes fact. It tells us how things feel.'[17] Hochschild's reflections about removing facts are helpful in pointing out the deeper narrative's seemingly fanciful territory – which may be at odds with an internally consistent and logical universe.

Probing the inconsistencies of your speaker's deeper narrative, in the first instance, may not be relevant and can come across as judgemental.

Immersing herself in communities in the US state of Louisiana over many years, Hochschild listened to people who held different political values from her own. Her ambition was to understand this paradox. Louisiana had been buffeted by a storm of environmental challenges, with land subsiding along the state's nearly 400 miles of low-lying, flat coastline. Severe hurricanes often battered the region. The state consistently ranked among the lowest in life expectancy, education and personal earnings. Yet many of these people doubted the science of climate change and had misgivings about federal aid.[18]

To genuinely listen across divides, Hochschild argues, we need to navigate what is often a chasm between our analytical capacity and our emotions. She coined the term *empathy wall* to describe this obstacle which can prevent us from deeply understanding another person and lead us to feel indifferent or even hostile to people who think differently. To climb over this wall, we need to understand how other people experience the world.

The sociologist built a relationship with a single mother, Sharon Galicia, who allowed Hochschild to shadow her on her rounds selling medical insurance.[19] Hochschild gained Galicia's trust by listening to her stories, without judgement. Through hearing Galicia's narratives, and those of others in her community, Hochschild made sense of their deeper narrative, 'to represent – in metaphorical form – the hopes, fears, pride, shame, resentment, and anxiety in the lives of those I talked with.'[20]

Hochschild describes her understanding of a deep story shared by many in this community – a play, she writes, that unfolds in scenes. Here's a taste:

> You are patiently standing in a long line leading up a hill, as in a pilgrimage. You are situated in the middle of this line, along with others who are also white, older, Christian, and predominantly male …
>
> Just over the brow of the hill is the American Dream, the goal of everyone waiting in line. Many in the back of the line are people of colour – poor, young and old, mainly without college degrees …
>
> The sun is hot and the line is unmoving. In fact, is it moving backward? You haven't gotten a raise, and there is no talk of one …
>
> Look! You see people cutting in line ahead of you! You're following the rules. They aren't … women, immigrants, refugees … – all have cut ahead of you in line. But it's people like you who have made this country great …
>
> *You feel betrayed.*[21]

I sense, in Hochschild's work, that she was able to clamber over the empathy wall and authentically tap into the communities' frustrations, their sense of vulnerability and anger, and convey it in this deeper narrative. When she checked if this story resonated with her new Louisiana friends and acquaintances, she received reactions like 'You've read my mind.' One man wrote in an e-mail:

'*I live your analogy.* We pay hundreds of millions of dollars in hard-earned taxes for these bureaucrats … to do their job and they do nothing of the sort. To add insult to injury these slackers jump the line to retire before the workers who pay their salaries can … and the rest of us are [still] waiting in line.'

When we are speaking with someone we oppose, engaging with their deeper narrative can help us make sense of them, empathise with them, find common ground or identify common values or aspirations. When you are in conflict, understanding what the other person stands for can be a pathway to building respect, even if you still disagree, as Arlie Hochschild found with the residents she met in Louisiana.

If a deeper narrative is punitive, for example *I don't feel I deserve to have my needs met*, the very process of unveiling it can also reduce its potency. Bringing such a narrative to the attention of the speaker can give the speaker a choice – play with this narrative, come to a different relationship with it or amend it. When my friend Sofiya came to acknowledge the taxonomy of pain she had experienced, it allowed her to flip this narrative on its head and comprehend how the pain has also positively shaped the person she had become. Challenging a destructive deeper narrative, however, is hard. You may need the help of a therapist or counsellor.

Walking a Tightrope

On one hand you are actively using your third ear to sense what's resonating for your speaker, and at the same time you want to keep being aware of what's going on in your own head, your own emotional baggage. Have you inadvertently introduced your own shadows, your own agenda when reflecting their deeper narrative back to them? Pre-listening to yourself and being alert to this possibility will help you avoid this pitfall. Do not assume that what is coming up for you is necessarily relevant or helpful for your speaker.

In other instances, especially when you disagree with your speaker, it may be hard to hear, let alone articulate, your speaker's deeper narrative, so you remain oblivious to it. For example, in the midst of feeling aggrieved and rejected by your partner, you may be unable to hear or reflect back the deeper narrative that they feel fundamentally unworthy of love.

You also need to be cautious about venturing into the territory of your speaker's deeper narratives. This caution echoes other guidelines in the world of Deep Listening: being wary of reflecting back unsaid emotions, especially ones which hint at your speaker's vulnerability; and exercising extra sensitivity if you have more power than your speaker, or you're in a professional setting. Deeper narratives are by their nature intimate, and so require you to treat them with respect and patience.

Moving through Time

After you circle through Steps One to Seven, you need to give plenty of time and space for this sense-making step. This can mean having multiple conversations with individuals and across communities.

In other contexts, when you are immersed in a tense personal conflict, or you feel it would be insensitive or inappropriate to speculate on your speaker's deeper narrative with them, you might find it helpful to imagine your speaker's deeper narrative before or after speaking to them. Here you can crystallise what you've understood from your speaker – just as I did as I walked through the early-morning fields after my conversation with the farmer Philip Davies. This process of imagining their deeper narrative may give you insights into their world which can help you develop more empathy.

If you create a deeper narrative about them before you meet, however, take care that this doesn't get in the way of your Deep Listening. Following the conversation, you might choose to go back to your speaker to check your understanding of their deeper story and see if it rings true for them, following the same approach as Arlie Hochschild when she recontacted the residents of Louisiana to check the story of waiting in line, and Dr Rita Charon when she sought confirmation from her patient that it was indeed death that was her primal fear.

You may even discover that their deeper narrative holds up a mirror for you. The practice of tapping into your speaker's deeper narrative can also help you become more acquainted with your own. Whenever you find yourself feeling just that little bit too antagonistic before, during or after meeting someone, you can pose the question, privately, What is my deeper narrative?

With complete honesty, you can ask yourself:

What's really going on here?
What is the overall feeling I have?
What will I know in a year's time that I don't know now, as I look back at this relationship/encounter?
What's really at stake for me here? Right now?

And let those questions sit with you. Witness what emerges. Perhaps share it with your speaker, as a hunch.

Listen to the Wind

Two years before his death, the poet John Keats wrote the following lines, highlighting the significance of meanings that we are accustomed to ignoring:

Or thou might'st better listen to the wind,
Whose language is to thee a barren noise,
Though it blows legend-laden thro' the trees.[22]

The invitation is to learn to listen to these winds. The answer might be blowing through them. If the conditions are right, attending to them can yield treasures for your speaker, your understanding and your relationship.

Go Deeper Takeaways

Use your third ear | Step back and let the whole of you listen to the whole of them. Be alert to the messages that travel from your speaker's unconscious to your own. Tune in to your physical sensations for clues.

What are their meta-feelings, the feelings behind their feelings | How are they making sense of their emotions?

Which perspective is your speaker using | *First, second* or *third person*, or universalising their thoughts.

Are they downplaying anything | What's unsaid? Trailing into silence can signal breakthrough thinking.

What values and unspoken needs lie underneath | Can you surface these, respectfully?

Be open to playfulness, embrace uncertainty and doubt | Let the meaning find you.

Reflect back to your speaker your hunch about their deeper narrative | Tread carefully with humility. Don't cling to your interpretation if they dismiss it.

Reflect on their deeper narrative before or after the encounter | If you feel unable to surface this together. Share if you feel appropriate.

Has your own deeper narrative entered the conversation? | What can you learn?

Go Deeper Challenge

This step is perhaps the hardest step in Deep Listening, so it's good to approach it in an experimental way. The idea is just to see what unfolds. This challenge is to surface a deeper narrative in two encounters:

First encounter: Choose someone with whom you have a straightforward relationship. As you reflect back, turn your attention to their deeper narrative. You may surface this together with them.

Second encounter: Choose someone with whom you disagree. Pay attention to their deeper narrative. This may emerge following the conversation as you reflect back on how you feel, and what might lie behind their or your feelings. You may choose not to share this deeper narrative with them.

Ask yourself: What's the question that I might ask myself about this encounter – if I had the courage? Notice if uncovering this deeper narrative changes your understanding of your speaker, your feelings towards them and the quality of your relationship.

PART THREE

NAVIGATING YOUR DEEP LISTENING JOURNEY

DEEP LISTENING ETHICS

When you Deep Listen to someone, you recognise their full self. As a person of value, as a bearer of equal rights, irrespective of their beliefs.[1]

During this powerful exchange through which your speaker feels truly heard, an environment of trust is created. A space where the speaker can lay down their guard. In this setting they may share things that they would ordinarily keep private, thoughts they have not previously acknowledged, even to themselves. They may become vulnerable. And so, integral to Deep Listening is an awareness of your ethical responsibilities.

When I created the BBC 100 centenary project, *Share Your Story*, we recruited over 100 staff ambassadors, many of them at an early stage of their career, to visit secondary schools and share stories of their personal journeys in order to inspire young audiences. Storytelling coach Alex Dalton listened to these ambassadors to help them craft an honest and compelling tale about facing a significant moment in their life – dropping out of university, for example, or their mother's ex-boyfriend setting fire to their house – creating the space for them to express how they navigated that difficult time. During these workshops, it was often the first time the ambassadors had shared their story with anyone. Dalton reflected on the process of helping these people go beneath the surface, exploring not just the events but why they unfolded and the feelings they evoked. 'If someone makes themselves vulnerable, you have a responsibility to care for them and not be cavalier about the information they have shared.'

Consider your broader responsibility as you listen, not as an obligation or a duty but as a capacity to be genuinely responsive to the other person, recognising your inherent connectedness as well as the differences between you. You might choose to ask yourself, what is the line between what your speaker shares voluntarily, what they think they wanted to say, what they felt encouraged to say and what they never meant to say.

If you feel, as you are listening, that a boundary has been crossed, and your speaker is sharing information that may compromise them in your eyes, you can ask: 'Are you sure you want to tell me the next bit?' Then pause. This gives them the opportunity to rein themselves in.

If your speaker has told you something which suggests that they or someone else may be in danger, you may need to break confidentiality – if they are at risk of self-harm, for example. In a professional relationship, you may need to sensitively point out this possibility prior to the conversation, and at the time. In personal relationships, let your speaker know you need to break confidentiality if this doesn't preclude you from getting the support that you or your speaker needs. If you know that your speaker is assuming dangerously incomplete information, or planning something unethical or harmful, do share your concerns. Your tone will naturally be respectful.

More broadly, if your speaker has experienced trauma, they may find it difficult to speak openly. Listening to someone without significant expertise – however helpful it is – is unlikely to solve deep-seated psychological problems.

There are a few other pointers that you might find helpful:

Does your speaker have any **vulnerabilities** you need to consider? For example, might the conversation lead them into a territory you are ill-equipped to handle?

If you're listening to someone to gather information, consider:

Repeated listening. You may want to Deeply Listen to someone more than once so that your speaker can absorb and reflect on what they have said, to produce a more meaningful, intentional response, which also enhances your understanding.

Consider the **impact of sharing** your speaker's information more widely. Will their more honest response be seen as a betrayal by other members of their community? What could be the impact on them?

You also have an ethical obligation to think about your own needs and the risks for you as a listener, including your right to be heard.[2]

DEEP LISTENING RISKS TO YOU

As you Deeply Listen, your empathy and openheartedness may start to feel natural. Your speaker will bask in the rich rewards, but there may also be hazards for you as a listener. There may be occasions when you need to define boundaries and protect yourself; being a container for other people can be exhausting. And there are risks if you feel that the person you are listening to is either manipulative or, in a different vein, wants to tell you something more than you are ready to bear.

Humanitarian worker Mohammad recounted that he often felt overwhelmed by the stories that he heard in the course of his work in Iraq. Mohammad was one of the 150 people living in Lebanon whom I trained in Deep Listening; he took a role in Mosul not long afterwards. He told me about a conversation with a male Iraqi taxi driver, who shared his experience of enduring 18 lashes as a form of punishment. His offence? Driving a woman in his car without a male companion, which was forbidden when the city of Mosul was under the control of the Islamic State group. Mohammad described how in the aid sector conversations can quickly reach a deep emotional level that staffers may not be prepared for.

'There is a dark side to Deep Listening. I know that at this time it is not safe for me to have these conversations. I need to be able to detach myself from other people's experience and suffering. Personally, I am not yet ready to master that emotional side. It's not that easy yet.'

Listening to Traumatic Stories

Mohammad's experience of recognising when *not* to Deeply Listen is a powerful reminder about the importance of practising Deep Listening safely, setting healthy boundaries and taking responsibility for your own well-being. Connecting at a deep level creates trust and can be a profound experience, as the natural membranes that separate you from another become more permeable. You are opening yourself – your inner world – to the voices and experiences of others.[1] We've evolved to care for others, so this can be hard. Mohammad was able to recognise when, for him, the risks were too great. But this could be more challenging if, for example, you're in a relationship in which you are experiencing or are at risk of experiencing domestic violence, or if your speaker has issues with gambling or substance abuse. You need to use your judgement.

Talking about traumatic experiences can be profoundly healing for the speaker.[2] Yet one study highlighted that listening to a distressed person sharing their stories of pain can be a burden, causing the listener's heart rate to increase. A listener may feel depressed, anxious and even traumatised, especially if they don't have the opportunity to talk about the listening experience to someone else.[3] Other research suggests that, in the long term, disclosure within a close relationship, listening, for example, to your partner talk about a trauma, may free you both from isolation and bring you closer.[4]

Not all listeners are equally affected and there are mindsets that can help protect you. If you are aware of where your responsibility towards your speaker ends, and understand that you're listening 'just to be there' rather than to take on responsibility for their healing, you can lower your risk. Research demonstrates the importance of being aware of the amount of time you spend listening to someone as they tell you about their distressing experience. Taking more frequent and longer breaks can help. You can also, if it feels right, tell your speaking partner about other sources of assistance.[5]

Knowing Too Much

Through Deep Listening, you may come to know things that you cannot unknow. You may have no choice but to act on what you've heard. The Samaritans, for example, sometimes need to contact the police or ambulance services, if they feel their caller is not able to make their own decisions.[6] You might learn of someone committing a crime. A striking example of the impact of listening and finding something out comes from Tennessee Williams's play *A Streetcar Named Desire*. Blanche tells her sister, Stella, that Stella's husband, Stanley, raped her. Stella then confides in a friend, 'I couldn't believe her story and go on living with Stanley.' Although Stella doesn't want to believe her sister, she cannot truly ignore what she has learned about her own husband.[7]

Too Young

Children can be harmed if they are coaxed into the role of a listener caregiver. The phenomenon known as *emotional parentification* describes a scenario in which a child takes on the emotional load of their own parent or caregiver, becoming that adult's confidant and even sole support. If this situation is prolonged, the child can suppress their own needs, which can have a major impact on their future psychological health.[8]

Protecting Your Solitude

While everyone is entitled to be heard, they don't all have the liberty to intrude upon your silence and solitude at a time that is not right for you. Nobel Prize-winning writer Wole Soyinka told me he wholly supported the idea of a right to be listened to, as long as it was also balanced by his right to be in solitude; he cherishes his alone time to think and write. If he has an idea for a poem, he'll scribble it quickly on a napkin. Interruptions are perilous. Unlike our eyes, our ears do not have lids, but we can metaphorically close our ear flaps by taking time away from listening.

Listening Limits

I'm often asked whether we should Deeply Listen to racists or homophobic people or others who peddle intolerant ideologies. Aside from the fear that we might be somehow contaminated by hearing these ideas, there's also a concern that we might be seen to endorse or respect these viewpoints.

I don't believe there are any people to whom we should *never* listen. But there are important provisos. There are situations in which I *don't* recommend Deep Listening:

- When listening will put you in danger physically or psychologically.
- When listening takes place in public, so you are being used to endorse extreme ideas or provide a platform for

them, or you're being used to legitimise prejudiced beliefs.
- When you fear that your conversation will be unfaithfully characterised, or recorded and used on social media for malicious intent.
- When your speaker's agenda is to manipulate you or catch you out.
- When your speaker has no intention of listening to you.

For many years UN climate negotiator Christiana Figueres held an open heart and mind as she listened to oil and gas industry leaders. 'They wanted to act with integrity even if it was a struggle, and our conversation was sincere and authentic,' Figueres reflected. She's finding it increasingly difficult, however, to genuinely listen to the people who are now leading these industries. Figueres believes that they are purely focused on maximising profits at the expense of the destruction of ecosystems and the pain of humanity. Figueres is aware of her red lines: sincerity and authenticity.

There are also questions that it is useful to ask yourself:

- Do I have the emotional energy for this?
- Have I listened to my own shadows first?
- Am I centred enough?

If you do not fear the first set of provisos, and you can answer positively to the second, you may want to Deeply Listen to someone with views you find abhorrent. Is it worthwhile? I believe it is, as long as you are in a fit state to do so. If you feel ready, follow the eight steps to maximise your chances of them feeling heard, of improving your relationship, as well as the likelihood of them being in a place to re-examine their own ideas and hear your perspective. Perhaps you need to develop your Deep Listening with less contentious people first. You might also ask yourself: What's the worst that can happen? And what support could help me listen in this situation? It's also completely legitimate if you don't feel ready or able to have this sort of conversation. Deep Listening is an opportunity, never a mandate. Does every single one of us have to listen to every single other person? Not by any stretch. And also, not on every occasion. Your time too is worthy of protection.

You may choose, after reflecting back 'objectionable views', to explain why you find these ideas offensive, upsetting or wrong, and the impact that hearing these views has on you and potentially on others too.

It's also not all or nothing. Perhaps you can listen to that person and avoid certain subjects. Most people believe what they're doing is the right thing, given their model of the world. When you Deeply Listen to someone, it is their intrinsic humanity that you give respect to, not what they believe or what they have done. You Deeply Listen to them just because they are human. You may discover that behind offensive words lies a terrified or even traumatised human being.[9]

QUESTIONS TO BEGIN

Which starter questions are most likely to unleash new thinking, inspire self-reflection and create insight? Those that come from a place of true curiosity, that draw on your respect for your speaker tend to yield the most meaningful responses. Zen Buddhist monk and teacher Shunryū Suzuki distinguished between *Beginner's Mind*, open, alert and receptive to surprises, to whatever is to come next, in contrast to *Expert's Mind*, which interprets everything through knowledge and experience.[1] Deep Listener's questions are asked with Beginner's Mind. They are not designed to assess or judge.

When you're considering what question to ask, there's no need to get hung up on your wording. After all, you can ask a beautiful question in complete silence, just in the way you pay attention. You can also choose to begin with a powerful question wrapped in a phrase which the speaker can answer in many ways, depending upon their needs:

I'm here to listen to you.

Here are a few other questions to inspire you when you Deeply Listen in different contexts:

- What's your story?
- What's on your mind?
- What would you like to think about?
- Would you like to talk about it or tell me about it?
- Where are you now in your thoughts?
- What makes you feel so passionately about ___?
- What matters most to you about ___?
- What's the impact of ___ on you/on others?
- If I was truly curious, what question would I be asking?
- There are many things that I'm still learning. What would you like to tell me?
- What are you assuming here? What might you be assuming that is stopping you from ___?
- Tell me a story about your relationship to the issue. Research has demonstrated that we listen better to stories,[2] so if someone tells you a story, it will be easier to Deeply Listen to them. If you ask them about a pivotal moment in their story, they will tell you a more compelling story, which is more likely to hold your attention.
- What did you learn, or learn about yourself, from that experience?

To encourage your speaker, you might also want to share something that makes you a little vulnerable. Vulnerability, it has been discovered, encourages others to talk more and feel more positive about an interaction.[3] When you are vulnerable, you signal that you accept yourself, so at some level, you are also open to accepting others.[4]

With a stranger, you might start with a question that lets the speaker reveal some of their humanity, making it easier to connect with them:

- What food reminds you of home?
- Tell me a story about your first name, your last name or your nickname.

When you use the Deep Listening steps, these seemingly superficial questions can unleash insights of extraordinary depth.

It can also be impactful to ask:[5]

- What in your life experience has led you to believe what you do?
- What is it that you think I don't get about you?
- What do you think is oversimplified about ___?
- How has ___ affected your life?

Questions to Ask Yourself:

What's Your Agenda?

What do you really want to get out of the exchange? For such a question to be meaningful, you need to be honest with yourself.

Often there are multiple factors at play. Disentangle and acknowledge to yourself these different threads, especially if they are contradictory. The more aware you are, the more you can be authentic. You can share with your speaker the reasons for your encounter, if it is at all unclear. You may also choose to share any ambiguities you are wrestling with.

Pride or Prejudice?

Sometimes life demands that you listen to someone you find highly annoying or for whom you feel contempt. Do they project any weaknesses or attributes that, at some level, you abhor in yourself? Are you making any generalisations based on the person's background, their religion or politics? Are your judgements accurate? Fair? Acknowledging these hidden biases gives you the freedom to move beyond them.

Are you in danger of falling into any of the listening traps or getting caught by your own shadows? You may, for example, be cultivating anger and resentment, sentiments that you're embarrassed to acknowledge as your own. You can choose whether to share these uncomfortable sentiments and even your feelings about holding them, but even acknowledging them to yourself can diminish their power to disrupt.

Your Turn to Speak

Listening is more powerful, as we've discussed, if you do so without expecting to be listened to in return, to prevent the act from being reduced to a transactional exchange. However, if you only listen and never speak it can be disempowering for you and frustrating for those who value your input. Never lowering your defences by sharing your own thoughts might also come across as aloof. Remember, Deep Listening doesn't mean abandoning your own voice. Once you've Deeply Listened to the other person and they feel truly heard, share your thoughts, even if they diverge from your speaker's. Authentic conversations thrive on respectful exchanges of ideas.

As a leader in a workplace, for example, your team relies on you to not only listen, but also provide direction and share insights. In a more personal context, you might say, 'I have something on my mind, and I'd love to be able to talk about it,' or 'There's something that I want to share, is now a good time?' The foundation of your request is made not because you have listened to them, but because they are important to you and you are important to them.[6]

When you do speak, you can draw upon and adapt Deep Listening principles to the role of a speaker while still honouring your own perspective and your right to share it. Try to genuinely respond rather than react, draw on the qualities of empathy and respect as you speak, and use silence to lower the temperature for everyone. Stay aware of your body language and your tone of voice. Where you can, acknowledge common beliefs, ambiguity and complexity, and if you feel safe, consider sharing something that makes you a little vulnerable.

The idea is to build on the rapport and trust that you've nurtured through being a Deep Listener to create more understanding and a truer connection.

HOW DID YOUR DEEP LISTENING GO?

Taking the opportunity to step back and reflect on your Deep Listening encounters might feel like a waste of time, even self-indulgent. But it's hugely helpful if you want to start listening with intention rather than on autopilot. You can reflect immediately after – even in scribbled notes – then unpack more when you have the space and time. And you don't have to restrict your reflection to your own listening.

Guiding Principles for Self-Reflection

Take the Time

Self-reflection doesn't happen automatically. You can't expect yourself to act differently if you don't set aside time and creative energy to consider how the conversation unfolded and to reflect on how that learning can inform your future encounters.

All Data is Useful

Any feedback from your speaker, whether elicited or spontaneously given, is powerful. When you Deeply Listen, you want the speaker to feel heard. Do they feel that they have been genuinely understood? Did they learn anything new? How did it feel to be listened to in this way? Witnessing your own feelings, both during the encounter and now as you consider how you felt, can also enrich your understanding and ultimately energise you for your next conversation.

Celebrate What Went Well

We've evolved to focus on what is going wrong in order to identify and protect ourselves from danger. This is essential to our survival, but it can lead you to give undue emphasis to lapses in understanding, leading you to blame yourself and to feel discouraged and unmotivated to continue. Instead of dwelling on what worked less well, start by identifying what you're proud of. That could be as simple as taking pride in setting the intention to try Deep Listening, or noticing when you were seduced by a Deep Listening trap. Research by psychologist Carol S. Dweck into the power of mindsets has demonstrated that believing you can improve your ability in practising a task or skill will make it more likely that you will do so.[1]

You can get caught in black-and-white thinking, believing that either you were outstanding or useless, trapped in the tyranny of perfection. If you judge yourself harshly for impulsively interrupting or arguing with your speaker or letting your mind wander, in future you will most likely protect yourself from your own judgements and 'fail' to notice these occasions or forget to set time aside for self-reflection. Instead, these faltering steps can be greeted with self-compassion and even humour. Getting caught in the traps and messing up are parts of everyone's journey.

Be Kind to Yourself

Bring the Step Four qualities to yourself: be curious, be empathetic, be aware of your self-judgements and bring respect. Also accept yourself with all your listening strengths and flaws, nurturing self-compassion. Recognise that you, in your ongoing Deep Listening journey, are in the process of becoming.

If your speaker has told you about something distressing, you may need to turn to a friend or get professional help, much like a coach or therapist turns to a supervisor. Someone else can help you make sense of what you've heard and discuss its impact on you, so that it doesn't affect your own well-being.

If an encounter doesn't go as well as you might have hoped, try listening to someone new. Research suggests that the quality of listening is determined not only by you, but also by the chemistry between you and your speaker.[2] Notice who around you is falling into one of the listening traps, and who is a beautiful listener, so you learn from others as well as place your own listening into context and refrain from judging yourself unduly harshly.

Questions to Reflect upon Afterwards

- What can I learn from this encounter?
- What might I try differently next time, if anything?
- Did I frame the encounter transparently and listen openly, authentically and honestly?

- What was the impact of Deep Listening on my speaker, on me, on our relationship? A deeper connection or was the relationship unchanged?
- Did I learn anything from the conversation that surprised me? Did my speaker have any new insights, any shift in thinking?
- How do I feel after the encounter? What does that mean? What am I making it mean?
- Have any ethical questions emerged from my Deep Listening? Am I proud of how I have addressed them? Is there anything else I could have done? That I still could do?

Meta-Reflections

In addition to reflecting on your individual conversations, you can also reflect on your wider Deep Listening journey. You may find it helpful to consider:

- How, if at all, has my listening improved?
- Is being aware of my listening while I am in a conversation becoming easier?
- Has my Deep Listening led to other changes in myself – in my perspective, assumptions, beliefs or values?
- Which skills and practices do I find easy? Which am I avoiding?
- What reoccurring challenges do I face when Deep Listening?
- What feedback have I received from my speakers? Should I be addressing any themes which have emerged? How might I do so?

- Are there specific contexts in which I listen well and others in which I don't? For example, can I bring the same thoughtfulness to my children and partner that I bring to my colleagues?
- Do certain encounters cause me to overreact, to become defensive? Can I keep a diary of these instances, comparing what was actually said and what I took it to mean? Can I listen to any shadows that reared their heads and understand their intention? Out loud?
- Who have I chosen/failed to listen to? The introverts who don't naturally speak up? Those who look different from me or have a different background?
- What am I learning from practising which might change my ideas of whom to listen to, challenge my prejudices, or alter my attitudes about speaking and listening?[3]

Contexts in Which to Practise Deep Listening

- When your partner gets home from work.
- On a journey.
- When a close friend, family member or colleague says something that they are struggling with. Can you hold back from offering advice or solving their problem?
- When a friend or relative has done something you deeply disapprove of, can you step back from sharing your judgements?
- At work, when you are having conversations with your boss, colleagues or people who report to you, your partners, clients or customers – even more so when there are competing agendas or charged disagreements.
- A conversation with a stranger.

- A taxi driver.
- Someone waiting with you at a bus/train/coach stop or on your journey.
- Someone seated near you in the doctor's or dentist's waiting room.

Times When Deep Listening May Be Especially Powerful

- When you are locked in a repetitive argument.
- When you sense unexpressed emotions.
- When you become aware that you are making simplified assumptions or value judgements.
- When you want to understand someone from a different perspective, for example if you are at odds with a neighbour or someone else in your community or beyond.
- When truly understanding someone is critical for you, for them or for your relationship.

As you improve your Deep Listening, you'll find that you become more aware of yourself and your *window of tolerance* will expand, the zone of comfort where you can effectively manage your emotions, stay listening and respond to what you hear in a healthy way.

Now that you've reflected on a Deep Listening conversation, you're empowered with more self-awareness. The invitation is to draw upon these insights in another encounter. Practice and reflection go hand in hand. Success will bring more motivation. Otherwise, you are at risk. At risk of holding knowledge whose worth remains unfulfilled. To know and not to act is not yet to know.

REFLECTIONS ON DEEP LISTENING CONVERSATIONS

When and to whom did you listen?

____

Which Deep Listening steps did you use?

____

How did you feel during the encounter?

____

What did you notice about yourself in the moment? (thoughts/feelings/responses)

____

What did you do well?

____

What was hard and what made it hard?

____

Reflecting now, what was the impact of the way that you listened on the speaker, on you, on your relationship?

____

What discovery or insight can you take forward in your practice?

____

CONCLUSION

In the course of this book, we've been exploring the many dimensions of Deep Listening: from creating the right environment to understanding what you're bringing to the encounter, to the sort of attention you give yourself and your speaker, the silence you embody, and the reflections you bring that help illuminate a deeper narrative. Yet there's a paradox. The book is divided into eight distinct steps to help you navigate your journey, an analytical division that may seem artificial. The separation between steps is at odds with the integrated way Deep Listening unfolds in practice, the heartfelt connection and understanding at the core of a Deep Listening encounter. Having read the stories and the guidance of the each of the steps, you're invited to draw on them to create your own integrated path.

Reading a book isn't enough, unfortunately, to master a new skill, let alone a new way of being. It takes practice and courage to look inside yourself and to be open to new ideas from elsewhere. You're not bound, however, to be the listener that you were last year, last week or last night. When you notice yourself becoming trapped by old habits – judging, assuming, interrupting (as I do frequently) – every moment is a fresh opportunity to become aware, to let that go, and to allow yourself to return to the rich spaciousness of being present.

It can also be hugely motivating to be Deeply Listened to by someone else. Gift this book to a friend so they can become a Deep Listener, and you too can experience being listened to in this way. Or even better, find a Deep Listening buddy so you can take turns playing the listener and the speaker. You can then enjoy the opportunity to practise this type of listening in a safe space while also experiencing the self-clarity that comes from being Deeply Listened to, which can be illuminating if you're grappling with a dilemma. And if you're about to have a challenging conversation, brief your buddy to role-play the other party, so you can practise with your shadows for real. I have been impressed by how even a two-minute briefing can be enough for someone to realistically play a role and bring up real challenges for the listener.

When you Deeply Listen as your real self, hiding nothing, you invite your speaker to explore their inner world, unhindered. Opening yourself to whatever unfolds for your speaker, you have the possibility to change something fundamental in your relationship, and in the way your speaker sees themselves. You might never know what new way of thinking or behaving will be unleashed, but it doesn't mean you can't feel uplifted by the possibilities.

Something outside yourself – nourishing your relationship or gaining a truer understanding – may have been your initial motivation to Deeply Listen. But as you practise and experience the wonder of I–thou encounters, you'll want more of them, and the benefits will start to feel intrinsic. Deep Listening relationships become an end in themselves, as the experience opens you to the pleasure of truly connecting with other people, with their stories and their humanity. As you listen in this different mode, you begin to become more interested in what others have to think and say. You may even contemplate that perhaps you can play a different role in the world. Consider introducing your favourite steps of Deep Listening into conversations with people who think differently, even strangers. Given the challenges our societies face – of division and polarisation – there's much at stake. But the doors we can unlock by nurturing deeper connections, despite our differences, open on a more inspiring future.

I've had the profound privilege of feeling truly held by Indigenous Canadians as they listened to me. I ask myself what would it have been like to grow up in a community where being listened to, and listening to others deeply, was familiar territory for everyone? And what would our society be like if Deep Listening principles were ingrained in everyone, from childhood? My experience of being listened to by these Canadians makes me ponder whether all of us were once Deep Listeners. If so, perhaps we can learn to be so again.

At the end of my conversation with my Russian-Ukrainian friend Sofiya, she concluded by crystallising what lies at the heart of Deep Listening:

'This time together enabled me to feel like I'm in the centre. Well, sometimes you feel quite peripheral. You sometimes feel like you're a small particle in the world, one that doesn't play any big role. And you would like to play your *full* role. In this conversation, it reminded me that I'm not a particle, I'm a universe. And all of us, we are all universes.'

ACKNOWLEDGEMENTS

It takes a village. I feel a huge sense of gratitude and privilege to have so many talented and generous people in my life. This includes both those who were already part of my journey and those I have connected with while researching and sharing the practice of listening.

Thank you.

I am immensely grateful to all of those who I have quoted or mentioned in the book's main text or in the endnotes, including those who have chosen to remain anonymous. You gave your time freely and shared your expertise generously. I spoke to many others who I wasn't able to feature, though your insights have played a significant role in shaping my understanding. These include: Vix Anderson, Tom Batty, Kieran White (coaches), Charlie Beckett (LSE), Peter Coleman (University of Leeds), Debbie Aung Din Taylor (Proximity Designs), Erin Dixon, Leslie Hunt-Dickie and Karen Joseph (First Nation Canadian leaders), Monica Nirmala and Kinari Webb (Health in Harmony), Mary Gordon (Roots of Empathy), Steve Mayo (PEARL), the late Mary Montague (peacebuilder), Alan Mullaly (former CEO, Ford Motor Company), John Sibi-Okiumu (actor) and Aina Vilcane (probation officer).

I have learned so much from the thousands of people who have participated in my Deep Listening workshops and those whom I have coached and mediated with. Your questions, reflections and ways of being have enriched my understanding of listening.

Studying with Professor Avraham Kluger was pivotal in introducing me to the wider academic research, while his illuminating listening provided valuable insights. I've learned a great deal from other listening experts and practitioners, in particular Raquel Arc, Jennie Grau, Jim Macnamara and Alex Gillespie and others in the Global Listening Movement. I've also been privileged to be part of the BBC Executive Coaching network for over a decade, and am especially grateful to Martin Vogel, Colin Tregear and Philippa Thomas. My understanding of listening in high-stakes conflict was greatly enhanced over a week spent in West Creek Ranch in Emigrant, Montana, at a conflict meditation retreat organised by the Solutions Journalist Network.

I am indebted to the BBC colleagues who worked with me directly on the Crossing Divides and Deep Listening projects, including Tessa Delauney, Estelle Doyle, Lourdes Heredia, Jacinta Dillon and Andrew McFarlane, all the many journalists who told powerful stories of engaging across divides, inspiring many millions of people among BBC audiences, and the support I received for these projects from Tim Davie, Tony Hall and Jamie Angus, among others. I've also collaborated closely with the British Council on many of the Deep Listening projects mentioned in the book, and it's been a pleasure to work with so many colleagues there, in particular Andrew Sheridan, Jane Grantham, Angelina Twomey and Maria Nomikou.

I am deeply appreciative of More in Common's Tim Dixon, Callista Small and Ed Hodgson for taking up the idea of a US and UK poll about listening – with such enthusiasm – and fine-tuning the questions with me. I am also grateful to Bobby Duffy at the King's College Policy Institute for providing me with an academic home.

I first met my agent, Esmond Harmsworth, when the book was merely an idea. My heartfelt thanks for his wisdom and encouragement through every stage of turning this idea into a book. Receiving guidance and insight from HarperCollins has been instrumental; editorially, and in many other ways, from Cyan Turan, Jane Sturrock, Katya Shipster, Georgina Atsiaris, Julia Pollaco, Nicky Gyopari, Lizzie Henry, Vanessa Bird and Yeon Kim, who created a cover that I love.

This is my first book, so taking part in two Arvon Foundation courses has been more than helpful, along with the feedback from two British Library writers in residence, Sita Brahmachari and Nii Parks. It has been lovely, if an early 7a.m. start, to be part of the Women's Writing and Journaling Circle.

Several friends offered insightful and thought-provoking edits and prompts on the whole manuscript or parts of it, including Andrew North, Andrew Lockett, Eric Nee, Francesca Unsworth, Anne Koch, Mark Easton, Susan Baer, Catalina Bronstein, Rozita Lotfi and Alan Reich. Friends Rosie Lonnon and Elizabeth Price have provided artistic inspiration and feedback. I am also deeply grateful for the support of Divya Prasad, Grace Whorrall-Campbell and Paul Norris in my research. Naturally, any errors are solely my own.

Migrating from working at the BBC to writing alone has been both energising and challenging. I want to acknowledge my brilliant group of friends, who have gifted me their kindness and support. In particular, and aside from those already mentioned, I'd like to thank Jo Rosenfelder, Bergit Arends, Charlotte De Vries Robbé, Karen Holden, The Moon Group,

Guy Stecklov, Dina Shiloh, Milton Nkosi, Jon Drori, Dougal Shaw, Adam Freudenheimer, Vincent Ni, Gillian Tett, Lucy Berthoud, Alice Black and Richard Steele for their sage advice and creative ideas.

And, most important of all, my family. Being endowed with sisters brings so many benefits, and I am truly blessed to have two: Daphne and Tamar have been an endless source of encouragement and feedback, on everything. And it's been wonderful to share updates with my late mother-in-law, Heli, and my mother, Judith, who has been unfailingly supportive and positive. Our adult children, Ben and Maya, left home during the writing of this book, perhaps not coincidentally, but they still contributed wise feedback. My husband, James, however, is still here, despite my periodic failures to listen. He is my greatest cheerleader, never wavering in his listening and his loving support. I am truly and deeply grateful.

ENDNOTES

Introduction

1 In October 2024, the NGO More in Common conducted a poll of over 2,000 adults in Great Britain. The sample was weighted to be representative of the population based on age, sex, General Election vote, ethnicity and education level. (https://www.moreincommon.com/media/aujdjnpi/listening.pdf)
2 Bussie, Jacqueline A. 'Reconciled Diversity: Reflections on our Calling to Embrace our Religious Neighbors', *Intersections*, Vol.33 (8) (2011)
3 Kluger, Avraham N., and Itzchakov, Guy. 'The Power of Listening at Work', *Annual Review of Organizational Psychology and Organizational Behavior*, Vol. 9 (1) (21 January 2022), pp.121–46

PART ONE – ARE YOU LISTENING?

What is Deep Listening?

1 Shay, Jonathan. *Achilles in Vietnam: Combat Trauma and the Undoing of Character*, Scribner, 2003, p.5
2 Schober, Michael F., and Clark, Herbert H. 'Understanding by Addressees and Overhearers', *Cognitive Psychology*, Vol.21 (2) (April 1989), pp.211–32 (describing *the autonomous view* of conversation)
3 Sturman, Janet L., ed. *The SAGE International Encyclopedia of Music and Culture*, 2019
4 The Center for Deep Listening at Rensselaer
5 O'Brien, Kerry. 'Listening as Activism: The "Sonic Meditations" of Pauline Oliveros', *New Yorker* (9 December 2016)
6 Berakoth 55b (https://halakhah.com/berakoth/berakoth_55.html)

7 Gilligan, Carol, and Eddy, Jessica. 'The Listening Guide: Replacing Judgment with Curiosity', *Qualitative Psychology*, Vol.8 (2) (June 2021), pp.141–51
8 Demorest, Amy. *Psychology's Grand Theorists: How Personal Experiences Shaped Professional Ideas*, Psychology Press, 2014, p.146
9 Kirschenbaum, Howard. 'Carl Rogers's Life and Work: An Assessment on the 100th Anniversary of His Birth', *Journal of Counseling & Development*, Vol.82 (1) (January 2004), pp.116–24
10 Carl Rogers lecture on Empathy, 1974. (YouTube 01-Carl Rogers on Empathy)
11 Kabat-Zinn, Jon. *Wherever You Go There You Are: Mindfulness Meditation in Everyday Life*, Hyperion, 1994, p.4
12 I have also been influenced by the host of thinkers who feature on the Waking Up meditation app. (www.wakingup.com)
13 Rogers, Carl R., and Farson, Richard E. *Active Listening*, Mockingbird Press, 1957, p.9
14 Tyler, Jo A. 'Reclaiming Rare Listening as a Means of Organizational Re-enchantment', *Journal of Organizational Change Management*, Vol.24 (1) (2011), pp.143–57

Why We're Not Listening – Eight Traps That Catch Us Out

1 Scene from *The Simpsons*. (YouTube: Homer Undivided Attention)
2 Hurwitz, Anat, and Kluger, Avraham N. 'The Power of Listeners: How Listeners Transform Status and Co-create Power', *Academy of Management Proceedings*, Vol.2017 (1) (August 2017)
3 Makiko Shinoda in conversation with the author
4 Bakhtin, M. M., and Emerson, Caryl. 'Problems of Dostoevsky's Poetics', *Theory and History of Literature*, Vol.8, University of Minnesota Press, 1984, p.81
5 Referenced by Mary Beard, 'The Public Voice of Women', *London Review of Books*, 20 March 2014
6 Santoro, Erik, and Markus, Hazel. 'How Do You Listen?: The Relationship Between How Men Listen and Women's Power and Respect in the U.S.', 10 May 2021. (https://doi.org/10.31234/osf.io/4ycf7)
7 Johnston, Michelle Kirtley, *et al.* 'Listening Styles: Biological or Psychological Differences?', *International Journal of Listening*, Vol.14 (1) (January 2000), pp.32–46

8 Adam Grant in conversation with the author
9 More in Common Survey with YouGov: 13 per cent of American women and 22 per cent of American men reported this motivation in taking an online course on Deep Listening. (https://www.moreincommon.com/media/aujdjnpi/listening.pdf)
10 Rilling, James K., *et al*, eds. 'Origins of Altruism and Cooperation', *Developments in Primatology: Progress and Prospects*, Springer Press, 2011, p.296
11 Lash, Amanda, *et al.* 'Expectation and Entropy in Spoken Word Recognition: Effects of Age and Hearing Acuity', *Experimental Aging Research*, Vol.39 (3) (May 2013), pp.235–53
12 Heingartner, Douglas. 'Now Hear This, Quickly', *New York Times*, 2 October 2003
13 Pikiewicz, Kristi. 'Submissive Listening, Therapeutic Listening and the Third Ear', *Psychology Today*, 17 August 2012
14 Amina in conversation with the author
15 Kveraga, Kestutis, *et al.* 'Top-down Predictions in the Cognitive Brain', *Brain and Cognition*, Vol. 65 (2) (November 2007), pp.145–68
16 Cooper-Cunningham, Dean. 'Is a picture really worth a thousand words? Posters In and About the British Women's Suffrage Movement'. *LSE Blogs*
17 Bathurst, Bella. *Sound: Stories of Hearing Lost and Found*, Profile Books, 2017, p.196
18 Rogers, Carl R., and Evans Farson, Richard. *Active Listening*, Mockingbird Press, 1957, p.6

How Deep Listening Will Enrich Your Life

1 Glenn, Cheryl, and Radcliffe, Krista. *Silence and Listening as Rhetorical Art*, Southern Illinois University Press, 2011, p.1
2 Solmsen, Friedrich. 'The "Gift" of Speech in Homer and Hesiod', *Transactions and Proceedings of the American Philological Association*, Vol.85 (1954), p.1
3 Tobin, Vincent Arieh. 'Moral Values in Ancient Egypt. Miriam Lichtheim', *Journal of Near Eastern Studies*, Vol.59 (3) (July 2000), pp.199–202
4 Glenn, Cheryl, and Ratcliffe, Krista. *Silence and Listening as Rhetorical Arts*, Southern Illinois University Press, 2011, p.1

5 Kane, Brian. *Sound Unseen: Acousmatic Sound in Theory and Practice*, Oxford University Press, 2014, Part 2: Myth and Origin of the Pythagorean Veil

6 Crossing Divides with Deep Listening for BBC100, *BBC News*, 2022 (https://www.bbc.co.uk/news/av/world-61984236)

7 Moin, Tia, *et al.* 'Deep Listening Training to Bridge Divides: Fostering Attitudinal Change through Intimacy and Self-insight', *Journal of Applied Social Psychology*, (6 February 2025)

8 Stern, Donnel B. 'Partners in Thought: Working with Unformulated Experience, Dissociation, and Enactment', *Psychoanalysis in a New Key*, Vol.12, Routledge, 2010, p.111

9 Wittenberg, Jonathan. *Listening for God in Torah and Creation: A Weekly Encounter with Conscience and Soul*, Hodder & Stoughton, 2023, p.17

10 Kant, Immanuel, *et al. Groundwork for the Metaphysics of Morals*, Cambridge University Press, 2008, pp.46–7

11 Honneth, Axel. 'Integrity and Disrespect: Principles of a Conception of Morality Based on the Theory of Recognition', *Political Theory*, Vol.20 (2) (May 1992), pp.187–201

12 Meg Bostrom, co-founder of Topos, in conversation with the author

13 Ignatieff, Michael. *In Consolation: Finding Solace in Dark Times*, Metropolitan Books, 2021, p.1

14 Gable, Shelly L., and Reis, Harry T. 'Good News! Capitalizing on Positive Events in an Interpersonal Context', *Advances in Experimental Social Psychology*, Vol.42, pp.195–257; also *Advances in Experimental Social Psychology*, Academic Press, 2010, p.245

15 Castro, Dotan R., et al. 'Does Avoidance–Attachment Style Attenuate the Benefits of Being Listened To?' *European Journal of Social Psychology*, Vol.46 (6) (October 2016), pp.762–75

16 Van Quaquebeke, Niels, and Felps, Will. 'Respectful Inquiry: A Motivational Account of Leading Through Asking Questions and Listening', *Academy of Management Review*, Vol.43 (1) (January 2018), pp.5–27

17 Pasupathi, Monisha. 'The Social Construction of the Personal Past and Its Implications for Adult Development', *Psychological Bulletin*, Vol.127 (5) (2001), pp.651–72

18 Rogers, Carl R. *On Becoming a Person: A Therapist's View of Psychotherapy*, Constable, 1967, p.19

19 Perrin, Christian, and Blagden, Nicholas. 'Accumulating Meaning, Purpose and Opportunities to Change "Drip by Drip": The Impact of Being a Listener in Prison', *Psychology, Crime & Law*, Vol.20 (9) (21 October 2014), pp.902–20

20 Bavelas, Janet B., *et al.* 'Listeners as Co-Narrators', *Journal of Personality and Social Psychology*, Vol.79 (6) (2000), pp.941–52

21 Bavelas, Janet, *et al.* 'Listener Responses as a Collaborative Process: The Role of Gaze', *Journal of Communication*, Vol.52 (3) (2002), pp.566–80

22 Baumeister, Roy F., and Leary, Mark R. 'The Need to Belong: Desire for Interpersonal Attachments as a Fundamental Human Motivation', *Psychological Bulletin*, Vol.117 (3) (1995), pp.497–529

23 Samuel, Kim. *On Belonging: Finding Connection in an Age of Isolation*, Abrams Press, 2022

24 Danvers, Alexander F., *et al.* 'Loneliness and Time Alone in Everyday Life: A Descriptive-Exploratory Study of Subjective and Objective Social Isolation', *Journal of Research in Personality*, Vol.107 (December 2023)

25 Greene, John O., and Herbers, Lauren E. 'Conditions of Interpersonal Transcendence', *International Journal of Listening*, Vol.25 (1–2) (31 January 2011), pp.66–84

26 Mihaly Csikszentmihalyi quoted in Greene, John O., and Herbers, Lauren E. 'Conditions of Interpersonal Transcendence', *International Journal of Listening* Vol.25, (1–2) (31 January 2011): p.69

27 Reis, Harry T., *et al.* 'Interpersonal Chemistry: What Is It, How Does It Emerge, and How Does It Operate?', *Perspectives on Psychological Science*, Vol.17 (2) (March 2022), pp.530–58

28 Mineo, Liz. 'Harvard Study, Almost 80 Years Old, Has Proved That Embracing Community Helps Us Live Longer, and Be Happier', *The Harvard Gazette*, 11 April 2017

29 Uchino, Bert N., *et al.* 'The Relationship between Social Support and Physiological Processes: A Review with Emphasis on Underlying Mechanisms and Implications for Health', *Psychological Bulletin*, Vol.119 (3) (1996), pp.488–531

30 Kluger, Avraham N., *et al.* 'Dyadic Listening in Teams: Social Relations Model', *Applied Psychology*, Vol.70 (3) (July 2021), pp.1045–99

31 Kalanit Ben-Ari, therapist, in conversation with the author

32 'Stephen Allan steps down from MediaCom after 12 years as Worldwide Chairman & CEO', 12 May 2020, exchange4media

33 Kirtley Johnston, Michelle, and Reed, Kendra. 'Listening Environment and the Bottom Line: How a Positive Environment Can Improve Financial Outcomes', *International Journal of Listening*, Vol.31 (2) (4 May 2017), pp.71–79
34 *Ibid.*
35 Hurwitz, Anat, and Kluger, Avraham N. 'The Power of Listeners: How Listeners Transform Status and Co-Create Power', *Academy of Management Proceedings*, Vol.2017 (1) (August 2017)
36 Adam Grant in conversation with the author
37 Kluger, Avraham N., and Zaidel, Keren. 'Are Listeners Perceived as Leaders?', *International Journal of Listening*, Vol.27 (2) (May 2013), pp.73–84
38 Grant, Adam M., *et al.* 'Reversing the Extraverted Leadership Advantage: The Role of Employee Proactivity', *Academy of Management Journal*, Vol.54 (3) (June 2011), pp.528–50
39 Itzchakov, Guy, *et al.* 'Learning to Listen: Downstream Effects of Listening Training on Employees' Relatedness, Burnout, and Turnover Intentions', *Human Resource Management*, 8 February 2022, pp.565–80
40 Tikva, Sigal Shafran, *et al.* 'Disruptive Behaviors among Nurses in Israel – Association with Listening, Wellbeing and Feeling as a Victim: A Cross-Sectional Study', *Israel Journal of Health Policy Research*, Vol.8 (1) (December 2019), p.76
41 Rogers, Carl R., and Farson, Richard. *Active Listening*, The University of Chicago, 1957, p.4
42 Kline, Nancy. *The Promise That Changes Everything: I Won't Interrupt You*, Penguin Books, 2020, p.24

Why the World Needs Deep Listening

1 2023 Edelman Trust Barometer – Navigating a Polarized World, p.16
2 Duffy, Bobby. *Generations: Does When You're Born Shape Who You Are?* Atlantic Books, 2021, p.5
3 More in Common poll carried out with YouGov. (https://www.moreincommon.com/media/aujdjnpi/listening.pdf)
4 A phrase coined by social cohesion NGO More in Common. (https://hiddentribes.us)
5 King's College London Policy Institute with the World Values Survey, 'UK Attitudes to Immigration: How the Public Became More Positive', 2023, pp.29–30

6 More in Common, 'Britain's Choice: Common Ground and Division in 2020s Britain, 2020', p.4
7 2023 Edelman Trust Barometer – Navigating a Polarized World, p.24
8 Van Bavel, Jay, and Packer, Dominic J. *The Power of Us: Harnessing Our Shared Identities for Personal and Collective Success*, Wildfire, 2022, p.32
9 Bruneau, Emile G., and Saxe, Rebecca. 'The Power of Being Heard: The Benefits of "Perspective-Giving" in the Context of Intergroup Conflict', *Journal of Experimental Social Psychology*, Vol.48 (4) (2012), pp.855–66
10 Hawraa Ibrahim Ghandour in conversation with the author
11 Nancy Kline in conversation with the author
12 Itzchakov, Guy, *et al.* 'Can High Quality Listening Predict Lower Speakers' Prejudiced Attitudes?', *Journal of Experimental Social Psychology*, Vol.91 (2020)
13 Meta-Gallup, 'The Global State of Social Connections', 2022
14 Danvers, Alexander F., *et al.* 'Loneliness and Time Alone in Everyday Life: A Descriptive-Exploratory Study of Subjective and Objective Social Isolation', *Journal of Research in Personality*, Vol.107 (December 2023)
15 Hannah Arendt, *The Origins of Totalitarianism*, Harcourt, 1976, p.474
16 Christiana Figueres, quoted in 'EU officials being trained to meditate to help fight climate crisis' by Robert Booth, *The Guardian*, 4 May 2022
17 Christiana Figueres in conversation with the author
18 More in Common poll. (https://www.moreincommon.com/media/aujdjnpi/listening.pdf)
19 Andžāns, Māris, 'Do Latvia's Russian-Speakers Blame Russia for the War in Ukraine?', Blog from the Davis Centre for Russian and Eurasian Studies, Harvard University, 28 June 2024
20 Rogers, Carl R., and Dorfman, Elaine. *Client-Centered Therapy: Its Current Practice, Implications, and Theory*, Constable, 1973, p.193
21 Drawing on ideas from Rogers, Carl R., and Farson, Richard. *Active Listening*, The University of Chicago Press, 1957, pp.3–4
22 Kalsched, Donald. 'Inner and Outer Democracy and the Threat of Authoritarianism: Reflections on Psychological Factors at Play in Our Polarized World', *Jungian Directory*, 19 September 2023
23 Suzuki, Shunryū, and Dixon, Trudy. *Zen Mind, Beginner's Mind*, Vol.15, Weatherhill Press, 2005, p.91

24 Itzchakov, Guy, *et al.* 'I Am Aware of My Inconsistencies But Can Tolerate Them: The Effect of High-quality Listening on Speakers' Attitude Ambivalence', *Personality and Social Psychology Bulletin*, Vol.43 (1) (January 2017), pp.105–20
25 More in Common poll carried out with YouGov. (https://www.moreincommon.com/media/aujdjnpi/listening.pdf)
26 Feedback from Pumulo Ngoma after the Deep Listening training
27 Hawraa Ibrahim Ghandour in conversation with the author
28 Schroeder, Tiffany. 'Are you listening to me? An investigation of employee perceptions of listening', Doctoral dissertation, Case Western Reserve University, 2016. (http://rave.ohiolink.edu/etdc/view?acc_num=case1465581382)
29 Graham, Renée. 'Once Again Women get Manterrupted', *Boston Globe*, 15 June 2017
30 Karpowitz, Christopher F., *et al.* 'Why Women's Numbers Elevate Women's Influence, and When They Do Not: Rules, Norms, and Authority in Political Discussion', *Politics, Groups, and Identities*, Vol.3 (1) (2 January 2015), pp.149–77
31 Baires, Natalia A., *et al.* 'On the Importance of Listening and Intercultural Communication for Actions against Racism', *Behavior Analysis in Practice*, Vol.15 (4) (December 2022), pp.1042–9
32 The Stuttering Foundation of America. (https://www.stutteringhelp.org/faq)
33 Rogers, Carl R., and Farson, Richard Evans. *Active Listening*, Mockingbird Press, 1957, p.11
34 Christakis, Nicholas A., and Fowler, James H. 'Social Contagion Theory: Examining Dynamic Social Networks and Human Behavior', *Statistics in Medicine*, Vol.32 (4) (20 February 2013), pp.556–77
35 Christakis, Nicholas A. *Blueprint: The Evolutionary Origins of a Good Society*, Little, Brown Spark, 2020; and in conversation with the author
36 Christiana Figueres in conversation with the author
37 Malcolm, Finlay, *et al.* 'Freedom of Speech in UK Higher Education: Recommendations for Policy and Practice', King's College London Policy Institute, September 2023

PART TWO – HOW TO DEEPLY LISTEN

Step One: Create Space

1 Paul Smyth, executive director of Politics in Action, in conversation with the author

2 Dhabhar, Firdaus S. 'The Short-Term Stress Response – Mother Nature's Mechanism for Enhancing Protection and Performance under Conditions of Threat, Challenge, and Opportunity', *Frontiers in Neuroendocrinology*, Vol.49 (April 2018), pp.175–92

3 Souza-Talarico, *et al.* 'Effects of Stress Hormones on the Brain and Cognition: Evidence from Normal to Pathological Aging', *Dementia & Neuropsychologia*, Vol.5 (2011), pp.8–16

4 Arnsten, Amy F.T. 'Stress Signalling Pathways That Impair Prefrontal Cortex Structure and Function', *Nature Reviews Neuroscience*, Vol.10 (6) (2009), pp.410–422

5 Many articles such as: Agarwal, Promila, and Farndale, Elaine. 'High–performance Work Systems and Creativity Implementation: The Role of Psychological Capital and Psychological Safety', *Human Resource Management Journal*, Vol.27 (3) (July 2017), pp.440–58

6 Edmondson, Amy C. *The Fearless Organization: Creating Psychological Safety in the Workplace for Learning, Innovation and Growth*, Wiley, 2018, p.15

7 Capilupi, Michael J., *et al.* 'Vagus Nerve Stimulation and the Cardiovascular System', *Cold Spring Harbor Perspectives in Medicine*, Vol.10 (2) (February 2020)

8 Bar, Moshe, *et al.* 'Very First Impressions', *Emotion*, Vol.6 (2) (2006), pp.269–78

9 Coleman, Peter T. *The Way Out: How to Overcome Toxic Polarization*, Columbia University Press, 2021, p.39

10 Peter Coleman in conversation with the author

11 Riedl, René. 'On the Stress Potential of Videoconferencing: Definition and Root Causes of Zoom Fatigue', *Electronic Markets*, Vol.32 (1) (2022), pp.153–77

12 Adam Grant in conversation with the author

13 Danziger, Shai, *et al.* 'Extraneous Factors in Judicial Decisions', *Proceedings of the National Academy of Sciences*, Vol.108 (17) (26 April 2011), pp.6889–92

14 Inclusive Meetings: The Autistic Self Advocacy Network's Community Living Summit (June 2019)
15 Christiana Figueres in interview with the author
16 Richard Jaffe, Zen Buddhist scholar, in conversation with the author
17 'Informal Dinner between Prime Minister Kishida and President Biden', Ministry of Foreign Affairs of Japan (9 April 2024)
18 Basu, A., *et al.* 'Attention Restoration Theory: Exploring the Role of Soft Fascination and Mental Bandwidth', *Environment and Behavior*, Vol.51 (9–10) (2019), pp.1055–81
19 Coss, Richard G., and Keller, Craig M. 'Transient Decreases in Blood Pressure and Heart Rate with Increased Subjective Level of Relaxation While Viewing Water Compared with Adjacent Ground', *Journal of Environmental Psychology*, Vol.81 (June 2022)
20 Gretchen C. Daily, professor of environmental science, in conversation with the author
21 Soyinka, Wole. *Selected Poems 1965–2022: A Retrospective*, Bookcraft, 2023

Step Two: Listen to Yourself First

1 Frost, Robert. *Witness Tree*, Henry Holt and Company, 1942, p.41
2 Kahneman, Daniel. *Thinking, Fast and Slow*, Penguin Books, 2012, pp.20–21
3 *The Voice in Your Head* by writer-director Graham Parkes. (https://vimeo.com/403146037)
4 Abrams, Jeremiah, and Zweig, Connie, eds. *Meeting the Shadow: The Hidden Power of the Dark Side of Human Nature*, Tarcher, 1991, p.3
5 Bly, Robert, and Booth, William C. *A Little Book on the Human Shadow*, Harper & Row, 1988, p.17
6 Abrams, Jeremiah, and Zweig, Connie, eds. *Meeting the Shadow: The Hidden Power of the Dark Side of Human Nature*, Tarcher, 1991, p.xvi
7 Gtsang-smyon, He-ru-ka, and Quintman, Andrew. *The Life of Milarepa*, Penguin Books, 2010, p.xxiii
8 Signell, Karen A. *Wisdom of the Heart: Working with Women's Dreams*, Ryder & Co, p.257
9 Christine Downing. In Abrams, Jeremiah, and Zweig, Connie eds. *Meeting the Shadow: The Hidden Power of the Dark Side of Human Nature*, Tarcher, 1991, p.66

10 Akhtar, Avad. *Homeland Elegies*, Tinder Press, 2021, Chapter VI

11 Brenner, Elizabeth G., Schwartz, Richard C., and Becker, Carol. 'Development of the Internal Family Systems Model: Honoring Contributions from Family Systems Therapies', *Family Process*, Vol.62 (4) (December 2023), pp.1290–1306

12 A very clear explanation of working with our inner parts by Mary-Anne Johnston is available at https://majohnston.wordpress.com/working-with-our-inner-parts/

13 Loch, Kelly. 'What is Self?' (https://ifsca.ca/wp-content/uploads/What-is-Self-Loch-Kelly.pdf)

14 Rogers, Carl R. *On Becoming a Person: A Therapist's View of Psychotherapy*, Constable, 1961, p.51

15 Sam Keen, 'The Enemy Maker' in Abrams, Jeremiah and Zweig, Connie, eds. *Meeting the Shadow: The Hidden Power of the Dark Side of Human Nature*, Tarcher, 1991, pp.197–202

16 Tara Brach in conversation with the author. More insights about anchors and working with trauma and fear from Tara Brach are available at https://www.tarabrach.com/working-with-fear/

17 Signell, Karen A. *Wisdom of the Heart: Working with Women's Dreams*, Rider, 1991, p.126

18 *Rumi: Selected Poems*, translated by Barks, Coleman, with Moyne, John, Arberry, A.J., and Nicholson, Reynold, Penguin Books, 2004

19 More about Corine Jansen's work on listening is available at https://corinejansen.com

20 Jones, Susanne M., *et al.* 'The Impact of Mindfulness on Empathy, Active Listening, and Perceived Provisions of Emotional Support', *Communication Research*, Vol.46 (6) (August 2019), pp.838–65

Step Three: Be Present

1 Schwartz, Richard. 'The Larger Self', *IFS Institute*

2 Miriam Rose Foundation. Words taken from a video available at https://www.miriamrosefoundation.org.au/dadirri/

3 Chadwick, David. *Crooked Cucumber: The Life and Teaching of Shunryū Suzuki*, Harmony/Rodale, 2011, p.301

4 Spinrad, T.L., and Eisenberg, N. 'Compassion in Children' in Cameron, D. C., *et al.*, eds., *The Oxford Handbook of Compassion Science*, Oxford University Press, 2017, pp.53–63

5 Williams, Mark. 'Effectiveness of School-Based Mindfulness Training', 2022 (https://arc-swp.nihr.ac.uk/news/effectiveness-school-mindfulness-training/)

6 Hanh, Thich Nhat. *The Miracle of Mindfulness: A Manual on Meditation*, translated by Vo-Dinh, Mai, Rider, 1993, p.30

7 This metaphor from listening authority Oscar Trimboli is available at https://www.oscartrimboli.com/greatlistenerstune/

8 Kabat-Zinn, Jon. *Wherever You Go, There You Are: Mindfulness Meditation in Everyday Life: A Guide to Your Place in the Universe and an Inquiry into Who and What You Are*, Hachette, 2023, p.9

9 Inspiration from a number of meditators, including Joseph Goldstein, on the Waking Up app. (www.wakingup.com)

10 Ma, Xiao, *et al.* 'The Effect of Diaphragmatic Breathing on Attention, Negative Affect and Stress in Healthy Adults', *Frontiers in Psychology*, Vol.8 (6 June 2017), p.874

11 Kabat-Zinn Jon. *Wherever You Go There You Are: Mindfulness Meditation in Everyday Life*, Hyperion, 1994, p.4

12 Robinson, Bryan E. 'The 90-Second Rule That Builds Self-Control', *Psychology Today*, 26 April 2020

13 Burkeman, Oliver. *Four Thousand Weeks: Time Management for Mortals*, Vintage, 2021, p.91

14 Pasupathi, M., and Billitteri, J. 'Being and Becoming through Being Heard: Listener Effects on Stories and Selves', *International Journal of Listening*, Vol.29 (2015), pp.67–84

15 The Policy Institute and Centre for Attention Studies, King's College London. *Do We Have Your Attention? How People Focus and Live in the Modern Information Environment*, February 2022

16 Skowronek, Jeanette, *et al.* 'The Mere Presence of a Smartphone Reduces Basal Attentional Performance', *Scientific Reports*, Vol.13 (1) (8 June 2023), p.9363

17 More in Common poll (https://www.moreincommon.com/media/aujdjnpi/listening.pdf)

18 Newport, Cal. *Digital Minimalism: Choosing a Focused Life in a Noisy World*, Penguin Books, 2020

19 Avraham Kluger in conversation with the author

20 The phrase, *Momento Mori*, 'Remember you must die,' with its skull or hourglass symbol, first became popular in 17th-century art, to create a similar impact

21 Tara Brach, in conversation with the author, prompted some of these questions

Step Four: Be Curious

1 'United Nations Myth Busters: The Facts on Climate and Energy'
2 Rogers, Carl R., and Farson, Richard. *Active Listening*, The University of Chicago, 1957, p.11
3 Susan Rice speaking at President Meles Zenawi's funeral. (https://www.youtube.com/watch?v=1_lx_apgRrY&ab_channel=NazretCom)
4 Kashdan, Todd, *et al.* 'The Five Dimensions of Curiosity', *Harvard Business Review*, 2018
5 Podcast available at https://therestispolitics.supportingcast.fm/
6 Kidd, Celeste, and Hayden, Benjamin Y. 'The Psychology and Neuroscience of Curiosity', *Neuron*, Vol.88 (3) (November 2015), pp.449–60
7 Wilde, Oscar. *An Ideal Husband*, Leonard Smithers and Co., 1894, Act 1
8 Informed by Gillespie, Alex. 'Semantic Contact and Semantic Barriers: Reactionary Responses to Disruptive Ideas', *Current Opinion in Psychology*, Vol.35 (October 2020), pp.21–5
9 Belser, Julia Watts. 'Strange Texts and Unexpected Pairings: Reflections on Pedagogy in Conversation with Eric Lawee', *Journal of Jewish Ethics*, Vol.3 (1) (1 January 2017), pp.63–7
10 Informed by Joseph Goldstein talk on the Waking Up app. (www.wakingup.com)
11 Wittgenstein, Ludwig, and Anscombe, G. E. M. *Philosophical Investigations*, Vol.3., Blackwell, 1994, Part 1
12 The Vuslat Foundation is behind the generouslistening.org initiative which champions this approach to listening
13 Bathurst, Bella. *Sound: Stories of Hearing Lost and Found*, Profile Books, 2017, p.199
14 Forkey, Heather, *et al.* 'Trauma-Informed Care', *Pediatrics*, Vol.148 (2) (1 August 2021)
15 Brown, Brené. *Atlas of the Heart: Mapping Meaningful Connection and the Language of Human Experience*, Vermilion, 2021. And Brené Brown website
16 Craik, Dinah Maria. *A Life for a Life*, Hurst and Blackett, 1859, p.169
17 Gary Friedman, conflict mediator, in conversation with the author

18 History of Ryoanji Temple Rock Garden (https://www.japan.travel/en/spot/1145/)
19 Rev. Daiko Matsuyama, deputy head priest of Zaizo-in Zen Buddhist temple, in conversation with the author
20 Kay, John. A. *Obliquity: Why Our Goals Are Best Achieved Indirectly*, Profile Books, 2010
21 Rogers, Carl. R., *On Becoming a Person: A Therapist's View of Psychotherapy*, Constable, 1961, p.55
22 Honneth, Axel. 'Integrity and Disrespect: Principles of a Conception of Morality Based on the Theory of Recognition', *Political Theory*, Vol.20 (2) (May 1992), pp.187–201
23 Buber, Martin. *I and Thou*, translated by Walter Kaufmann, Free Press, 2023. My explanation of *I–it* and *I–thou* also draws on Cooper, Mick, *et al.* 'Dialogue: Bridging Personal, Community, and Social Transformation', *Journal of Humanistic Psychology*, Vol.53 (1) (January 2013), pp.70–93
24 Uri Hasson in conversation with the author
25 Stephens, Greg J., *et al.* 'Speaker–Listener Neural Coupling Underlies Successful Communication', *Proceedings of the National Academy of Sciences*, Vol.107 (32) (10 August 2010), pp.14425–30

Step Five: Hold the Gaze

1 Foucault, Michel. *Power/Knowledge: Selected Interviews and Other Writings 1972–1977*, Harvester Press, 1980, p.155
2 Koithan, Mary. 'Gazing with Soft Eyes: Envisioning a Responsive, Integrative Healthcare System', *Global Advances in Health and Medicine*, Vol.4 (3) (May 2015), pp.7–8
3 Farroni, T., *et al.* 'Eye Contact Detection in Humans from Birth', *Proceedings of the National Academy of Sciences USA*, Vol.99 (2002), pp.9602–5
4 Goodwin, Charles. 'Conversational Organization: Interaction between Speakers and Hearers', *Language, Thought, and Culture: Advances in the Study of Cognition*, Academic Press, 1981, pp.58, 61
5 Cavallo, Andrea, *et al.* 'When Gaze Opens the Channel for Communication: Integrative Role of IFG and MPFC', *NeuroImage*, Vol.119 (October 2015), pp.63–9

6 Simon Baron-Cohen in Zhou, Chu, *et al.* 'Direct Gaze Blurs Self–Other Boundaries', *The Journal of General Psychology*, Vol.145 (3) (3 July 2018), pp.280–95

7 Zhou, Chu, *et al.* 'Direct Gaze Blurs Self-Other Boundaries', *Journal of General Psychology*, Vol.145 (3), (3 July 2018), pp.280–95

8 Bavelas, Janet B., *et al.* 'Listener Responses as a Collaborative Process: The Role of Gaze', *Journal of Communication*, Vol.52 (3) (1 September 2002), pp.566–80

9 Blue, Arthur W., *et al.* 'Through Silence We Speak: Approaches to Counselling and Psychotherapy with Canadian First Nation Clients', *Online Readings in Psychology and Culture*, Vol.10 (3), (1 September 2015)

10 Kline, Nancy. *The Promise That Changes Everything: I Won't Interrupt You*, Penguin Books, 2020, p.37

11 Bahl, Nancy, and Ouimet, Allison J. 'Smiling Won't Make You Feel Better, But It Might Make People Like You More: Interpersonal and Intrapersonal Consequences of Response-Focused Emotion Regulation Strategies', *Journal of Social and Personal Relationships*, Vol.39 (7) (June 2022), pp.2262–84

12 Kraft, Tara L., and Pressman, Sarah D. 'Grin and Bear It: The Influence of Manipulated Facial Expression on the Stress Response', *Psychological Science* Vol.23 (11) (November 2012), pp.1372–78

13 Bahl, Nancy, and Ouimet, Allison J. 'Smiling Won't Make You Feel Better, But It Might Make People Like You More: Interpersonal and Intrapersonal Consequences of Response-Focused Emotion Regulation Strategies', *Journal of Social and Personal Relationships*, Vol.39 (7) (June 2022), pp.2262–84

14 Beukeboom, Camiel J. 'When Words Feel Right: How Affective Expressions of Listeners Change a Speaker's Language Use', *European Journal of Social Psychology*, Vol.39 (5) (August 2009), pp.747–56

15 Austen, Jane. *Pride and Prejudice*, T Nelson & Sons Ltd., 1900, p.169

16 Mehrabian, Albert, and Wiener, Morton. 'Decoding of Inconsistent Communications', *Journal of Personality and Social Psychology*, Vol.6 (1) (1967), pp.109–14

17 Mehrabian, Albert, and Ferris, Susan R. 'Inference of Attitudes from Nonverbal Communication in Two Channels', *Journal of Consulting Psychology*, Vol.31 (3) (1967), pp.248–52

18 Lapakko, David. 'Three Cheers for Language: A Closer Examination of a Widely Cited Study of Nonverbal Communication', *Communication Education*, Vol.46 (1) (January 1997), pp.63–7
19 Adam Grant in conversation with the author
20 Kraus, Michael W. 'Voice-Only Communication Enhances Empathic Accuracy', *American Psychologist*, Vol.72 (7) (October 2017), pp.644–54
21 Chuenwattanapranithi, Suthathip, *et al.* 'The Roles of Pitch Contour in Differentiating Anger and Joy in Speech', *International Journal of Signal Processing*, Vol.3 (2) (2007)
22 Hostetter, Autumn B. 'When Do Gestures Communicate? A Meta-Analysis', *Psychological Bulletin*, Vol.137 (2) (2011), pp.297–315
23 Vrij, Aldert, *et al.* 'Pitfalls and Opportunities in Nonverbal and Verbal Lie Detection', *Psychological Science in the Public Interest*, Vol.11 (3) (December 2010), pp.89–121
24 Guerrero, Laura K., *et al. Close Encounters: Communication in Relationships*, Sage Publications, 2014, p.17
25 Wilde, Oscar. *An Ideal Husband*, Leonard Smithers and Co., 1894, p.13

Step Six: Hold the Silence

1 Hempton, Gordon, and Grossman, John. *One Square Inch of Silence: One Man's Quest to Preserve Quiet*, Free Press, 2010, p.2. Gordon has created a sanctuary for silence in the Olympic National Park, possibly the quietest place in the United States. (https://onesquareinch.org/)
2 Goodman, Paul. *Speaking and Language: Defence of Poetry*, Random House, 1972, p.15
3 Parke, Michael, *et al.* 'How Strategic Silence Enables Employee Voice to Be Valued and Rewarded', *Organizational Behavior and Human Decision Processes*, Vol.173 (November 2022)
4 This dialogue is based on Gregg, Dorothy. 'Reassurance', *American Journal of Nursing*, Vol.55 (2) (February 1955), pp.171–4
5 Burkeman, Oliver. *Four Thousand Weeks: Time Management for Mortals*, Vintage, 2021, p.176
6 Robert Grodin in Burkeman, Oliver. *Four Thousand Weeks: Time Management for Mortals*, Vintage, 2021, p.177
7 Bernardi, L., *et al.* 'Cardiovascular, Cerebrovascular, and Respiratory Changes Induced by Different Types of Music in Musicians and

Non-Musicians: The Importance of Silence', *Heart*, Vol.92 (4) (9 December 2005), pp.445–52

8 Curhan, Jared R., *et al.* 'Silence Is Golden: Extended Silence, Deliberative Mindset, and Value Creation in Negotiation', *Journal of Applied Psychology*, Vol.107 (1) (January 2022), pp.78–94

9 *Ibid.*

10 Kahneman, Daniel. *Thinking, Fast and Slow*, Penguin Books, 2012, pp.20–21

11 Weis-Rappaport, H., and Kluger, A. N. 'The Effects of Listening with "Time-Sharing" on Psychological Safety and Social Anxiety: The Moderating Role of Narcissism and Depression', *Journal of Social Psychology*, (27 December 2022), pp.1–12

12 Prochnik, George. *In Pursuit of Silence: Listening for Meaning in a World of Noise*, Anchor Books, a division of Random House, Inc., 2011, p.11

13 Nancy Kline, coach, in conversation with the author

14 Guidance for silence at Gaia House (https://gaiahouse.co.uk)

15 Ury, William. *Getting Past No: Negotiating with Difficult People*, Bantam Books, 1991, p.2

16 ADHD Symptom Spotlight: Interrupting (Updated July 22, 2024)

17 Nancy Kline in conversation with the author

Step Seven: Reflect Back

1 Hollingsworth Whyte, William. *Is Anybody Listening?*, Time Inc., 1950 (verified on microfilm) referenced in http://quoteinvestigator.com/2014/08/31/illusion/

2 Carl Rogers, lecture on Empathy 1974 (YouTube 01-Carl Rogers on Empathy)

3 Gary Friedman and Catherine Conner, mediators at the Center for Understanding in Conflict, in conversation with the author

4 Friedman, Neil. 'Experiential Listening', *Journal of Humanistic Psychology*, Vol.45 (2) (April 2005), pp.217–38

5 Eugene Gendlin, in Friedman, Neil. 'Experiential Listening', *Journal of Humanistic Psychology*, Vol.45 (2) (April 2005), pp.217–38

6 Gilligan, Carol, and Eddy, Jessica. 'The Listening Guide: Replacing Judgment with Curiosity', *Qualitative Psychology*, Vol.8 (2) (June 2021), pp.141–51

7 Friedman, Neil. 'Experiential Listening', *Journal of Humanistic Psychology*, Vol.45 (2) (April 2005), pp.217–38
8 This dialogue is based on a conversation between a machinist and a foreman in Rogers, Carl R., and Farson, Richard Evans. *Active Listening*, Mockingbird Press, 1957, p.9
9 Carl Rogers lecture on Empathy, 1974 (YouTube 01-Carl Rogers on Empathy)
10 Friedman, Neil. 'Experiential Listening', *Journal of Humanistic Psychology*, Vol.45 (2) (April 2005), pp.217–38
11 Indre Viskontas, neuroscientist and musician, in conversation with the author
12 Rogers, Carl R. *On Becoming a Person: A Therapist's View of Psychotherapy*, Constable, 1961, p.53
13 Friedman, Neil. 'Experiential Listening', *Journal of Humanistic Psychology*, Vol.45 (2) (April 2005), pp.217–38
14 Levine, Linda, *et al.* 'Remember Children's Emotions: Sources of Concordant and Discordant Accounts between Parents and Children', *Developmental Psychology*, Vol.35 (3) (1999), pp.790–801
15 Bruneau, Emile G., and Saxe, Rebecca. 'The Power of Being Heard: The Benefits of "Perspective-Giving" in the Context of Intergroup Conflict', *Journal of Experimental Social Psychology*, Vol.48 (4) (2012), pp.855–66
16 Friedman, Neil. 'Experiential Listening', *Journal of Humanistic Psychology*, Vol.45 (2) (April 2005), pp.217–38

Step Eight: Go Deeper

1 David Grossman in a lecture at the 92nd Street Y, 2017 (https://www.facebook.com/92ndstreetY/videos/10154738871168884/)
2 Steiner, George. *After Babel: Aspects of Language and Translation*, Oxford University Press, 1975, p.172
3 Friedman, Neil. 'Experiential Listening', *Journal of Humanistic Psychology*, Vol.45 (2) (April 2005), pp.217–38
4 Hansen, Flemming. 'Distinguishing between Feelings and Emotions in Understanding Communication Effects', *Journal of Business Research*, Vol.58 (10) (October 2005), pp.1426–36
5 Rogers, Carl R. *On Becoming a Person: A Therapist's View of Psychotherapy*, Constable, 1961, p.204

6 Pugh, Allison J. 'What Good Are Interviews for Thinking about Culture? Demystifying Interpretive Analysis', *American Journal of Cultural Sociology*, Vol.1 (1) (February 2013), pp.42–68
7 Lipari, Lisbeth. 'Listening, Thinking, Being', *Communication Theory*, Vol,20 (3) (20 July 2010), pp.348–62
8 Gilligan, Carol, and Eddy, Jessica. 'The Listening Guide: Replacing Judgment with Curiosity', *Qualitative Psychology*, Vol.8 (2) (June 2021), pp.141–51
9 Barish, Samoan. 'Lend Me Your Ear: An Exploration of Clinical Listening', *Clinical Social Work Journal*, Vol.3 (2) (June 1975), pp.75–84
10 Gilligan, Carol and Eddy, Jessica. 'The Listening Guide: Replacing Judgment with Curiosity', *Qualitative Psychology*, Vol.8 (2) (June 2021), pp.141–51
11 Reik, Theodor. *Listening with the Third Ear: The Inner Experience of a Psychoanalyst*, Jove Publications Inc., 1977, pp.144–5
12 *Ibid.*
13 Moral Foundations Theory (https://moralfoundations.org/). And Haidt, Jonathan, ed. *The Righteous Mind: Why Good People Are Divided by Politics and Religion*, Vintage Books, 2013
14 Graham Jesse, *et al.* 'Moral Foundations Theory: The Pragmatic Validity of Moral Pluralism', *Advances in Experimental Social Psychology* (4 December 2012)
15 Charon, Rita. *The Principles and Practice of Narrative Medicine*, Oxford University Press, 2017, p.166
16 *Ibid.*, p.169
17 Hochschild, Arlie Russell. *Strangers in Their Own Land: Anger and Mourning on the American Right*, The New Press, 2018, p.135
18 *Ibid.*, p.9
19 *Ibid.*, p.xiii
20 *Ibid.*, p.135
21 *Ibid.*, pp.136–40
22 Keats, John, and Sheats, Paul D. *The Poetical Works of Keats*, 'The Fall of Hyperion – A Dream', Houghton Mifflin, 1975, p.238

PART THREE – NAVIGATING YOUR DEEP LISTENING JOURNEY

Deep Listening Ethics

1 Gilligan, Carol, and Eddy, Jessica. 'Listening as a Path to Psychological Discovery: An Introduction: The Listening Guide', *Perspectives on Medical Education*, Vol.6 (2) (27 March 2017), pp.76–81

2 This chapter has drawn on Professor Alex Gillespie, coach Nancy Kline and coach Sarah Rozenthuler in conversation with the author

Deep Listening Risks to You

1 Gilligan, Carol, and Eddy, Jessica. 'The Listening Guide: Replacing Judgment with Curiosity', *Qualitative Psychology*, Vol.8 (2) (June 2021), pp.141–51

2 Lewis, Tiffany, and Manusov, Valerie. 'Listening to Another's Distress in Everyday Relationships', *Communication Quarterly*, Vol.57 (3) (25 August 2009), pp.282–301

3 *Ibid.*

4 Stein, Jacob Y., *et al.* 'Self-Disclosing Trauma and Post-Traumatic Stress Symptoms in Couples: A Longitudinal Study', *Psychiatry*, Vol.80 (1) (2 January 2017), pp.79–91

5 Lewis, Tiffany, and Manusov, Valerie. 'Listening to Another's Distress in Everyday Relationships', *Communication Quarterly*, Vol.57 (3) (25 August 2009), pp.282–301

6 Samaritans (https://www.samaritans.org/about-samaritans/our-organisation/our-safeguarding-policy/)

7 Williams, Tennessee. *A Streetcar Named Desire*, New American Library Inc., 1947, p.153

8 Hooper, Lisa M. 'Expanding the Discussion Regarding Parentification and Its Varied Outcomes: Implications for Mental Health Research and Practice', *Journal of Mental Health Counseling*, Vol.29 (4) (1 October 2007), pp.322–37

9 The author's ideas on this question have been deepened through conversations with Ruth Turner, senior director at the Forward Institute; Alex Evans, executive director at Larger Us; and Tanya Israel, psychologist

Questions to Begin

1 Fischer, Norman. *Taking Our Places: The Buddhist Path to Truly Growing Up*, HarperCollins*Publishers*, 2006, p.45
2 Itzchakov, Guy, *et al.* 'If You Want People to Listen to You, Tell a Story', *International Journal of Listening*, Vol.30, (3) (1 September 2016), pp.120–33
3 Traeger, Margaret L., *et al.* 'Vulnerable Robots Positively Shape Human Conversational Dynamics in a Human–Robot Team', *Proceedings of the National Academy of Sciences*, Vol.117 (12) (24 March 2020), pp.6370–75
4 Avraham Kluger in conversation with the author
5 Powerful questions for journalists and others to ask can be found in Amanda Ripley 'Complicating the Narratives', *Medium*, June 27, 2018. More questions and ideas from Solutions Journalism are at https://s3.amazonaws.com/sjn-static/CTN_Interview_Qs.pdf
6 Kalanit Ben-Ari, therapist, in conversation with the author

How Did Your Deep Listening Go?

1 Dweck, Carol D. *Mindset: How You Can Fulfil Your Potential; Business, Parenting, School, Relationships*, Robinson, 2012
2 Kluger, Avraham N., *et al.* 'Dyadic Listening in Teams: Social Relations Model', *Applied Psychology*, Vol.70 (3) (July 2021), pp.1045–99
3 Reflections also drawn from Passmore, Jonathan, ed. *The Coaches' Handbook: The Complete Practitioner Guide for Professional Coaches*, Routledge, 2021, p.389

INDEX

A
acoustics 93, 97
Active Listening 27–8
ADHD (attention deficit hyperactivity disorder) 150, 193, 225
advice, offering 18, 26, 34, 36–8, 303
affective polarisation 67
agency 37–8, 54
agendas, navigating 18, 90, 108, 129, 162, 184, 191, 217, 231, 233, 234, 238, 247, 250, 269, 274, 291, 295, 303
Akhtar, Ayad 119
Alex 143–4, 259–60, 268–9
Ali, Muhammed 87
Ali, Rashad 169–70, 176, 180
alienation 68
Allen, Stephen 59–60
Amina 41, 213–14
anchors, returning to your 124, 131, 152, 155
Angelo 232–3
anger 74, 108, 111, 126, 138, 146, 148, 149, 167, 188, 198–9, 203, 248, 252, 258, 273, 296
anxiety 68, 89, 149, 179
approval 72–5, 173
Arendt, Hannah 68
arrogance 34, 166, 225
assertiveness 35
assumptions 4, 8, 35, 57, 62, 67–8, 75, 181, 185, 229, 232, 238, 302, 304
attention 3, 100, 115, 117, 137, 149, 150, 204, 221, 225, 240, 242, 293, 294, 307
  ADHD and 193
  applying creative attention 101
  centring with breath 18, 140
  creating warmth with 141
  directing to an anchor 152
  disruptive shadows and 110
  empathetic attention 195
  focusing your 19, 24, 27, 56, 90–1, 145, 182, 233
  the gaze and 192
  impact of smartphones on 153
  Japanese tea ceremonies 98
  nature's soft fascination 102
  not giving real attention 29–30
  paying attention to the present moment 147
  paying attention to tone of voice 203
  paying attention to your thoughts 43
  quality of our attention 40
  receiving 178, 179
  withdrawing your 34
attentiveness 58
attitude extremity 68, 72, 90
Austen, Jane, *Pride and Prejudice* 198–9, 202
authenticity 3, 6, 12, 18, 57, 58, 59, 62–3, 76, 79, 85, 123, 173, 197, 242, 269, 291, 295
  authentic curiosity 163–5, 167, 234
  authentic respect 180
  and the exchange of ideas 296
  power of authentic reflections 251–2, 253
authority 32–3, 90, 116–17, 267
  authoritarianism 68
awareness 122, 129, 149

cultivating 141, 156
of judgements 160
and presence 135–7, 143, 210
self-awareness 6, 53–4, 152, 183, 304
awkward silences 212, 215, 224–5, 226

B
backchannel responses 56
Barish, Samoan 261
Bathurst, Bella 43, 171
Bavelas, Janet 55–6
BBC 1, 5, 8, 37, 61, 85, 103, 118, 143, 146, 159, 162, 184
Crossing Divides Across the Globe 5, 9, 48–50
Share Your Story 283–4
becoming, process of 177–8, 301
beliefs 63, 67–8, 72, 75, 78, 180, 212, 230, 231, 245, 246, 247, 261
belonging 75, 173, 249
bias 223, 227, 245–6, 296
Biden, Joe 99
Billie 211–12
Bjorn 236–7, 241, 251
Blair, Tony 164, 165
Bly, Robert 111–12
bodily sensations, tuning in to 146
body language 96, 188, 193–7, 198, 199, 205, 206, 239, 297
Bolsonaro, Jair 45
boredom 132, 150–1, 156, 211
boundaries 52, 79, 168, 172–3, 185, 253, 262, 284, 287, 288
Brach, Tara 124
the brain 39, 42, 43
fMRI scan 183
the gaze and 191
and the parasympathetic nervous system 87
thumb circling and 146
breath: 4–7–8 breath 145, 157
centring with the breath 18, 124, 136, 140, 145, 156, 157, 244
British Council 5, 48–50, 70–1
Brown, Brené 173
Bruneau, Emile 249–50
Buber, Martin 166, 182
Buddhism 12, 27, 72, 99, 175–6, 196, 293
Burkeman, Oliver 150, 216
Bushreida, Rana 49–50
Bussie, Jacqueline 6

C
Cambria, Jack 147–9
Campbell, Alastair 146, 164–5
care 267
Cash, Fermina Lopez 194–5
celebrations 52–3
central nervous system 87
centring 145–6, 156, 160, 161
with the breath 18, 124, 136, 140, 145, 156, 157, 244
Charon, Dr Rita 270–1, 276
chattering, intrusive internal 147–9
cheering people up 38, 247–9
chemistry, interpersonal 58
children and childhood 90–1, 100–1, 103, 111–12, 127, 178–80, 247–9
childhood shadows 115–19, 129–30, 131
connection between emotions and physical expressions 199
emotional parentification 289–90
lack of sharing in 4
Christakis, Nicholas 77
citizenship 78
climate change 66, 69–70, 97, 160, 165, 184, 247, 256–7, 269, 272, 291
Clinton, Bill 87
clues, being alert to 258–62
coaching 54, 61, 89, 104, 110, 143, 171–2, 177, 192, 203, 222–3, 226, 234, 238, 241
Coleman, Peter 89–90
collaboration 37, 55–6, 87, 188
colour of lighting 94, 105
comfort 18, 52, 87, 89, 91–7, 106, 135, 215, 222
comfort zones 84, 304
creating comfort, physically 91–2
feeling safe with someone 174
communication, non-verbal 11
companionable silences 215
compassion 122, 126, 127, 129, 131, 181, 287, 301
confidentiality 89, 284
confirmation bias 245–6
confrontation 30–1, 162
connections 4, 25, 49, 53, 57–8, 87–9, 95–6, 103, 108, 136, 155, 168, 170, 172, 182, 212, 217, 288
consciousness 122
consolation 52
contagious listening 77–8

contexts to practice Deep Listening 303–4
contracting 89–90
control 32–3, 37, 53, 189, 213–14, 217
controversial subjects 72, 181, 290–2
conversations, 'winning' 31
core beliefs 67–8
cortisol 145
counselling 89, 123, 240–1
Craik, Dinah Maria 174
curiosity 40, 43, 58, 59, 63, 127, 129, 159–86, 190, 293, 301
  authentic curiosity 163–5, 167, 234
  cultivating 126, 161–8
  lack of 28
  muted curiosity 166

D

Dadirri 136–7
Dalton, Alex 283–4
Davies, Philip 159–60, 165, 184, 256–7, 269, 275
deeper narratives 255–79
depression 68, 219, 227, 268
Difficult Conversations Lab 89–90
digital disconnect, avoiding 95–6
Digital Minimalism 153
disagreeable ideas, reflecting back 245–50
disagreements, listening when you disagree 46–7, 49–50, 152, 164–5, 177, 181, 245–50, 266, 275
distraction: as diminishers of speaker's experience 54, 152, 296
  distracted listening 23, 28, 56, 63
  external distractions 93, 96, 149–50, 156
  internal distractions 110, 125, 148–9, 150, 156
  messages in 150–1
  mobile phone as a distraction 18, 100, 153–4, 221
  staying present despite distractions 18, 143, 150, 151–2
  supercharged distractions 153–4
Dōgen Zenji 72
domination, of conversations 32–3, 35
Downing, Christine 116
Druze 197–8
Dweck, Carol S. 300

E

Edmondson, Amy 86
Egyptians, ancient 47
electrifying stillness 195
embarrassment 85, 111, 211, 296
embodied messages, decoding 197–200
emotions 89, 112, 119, 129, 137, 183, 258–9, 271, 274
  emotional closeness 51, 53, 59
  emotional parentification 289–90
  emotional reflections 239–42, 253
  emotional state 125, 138, 170
  empathy and 168
  meta-reflections 241–2, 253
  negation of 248–9
  reflecting back 253, 258–9
  reframing negative 167
  strong emotions 108, 115, 120, 123–4, 127, 148, 199
  taking note of 148–9, 168, 237, 253
  as transient waves and ripples 137
empathy 26–7, 43, 54, 55, 58, 63, 125–6, 160, 182, 184, 185, 188, 190, 195, 197, 225, 287, 297, 301
  embodying empathy 168–71
  empathy with boundaries 172–3
  'empathy wall' 272–4
  'I've Been There' empathy 171–2
enthusiasm 33–4
ethics, Deep Listening 283–5, 287–9
expertise trap 33–4
extreme views 12, 65, 68, 75, 90, 169–70, 290–1
eye contact *see* gaze

F

facial expressions 56, 94, 187–93, 196–7, 201–2, 203, 239
fairness 3, 267
feebleness, silence as hallmark of 35
feedback 166, 223, 300, 302
feelings 258–9, 277
  meta-feelings 258–9, 277
  see also emotions
feels-as-if-story 271–4
femininity, passive 35
Fielden, Lara 140–1, 221
fight or flight 86, 146
Figueres, Christiana 69–70, 78, 97, 247, 291
firefighters (sub-personalities) 120, 121, 122, 131

flow, evoking a state of 57
Foucault, Michel 189
framing 89–90
Freud, Sigmund 262
Friedman, Gary 174
Friedman Neil 245, 252
Frost, Robert 108, 109

G

Galicia, Sharon 272
gaze 205, 221
  directing the gaze 191
  the gaze window 192
  holding the gaze 187–206
  mutual gaze 191
  quality of the gaze 190–1
  virtual conversations and 96
gender 34–5
generosity 77
gestures 203–4, 239
Ghandour, Hawraa Ibrahim 67, 75, 187–8
goals, desire to achieve 30–1
Gonsalves, Megan 181
Goodman, Paul 210–11
Gormley, Antony 112–14, 142–3, 182
Graham, Renée 76
Grant, Adam 35, 60–1, 96, 202
Greeks, ancient 47
grief 52–3, 108, 119–20, 195
Grono, Nick 39–40
Grossman, David 255

H

Haidt, Jonathan 266–7
Hannah 207–9
happiness, and healthy relationships 58
harm, avoiding 267
Hasson, Uri 182–3
heart's intention 151–2
Hempton, Gordon 209
Heron, Larissa 133–5, 136, 137, 138, 155, 216
Hizb ut-Tahrir 169–70
Hochschild, Arlie 271–4, 276
Holder, Brenda 133–5, 136, 137, 138, 144, 155, 216
Homer 34, 47
Honneth, Axel 51, 181
Hoshina, Machiko 98–101
Hussein, Saddam 165

I

I-it and I-thou encounters 182–3, 185
ichigo ichie 99, 104
ideological polarisation 66–7
inclusion 76–7
indifferent listening 161–3
Indigenous cultures 76, 133–5, 136–7, 193, 216, 309
inner voices *see* shadows
inoculation, Deep Listening and 69–71
inspiration: inspiration to become still 142–3
  spaces to inspire 98–9
instincts 262–4
insula 183
intentions, clarifying 105
intergenerational: dynamics 45–6, 65, 73
  shadows 119, 135
Internal Family Systems Therapy 120–2
International Journalism Festival 236–7, 241, 251
interpersonal chemistry 58
interruptions 209, 214, 218, 219, 221, 223, 225, 290
intimacy, fear of 53
Iskander, Maryana 167, 181, 225
Islam 67, 151, 197
Itzchakov, Guy 49

J

James, Henry 270
Jansen, Corine 125–6, 129–30, 215
Japanese tea ceremony 98–101, 104
jiu-jitsu 199–200
Joe 30–1
journalism 38, 62–3, 151–2, 162–3, 269–70
  International Journalism Festival 236–7, 241, 251
joy, sharing 52–3
Judaism 25, 151
judgements 42–3, 55, 67, 71, 160
  letting go of 173–5, 177, 178, 185
  and reflecting back 244
  silence and 216
Jung, Carl 26, 111, 120
Jungian analysis 115, 116

K

Kabat-Zinn, Jon 27, 144
Kahneman, Daniel 109, 218

Kant, Immanuel 51
Kasriel, Harry 7, 107–8, 135
Kasriel, Judith 154, 155, 178
kavanah 151
Kay, John 176
Keats, John 277
Keen, Sam 122–3
Kelly, Loch 122, 128–9
Kentridge, William 103–4, 265–6
Khan, Akram 117–19, 126, 154–5, 199–200
kindness 77, 171, 301
King, Dr Martin Luther 216
Kline, Nancy 62, 67–8, 195

L

labelling people 42
Latvia 70–1
leadership 9, 28, 39, 59–60
  curiosity as an important quality of leadership 167
Lesinko, David Ole 91–2, 93, 99
liberty 267
lighting, to enhance listening 93–4, 97, 105
limits, listening 290–2
Lina 36
lip-service listening 39
listening: enrichment due to 54–5
  listening as collaboration 55–6
  listening to yourself first 107–32
  standard listening 6, 23–4, 39
  what Deep Listening is 6, 17–28
  why we're not listening 29–43
  why the world needs Deep Listening 65–79
loneliness 57, 68–9
loyalty 267

M

Maasai community 91–2, 99
McCartney, Paul 88
Mandela, Nelson 1–3, 5, 90
manipulation, risks of 287, 291
Maria 218–19, 220
Mark 116–17
masculinity, dominating 35
meaning: creation of 231
  waiting for it to reveal itself 265–6
Mediacom 59–60
mediation 62, 89, 241
medicine, Narrative Medicine 270–1
meditation 27, 128, 138–40, 141, 145–6, 157, 221
Medusa 189
Mehdi 170
Mehrabian, Albert 200–2
memories 53–4, 108
men, role in conversations 34–5
Meredith 262
meta-feelings 258–9, 277
meta-reflections 241–2, 253, 302
Milarepa 112–14
Miller, Fiona 165
mindfulness 27, 102, 126, 141, 144–6, 156, 221
mindsets, power of 300
Minogue, Kylie 117–18
mobile phones, as digital distraction 18, 100, 153–4, 156, 221
Mohammad 287–8
moral values 267–8
motivation 151–2
Munro, Alice 270

N

narratives: authentic narratives 62–3
  deeper narratives 255–77
nature 101–3, 105
neuroplasticity 43
neuroscience of listening: judgement and neuroplasticity 42–3
  neural entrainment 183
  self-awareness 107–32
Newport, Cal 153
Ngangikurungkurr community 136–7
Ngoma, Pumulo 73
niyya 151
non-verbal communication 11, 187–206, 239, 240, 253
notes, taking 234–5
noticing, failure to notice 108–9

O

obedience, listening as 40–1, 213–14
obliquity, the path of 176–7
The Odyssey (Homer) 34
Oliveros, Pauline 24
once-in-a-lifetime exchanges 99–100, 106
openheartedness 287
openness 58
oppression, challenging 267

P

Packer, Dominic J. 66
parasympathetic nervous system 86–7
parents 57, 90–1, 100–1, 103, 111–12, 166, 178–80, 213–14, 247–9
  emotional parentification 289–90
  intergenerational shadow 119–20
Paris Climate Agreement (2015) 69–70, 97
Parsons, Vicken 142
pauses, transformational 220–2, 227
Paxman, Jeremy 146
Person Environment Activity Research Laboratory (PEARL) 92
personalities, sub- 120–2, 131
perspective 217, 260–1, 277
  broadening perspectives 224
  competing perspectives 70–1
  multiple perspectives 72, 175–6, 185
physical conditions, speaker's 97
physical safety 91–105
Platon 87–9, 193–5
playful spaces 103–4, 106
polarisation 4, 65–8, 79, 89–90, 122
  affective polarisation 67
  ideological polarisation 66–7
  and importance of interactions 7
  Iranian participant's reflections 74–5
  Latvia case study 70–1
Police Service of Northern Ireland 83–5
political differences 45–7, 65
posture 239
power dynamics 3, 41, 75, 83–5, 87–9, 90, 180, 189, 213–14, 227, 232–3, 249–50, 275, 283
preconceptions, effect of our own 25
prefrontal cortex 86
prejudice 71, 108, 296
presence 133–57
  awareness and 135–7
  being fully present when it matters 138–40
  bonding benefits of 137–8
  and distracted listening 23
  distractions as diminishers of speaker's experience 54, 152, 296
  embodying stillness 145–6
  external distractions 156
  inspiration to become still 142–3
  internal distractions 148–9, 150
  intrusive external distractions 149–50
  intrusive internal chattering 147–9
  messages in distractions 150–1
  staying present despite distractions 150
  stillness in everyday rituals 144–5
  supercharged distractions 153–4
  taking time to move into stillness 143–4
presumptions 57
Prochnik, George 220
psychological safety 25, 53, 85–91, 105
psychotherapy 26, 120–2, 128–9
public speaking 177
Putin, Vladimir 88
Pythagoras 47

Q

questions, starter 293–7

R

reactiveness 46, 167
reciprocal listening 58–9, 296–7
recognition, need for 50–2
reflecting back 229–54, 258–9, 270, 271, 278
  emotional reflections 239–42, 253
  meta-reflections 241–2, 253
  power of authentic reflections 251–2, 253
  reflecting back disagreeable ideas 245–50
  selective reflecting 247–9
  striking the right note 242–5
  what to reflect back 235–9
Reik, Theodor 262–3
rejection, silence as a sign of 219
relating well 57–8
repeated listening 285
respect 43, 76, 126, 160, 178–81, 182, 185, 190, 217, 245, 297, 301
The Rest is Politics 164–5
Ribeiro, Ana Luiza 45–7, 232–3
Ribeiro, Manoel 45–7
Ricard, Matthieu 27
Rice, Susan 163
rights to be listened to 78–9
risks of Deep Listening 166, 173, 285, 287–92
rituals: Japanese tea ceremony 98–101
  stillness in everyday rituals 144–5
Rogers, Carl 26–7, 43, 55
  accepting your shadows 122
  Active Listening 27

emotional reflections 240
empathetic reflection 230
multiple perspectives 72
principles of Deep Listening 161
in the process of becoming 177
psychological safety 71
treating thoughts of another 244–5
roles 32, 34–5
Romans 47
Rose 211–12
Rumi 125
Russia 70–1
Ryoan-ji Temple, Kyoto 175–6

S

Sabancı, Vuslat Dōgan 168
safety 185
places of 85–91, 104, 124, 173
psychological safety 85–91, 105
silence of listening as place of 215
The Samaritans 143–4, 259–60, 268–9, 289
Samuel ben Nahmani 25
sanctity, valuing 267
scaling Deep Listening 78
Schwartz, Richard 26, 120, 121–2, 136
scripts, breaking out of 233–4
seating 94–5, 97, 105
Self 121–2, 131
self-awareness 6, 53–4, 152, 183, 304
self-compassion 301
self-discovery 37
self-esteem, boosting 53
self-expression 47–8
self-reflection 49, 299–305
meta-reflections 302
questions to reflect upon afterwards 301–2
striking the right note 242–5
sense-making 265–6
shadows: accepting your 131
appreciating your shadows 130
childhood shadows 115–19
dancing with shadows who interrupt 128–30
decoding shadows 111–12
disruptive shadows 108, 109–11, 128–30
exploring your shadows 112–14
giving shadows a voice 127–8
giving yourself space 125–7
how to handle 123
inherited shadows 119–20, 131
intergenerational shadows 119–20, 135
returning to your anchor 124
shadow signs 114–15, 131
shadows in conflict 122–3
sub-personalities 120–2, 131
welcoming shadows 124–5
Shaheem, Kareem 151–2
shame 85, 111, 124, 173
Shinoda, Makiko 33
Signell, Karen 115, 124–5
silence 278, 297
benefits of for both sides 222–4
controlling forms of 213–14
easing into 224–6
elevating your connection 217
as hallmark of feebleness 35
holding the silence 207–27
resistance to 211–13, 226
silence of Deep Listening 214–17
'Silence is Golden' 217–20, 225
spectrum of 210–11
trailing into silence 261–2
transformational pauses 220–2, 227
using the presence of 209
Simpson, Homer 29
The Simpsons 29
smiles 56, 202, 238
spontaneous 196–7
Smyth, Paul 83, 84–5, 87
social cohesion 76–7
social contagion 77–8
Sofiya 17–23, 53, 57, 192, 203, 231, 274, 309
solitude, protecting your 79, 290
Soyinka, Wole 70, 102, 290
space, giving yourself 125–7
spaces: playful spaces 103–4, 106
spaces to inspire 98–9
testing perfect spaces 92
spatial equality 97
speakers: benefits of listening on the speaker 50–4
the listener as speaker 296–7
stammers 76–7
standard listening 6, 23–4, 39
starter questions 293–7
status, desire to enhance 30–1
Steiner, George 257
Stern, Donnel 50–1
Stewart, Rory 164–5

stillness 160, 221
  electrifying stillness 195
  embodying stillness 145–6
  in everyday rituals 144–5
  inspiration to become still 142–3
  taking time to move into stillness 143–4
strangers 53, 122–3, 135, 191, 294
  promoting interactions between 94–5
  talking to 49
stress 86
stress hormones 145
sub-personalities 120–2, 131
subjects, controversial 72
successes, celebrating 300–1
suffragettes 42
superior temporal gyrus 183
Suzuki, Shunryū 138, 293

T

Taylor, Jill Bolte 148
tea ceremonies 98–101, 104, 143–4
TED talks 47–8, 177
'tell me more' 232–3
texture 190
therapy 89, 123, 240–1
Thich Nhat Hanh 143–4, 196
the third ear 262–4, 274, 277
thumb circling 146
time: best times to listen 96–7
  lack of 38–40
  moving through time 275–6
  regular listening times 90–1
  taking your time 299
tolerance, window of 59, 304
Topos Partnership 51–2
trauma 269, 284–5
  and creation of shadows 119–20, 131
  deriving comfort from shared experience 171–2
  intergenerational trauma 135
  listening to traumatic stories 288–9
  seeking support for 123
trust 58, 88, 105, 193, 195, 217, 238, 243, 288
truth, open to a new 232–3
Tyler, Nick 92–5, 103

U

UK Forward Institute 9
unconsciousness 111, 115, 123, 253, 262, 263, 265
Ungunmerr-Baumann, Miriam Rose 136–7
university students 78
Ury, William 224
Ustinova, Ilona 71

V

vagus nerve 87
values 266–8, 278
Van Bavel, Jay 66
virtual conversations 95–6
voice, tone of 201, 202, 238, 297
  reading 203
  striking the right note 242–5
The Voice in Your Head 109–10, 130
vulnerability 285, 294

W

Waldron, Reece 76–7
walking, listening while 103
Weinstein, Netta 49
the whispering 261
'whispers' 90–1
Wikimedia Foundation 167, 181
Wilde, Oscar 166, 205
Will 264
Williams, Tennessee, *A Streetcar Named Desire* 289
Willie 107–8, 151
window of tolerance 59, 304
'winning' conversations 31
women: failure to listen to 76
  role in conversations 34–5
words, unsaid or downplayed 259–60
work: Active Listening training 28
  feeling of safety in the 85, 86
  framing conversations at 89
  link between gender and assertiveness 35
  polarisation at 65
  speaking up in meetings 33
  tuning in at work 59–62

Y

Yalda 74–5
YourLifeCounts.org 123
Yuko, Mrs Kishida 99

Z

Zenawi, Meles 161–3